BONNES

VACANCES!

A crazy Family Adventure in the French Territories

Rosie Millard

summersdale

Summersdale Publishers Ltd
46 West Street
Chichester
West Sussex
PO19 1RP
UK

www.summersdale.com

Printed and bound in Great Britain

ISBN: 978-1-84953-149-8

Extracts from *France's Overseas Frontier: Départements et Territoires d'Outre-Mer* by Robert Aldrich and John Connell (Cambridge University Press, 2006) are reproduced by kind permission of the authors.

Substantial discounts on bulk quantities of Summersdale books are available to corporations, professional associations and other organisations. For details contact Summersdale Publishers by telephone: +44 (0) 1243 771107, fax: +44 (0) 1243 786300 or email: nicky@summersdale.com.

To Pip

Rosie Millard is a well-known journalist across the spectrum of the British press and commentator on television and radio. She was the arts correspondent for the BBC for ten years and regularly writes for *The Daily Telegraph* and the *Financial Times*. She lives in central London with her TV producer husband Pip Clothier and their four young children.

www.rosie-millard.co.uk

Contents

Our

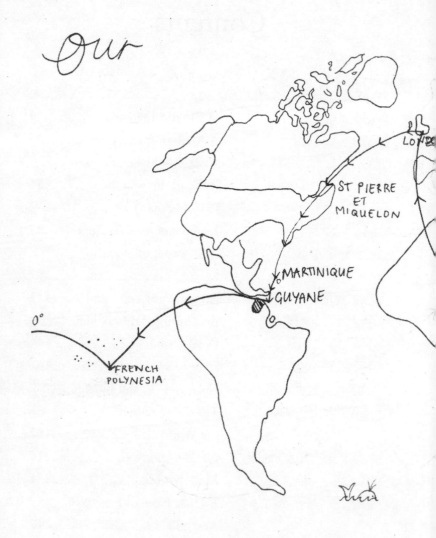

ST PIERRE
ET
MIQUELON

LONDON

MARTINIQUE

GUYANE

0°

FRENCH
POLYNESIA

Trip

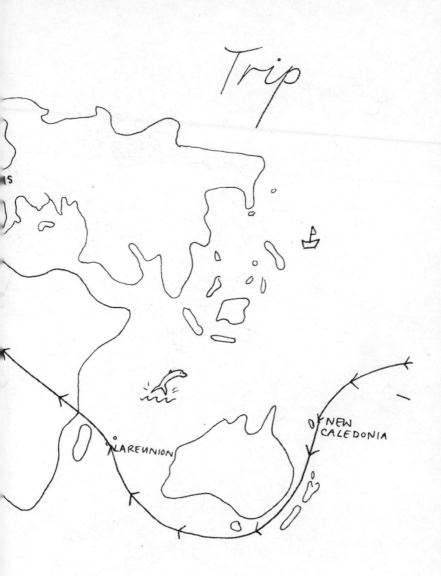

LA REUNION

NEW
CALEDONIA

St. Pierre et Miquelon

Miquelon

L'Anglade

St. Pierre

CHAPTER ONE

'A Bit Too French'

Honey's diary: *I had a backpack and Lucien had the same.
Gabriel had two backpacks. Mummy had O so much and
Daddy O so much, he had as much as Mummy had. Then
we walked to the stashon and hoped on the Choob. Then we
went to the airport and we had to go in a thing that sees if
you'v got any thing dandrous in your pocket.*

Twenty-seven hours and three flights after leaving London, we
drop down through banks of white fog in a tiny French mail
plane, and land on a French airstrip. When the propellers stop
whirring, I'm the first to leap off the plane. All right, there's jet
lag, since we have crossed about six time zones, but what is jet
lag when you have surmounted the insurmountable?

Above the wind, I shout something along these stirring lines
to Pip, who is coming off the plane rather slowly, since he is
carrying quite a few bags. He rolls his eyes in response. I rather
fear he has lost the will for words. 'Look, look!' I yell to the
children, who have just stumbled sleepily down the stairs.
There it is. The *bleu, blanc, rouge – le tricolore –* whipping
away in the chill Atlantic breeze.

After two years of planning, we have finally arrived. Saint Pierre et Miquelon, the most minuscule of France's overseas domains, is a rocky, fog-bound speck in the Atlantic. It has no landmarks and no grand city. It is known chiefly for publishing stamps, and for the fact that Al Capone visited it, briefly, in the 1920s. Yet this moment, touching down at Saint Pierre Pointe Blanche, is our entry point into the world's most bizarre parallel universe.

If you have an atlas, the *départements et territoires d'outre-mer* are the tiny pieces of land scattered right across the globe, identifiable by the enigmatic two-letter postscript (Fr). They are a collection of islands and jungles which are directly nurtured by Paris. They account for only 1 per cent of France's former colonies, but these 76,000 square kilometres, which stretch over three oceans and five continents, ensure the continuing presence of a miniature Gallic empire still seemingly loyal to the beat of the Marseillaise.

Who are these English people on the French tarmac? My husband Pip, a TV director who doesn't speak French. He has a French *sounding* surname (Clothier) but is as English as they come. He loves cricket, politics and West Ham, and is a great cook. He is smart and funny, and he's thrown his lot in with me. What this has meant over the years, is if we decide to do something together, then after an inordinate amount of bathtime chatting about it, we venture off and do it. That's the sort of person he is. I'm lucky.

There is our eldest son Gabriel, nine, who has an intense curiosity about life, but whose adventures are dogged by intense travel sickness. Then there is Honey, six, a modern-day Pepys in hair slides, a well-organised child, who finds nothing more satisfying than spending a morning tidying her bedroom and writing her diary. Bringing up the rear is Lucien, four, a child who regards France as a wholly annoying presence in his otherwise enjoyable life. He will not speak French. He dislikes *le tricolore* with a vengeance. He cries when I play him French pop music, and he's even gone off *The Magic Roundabout* after I told him the iconic show was of Gallic descent. Lucien does not want to be here. He wants to be sitting on his mother's knee. In London.

Our eldest daughter Phoebe, twelve, is not with us. We have left her behind for the first half of the trip; I was too frightened to negotiate six weeks off school with her headmistress, who is rather stern. So she is staying with her great friend Eve. A month or so before we left, I rang Sarah, Eve's mother, and had the following halting conversation. Well, my side of it was halting. Actually, I was dreading it.

'Hello, Sarah, it's Rosie. Er, you know we are planning on taking, um, three or four months to voyage around the French-speaking world?'

'Yes, yes, I think I do. How wonderful.'

'Only thing is, Sarah, [deep breath] I don't think we can take Phoebe with us at the start, because, er, she'll miss too much school.'

'Oh, would you like her to come and stay with us?'

'Yes!'

'No problem.'

'Really? Thanks very much!'

That was the conversation. I sat down shaking slightly.

Other moments during the 24-month planning operation prior to our arrival at Saint Pierre Pointe Blanche didn't go so smoothly. This was the trip No One Wanted Us To Make.

I had envisaged our journey could be the subject of a fantastic television programme: *How to Go Around the World Without Ever Leaving France*; or *How to Understand the French (in*

Hot Places). At first, it looked as if this plan would be a piece of cake to galvanise into action.

The timing was in our favour. I say 'our' favour but really I suppose going away was my idea. It was not something I insisted on, stamping my foot in a spirit of dogged individuality. Pip and I are both happy with risk; we enjoy slinging mad ideas at one another and seeing how the other half accepts it. Anyway, one night Pip had just returned home after an intractable meeting with a television executive.

Our chat went something like this:

'God I hate the television world sometimes,' says Pip.

'Imagine leaving all this behind and going on our big adventure.'

'What, you mean the mid-life crisis one?'

I look at him quizzically.

'No, no. You know, the trip we talked about ages ago? About overseas France. You must remember. When our old friend Peter came over and talked to us about Saint Pierre et Miquelon. And then we found out about Martinique, Guyane and Polynesia! Come on, don't you recognise these names? Nouvelle Calédonie? You must remember! You know, the place that's two o'clock off the coast of Brisbane? And La Réunion in the Indian Ocean.'

'Hmm, Polynesia might be all right. But what is Saint Pierre et Miquelon? I remember Peter saying it was a fog-bound dump. And where the hell is Guyane? It sounds dreadful. Isn't that where Papillon was incarcerated and Alfred Dreyfus spent five years in solitary?'

'Yes, but that's all in the past,' I say.

I can sense him weakening.

'Just imagine! Think of the waves crashing on the beaches of La Réunion! We always said, didn't we? That when we were in our forties we would go around the world one day?'

'It is the mid-life crisis trip, then.'

Was it a crisis? Not overtly. Everything in the garden was good: job, children and house were all in order, parents not yet doddery, children not yet stroppy. The days, weeks, months spun round. That, of course, was the catalyst.

My plans were hatched in the artificial heat of the sauna at the Virgin gym in North London. In my steamy bunker, in the subterranean depths of London N1, lights and a tape of noises supposedly sourced in a rainforest played on an eternal loop.

'Squawk! Howl! Tweet tweet! Caw caw! Yaaagh! Squawk! Tweet,' and so on. A green light flickered over the pine benches, imitating the equatorial sun shining through many thousands of leaves. I would sit in the sauna, thinking of my future. I projected the years ahead so deeply that at one time I was practically blowing out eighty candles on my birthday cake.

I suppose Virgin's idea was that its clients should lie back on fluffy towels, away from worries about money, work and childcare, and imagine being in the middle of a rainforest. I don't think the Virgin Gym envisaged for one second that one of its clients would actually take them at their word, cancel their membership and travel to a real rainforest. Yet I was that client.

Then I would remind myself about what my parents did once in the mid 1970s, which was, essentially, to up sticks and cart their family to the middle of nowhere in Africa. This was the era of heroic flares, the three-day week, the OPEC petrol crisis and The Three Degrees singing 'When Will I See You Again'. My parents, both doctors, decided to do some medicine which mattered. My father got a job in a former mission hospital which had only three doctors and about a hundred nurses. My mother agreed to work alongside him. I was nine. And so one day, my mother turned around to us four children sitting in the back of the family Cortina and casually announced that next week we were all off to Africa: 'For a year.'

The house was packed up. The dog was sent off to live with some friends. The car was sold. We boarded a UTA jumbo for Jo-burg, from whence we voyaged to a former mission hospital in one of the South African 'homelands' – basically an arid dump where Africans were forced to live. It was the most astonishing, demanding adventure.

'Why can't we be like that?' I ask Pip one day after a session in the Virgin sauna.

'Like what?'

'Like Moth and Foth. Adventurous. Daring. Living for the moment, not for our pensions.'

'What about work?'

A pause. I think about how my parents managed this potential hurdle.

'We'll take our work with us!' I exclaim, in a moment of inspiration.

'How?'

'We'll film the trip. You're a TV producer. I'm a reporter. We'll make documentaries about the French and their ambition to project their nation across the globe via their hidden empire. I bet no one has ever heard of Saint Pierre et Miquelon.'

'What will we do with the children? Shall we leave them behind? Take them with us? Will we have to take a nanny?'

'God, no. We won't have any money, will we? But we can't very well leave them behind. We'll take them with us. That's part of the point. Anyway, being with us on their own will be good for them. They can just play around our feet while we're filming. And they'll see... they'll see a different world. Think how much they'll learn!'

With the vision of a giant picture of my family – who knows, wrapped in a *tricolore*? – gracing the cover of the *Radio Times*, I did the rounds: the BBC, Channel 4, ITV, Channel 5, as well as Radio 4 and a variety of oddball cable channels.

Each meeting took about eight weeks to arrange. At each meeting, every executive gave me a hot drink, widened their eyes, nodded their head, smiled a lot and then proceeded to list a host of reasons why my brilliant idea was, well, rubbish. In their view. Broadly speaking, there was one main sticking point.

'It's just too French.'

'Too long a trip and, you know, it's a bit too French.'

'Too short a trip... and the programmes would be far too French.'

And so on. It wasn't the fact that we were going around the world. Actually, that was quite acceptable. Hazardous family experiences are all the rage on British television these days. No, the main problem was that it was, ahem, too French. The executives, or at least most of them, clung to the innate British mistrust of les Frogs and pulled the drawbridge up behind them.

Undeterred, we pitched it to the French. I composed a series of begging letters in that formal eighteenth-century style that the French seem to require for correspondence. That would surely be the answer; an English point of view on the French. We achieved perfection in the style of the letters, as our French next-door neighbour kindly did them for us. We did not receive a single response.

The only place that seemingly was not scared of the French was the Travel Channel – a small but energetic outfit that doesn't even broadcast to France. But it's very big in Dubai and South Africa. They thought it was a capital idea. So, we got a commission. We are making six documentaries about the French overseas empire for the Travel Channel. There'll be no money in it, but at least it's a commission.

'And that means we'll get lots of politicians talking to us,' says Pip, who is a serious documentary maker.

I'd better brush up on my language skills, I think nervously. I speak French like a sort of enthusiastic exchange student, not a Brussels-based foreign correspondent.

We write more letters, this time in cobbled-together French, being too embarrassed to ask the neighbour again. We try to contact all the French politicians living out across the world in these far-flung territories. Again, none of them reply.

'This letter isn't ingratiating enough!' I shout at Pip. 'It's not courteous enough!' I fling open an art history book I have been thumbing through in the bath. Standing dripping on the bathmat, I quote directly from it.

'This is what Paul Gauguin did when he wanted to go to French Polynesia! Listen to this, written on 15 March 1891:

'"Dear Minister," [this is the French Minister of Fine Arts]

'"I would like to go to Tahiti to make a series of paintings to capture the character and light of this country. Sir, I have the honour of requesting that you grant me official creditation... which although unsalaried would nevertheless, by the advantages it would proffer, facilitate my studies..."'

The request was endorsed by the Ministry of Public Education eleven days later.

I look at my husband. 'You see? He talks of *honouring*. He talks of *requesting*. He talks of *proffering*. Basically, he's grovelling. That's what we need to do!'

'Yes, well even he knew there was no money in it,' says Pip. He pauses for a moment. 'And didn't he DIE out there? Of syphilis?'

'That is a minor detail,' I say, stalking away to find a towel.

We will later discover what an awful time poor old Gauguin eventually had. Right now, with the wind in our sails from the Travel Channel, it's all gung-ho optimism.

'Look, even Gauguin's *mates* felt like escaping Europe,' I cry, after finding yet another reason for us to go from the annals of the past, namely a letter to Gauguin from his friend Émile Bernard, written in June 1890, "Oh to leave without having to worry about anything, far far away. To leave the abominable life in [Europe], its boors, its layabouts, its moaners, this plague-stricken breed."

'Yes, well,' says Pip reasonably. 'Nobody has the plague in Europe at the moment.'

Never mind. We hire a French researcher, Noemie, whose father is a gendarme in Guyane (known in the UK as French Guiana), South America. So she knows how things are done. She sends out an entire dossier of emails in perfect French. No one writes back to her, either. What is it about the French and their fear of correspondence?

'I don't think they quite believe you are going to do these visits,' says Noemie. 'No English people have ever done this before. Certainly not with four children. *Mais, tant pis,*' ('Too bad') she says with perfect French insouciance. 'We will continue.'

We eventually move into a mindset that we are going to go on this trip, whether anybody wants us to or not. The more people ignore us, the keener I become.

I find the only English-language book in existence on the subject of France's overseas domains. *France's Overseas Frontier* is by Professor Robert Aldrich and Professor John Connell from Sydney University. I take Aldrich and Connell on the bus. I take them to the bath. I take them to bed. I become an anorak about the French *départements et territoires d'outre-mer*, or DOM-TOMs.

I start to talk about them to everyone I meet. I'm now not wholly surprised to discover that the only person I meet who has heard of them is Boris Johnson.

I start to surround myself with positive people who say inspiring things like: 'It's the things you don't do that you regret the most, not the things you do do.' It is utterly vital to do this, if you are planning a mad trip, as everyone else will want to put you off going. Don't listen to them, is my advice.

Then, one day, I pick up the phone. And with my heart in my mouth, I buy the air ticket. This is the passport that will take us to all of these far-flung places. Its extreme bargain-basement nature means frequently boarding planes at 05:00 in the morning, but never mind. It just adds to the excitement.

'We're going,' I say to Pip.

'We're going,' I say to my parents, who cheer from a safe distance.

'We're going,' I say to the children.

We crack open a bottle of cheap red wine and toast the future.

Needless to say, our offspring don't see this move in quite such a positive light.

They are deeply suspicious of France, recognising it as a dangerous force that has seduced and encouraged their mother to bend away from normal British life: deliveries of *The Times*, conversations about interest rates and schools, summer holidays in Cornwall and shouting about when they will sit down and do some piano practice. Of course, this is part of the reason I'm suddenly keen to get away. I feel I'm so immersed in the world of London, the media and what Mini Boden has in its upcoming spring catalogue that it's become unhealthy. I need to shake England out of my hair for a bit. And replace it with France.

My Gallic fascination has always been part of my character. But recently, I'll admit, it has got somewhat out of control. This is not a weekend jaunt to Paris I've suggested; this is a global odyssey around the francophone world. When we were still in London, to get into the swing of things, I would encourage everyone to sometimes have breakfast *quand tout le monde parle français*. I would beg my children to join in, offering them *la confiture et les Cheerios*, to a response of total silence. I even paid for a charming French gentleman, Gerard, to cycle round to the house and indulge them in conversation once a week. It was a disaster. They flatly refused to talk to him and, out of embarrassment, I ended up having the conversational lessons myself.

'It's because our mother is MAD,' say the children when anyone asks why we are determined to do this adventure. 'She listens to Jacques Brel in the bath! She loves the smell of rat poison on the Paris Metro! She wants us to all speak French! At breakfast!'

I don't really understand it fully myself. Why is it that I only have to hear a couple of tourists on the London Underground say *'Où est Leicester Square?'* (one of those tricky British names which flummox the French), and my heart starts to race madly.

Is it the melodious, beautiful language? The perfect food? The elegant adults and their perfectly kitted-out children? The idiosyncratic cars, the poetry, the art, the films, the tragic narratives in the dire pop songs; or the fact that when in France, you are never more than 20 metres from a chemist offering an enema? It is all of these things, and more. (Well, maybe not the enema, but I certainly love spending a good 40 minutes in a Parisian pharmacy.)

My fundamental love of France kicked off when my parents took the family to Paris one rainy spring weekend when I was sixteen. We went up the Eiffel Tower, walked around the Louvre, ate in bistros and did a bit of shopping in Printemps. Paris, under her cool grey light, captured my heart.

My younger sister and I shared a bedroom in a modest B&B in the Latin Quarter, somewhere near the Pantheon. Our window looked straight onto the houses on the opposite side of the narrow street. The most exciting thing about our lodging was that every morning in one of the flats in the block opposite ours, a naked man could be seen ironing his socks. Naked, and ironing. We found both events absolutely hilarious.

I believe that this explicit introduction identified Paris in my mind as a hive of rather joyous naughtiness, a view wholly confirmed courtesy of a sexy weekend, again in the Latin Quarter, when I was nineteen with my then boyfriend (who, rather thrillingly, was in an eighties boy band, Curiosity). After him, I went to the top of that particular ladder and experienced love with a real Frenchman. He was slight, sexy and sullen.

It took me quite a while to get past the excitement of having a relationship with an actual Parisian and figure out that the relationship itself was fundamentally flawed, thanks in no small part to the fact that he had absolutely no sense of humour.

I didn't go to Paris much after that, or France. I was too busy falling for other countries; Italy, Greece, America. Then I was working. Then I was having children. And then, fifteen years later, on a bitter January day in 2002, I was sent by the BBC to report on Yves Saint Laurent's swansong on the catwalk; his final show.

It was at the Centre Georges Pompidou. I was not sitting on the gilt chairs next to Catherine Deneuve; we, the British media, knew our place. We were all outside in the freezing chill air, standing on the red carpet and grabbing interviews with the fashion world as it swayed past us on impossibly high heels. But amid the shouting and the rush, I remember looking at Paris with astonishment.

I'd forgotten all about her severe beauty. The leafless trees, pruned to the nearest centimetre of accuracy, the slate-grey light bouncing off the Haussmann architecture, the smell of the Metro. How could I have forgotten? I'd been backpacking in Greece and sightseeing in New York, yet all the time here was Paris, the most elegant, arresting and demanding city on the planet. I was seduced afresh. I had been given a small but not insignificant amount of money. I put it down as a deposit on a tiny flat in Pigalle. I rented the flat out to tourists and used it myself. I started to dream of living there.

'The general stereotype of the French… is of a voluble, excessively excitable… and somewhat lecherous personality,' ran a wartime document published in Britain. In some people's minds, that viewpoint has not changed one iota.

Equally, many people regard France as a country full of people who are at best flighty and unhygienic, and at worst corrupt, with a nasty habit of going on strike.

But put aside these elements of francophobia. Even forget about Paris, just for a moment. For as I began to reclaim my own, early love for France, I discovered there was another France; a hidden France, several time zones away from Paris.

When I discovered the existence of the DOM-TOMs, I was intrigued and engaged. Any aspect of French life interested me, but this more than most. Something about their wildly distant positions on the globe, alongside a clear determination to remain French, rather touched me. I determined to visit them. Well, perhaps not the uninhabited Antarctic ones, and those in the South Pacific which you can only get to by container vessel, but certainly the rest. And I wanted my children to come with me. I had a notion that the trip could be something crucial in the progress of their childhood, an experience of life outside the anglophone bubble, a challenge which they would never forget. Indeed. They would witness a unique world of croissants in the jungle, newly married French brides tipping out of Air France jets for a honeymoon visit, and crumpled copies of *Le Monde* blowing around in a South Pacific typhoon. That was what I hoped. Yes, it was hopelessly romantic. It was also something which harked back to what I had had as a child. I wanted to give it to my children, and I wanted to reclaim it for myself; a sense of wilderness, of freedom, of intrepid adventure without an obvious safety net.

It was a vision which led us to arrive in the freezing wind on the unwelcoming island archipelago of Saint Pierre et Miquelon, somewhere in the North Atlantic.

Now as I watch them clambering off the tiny Air Saint-Pierre twin-prop plane, struggling through the wind which has come straight off glaciers in the Atlantic Ocean, it occurs to me that I have been monstrously selfish; I have imposed my deepest wishes on the family unit, and wrenched my children away from their contented and risk-free life to fulfil a madcap idea of my own. Do I feel bad about this? Not yet.

It may be June, but it is freezing. We are all wearing our cold weather wardrobes, namely sweatshirts and thin cagoules. Never mind. I bet Sir Ranulph Fiennes didn't let a bit of chilly air spoil his enthusiasm, and I'm determined not to rub the polish off this momentous occasion.

Pip is shouldering a backpack so vast it makes him stagger. Everyone else is pulling or carrying at least two bags, even little Lucien. My own assembly of bags, rucksacks and various zipped receptacles are so heavy that once I hoist them up onto my shoulders, I fear they may cut off the blood supply to my arms. I don't care.

We walk towards the shiny modern airport, where inside everything positively gleams with glossy promotion of the French lifestyle; Perrier, Renault, Chanel, champagne. I photograph a plaque attesting to the fact that President Chirac arrived here in September 1999.

'Imagine!' I say to the children. 'President Chirac came here!' They look deeply unimpressed.

'Actually, you know this is not a *département d'outre-mer*, or even a *territoire d'outre-mer*. It's something between the two,' I continue. 'It's an overseas collectivity!'

Nobody responds.

There are no taxis outside, even though I thought we had booked one. After about ten minutes, which feels like an hour, a third of the island's cab population rolls up. We hire them both.

On our way to Saint Pierre, the only town on the eponymous island, we pass rather a lot of important-looking shiny 4x4 jeeps. The terrain is what is called 'rugged' in brochures and looks rather like the Scottish Highlands; scrub bushes, heather, cliffs, rocks. Small buildings crouch on the rocky earth, hugging the coast as if the freezing sea water of the North Atlantic is some comfort. There are no trees. Seagulls wheel and cry above us in the fresh, windy air.

Twenty minutes later, I'm still excited and we are standing in the middle of the tourist office with our thirteen pieces of luggage. We have arrived! Roll on the filming schedule! I can't believe it! Sadly, neither can the tourist office.

No one, it appears, is ready for us. No one knows who we are. Or why we are here. I realise that, foolishly, I had been expecting a welcoming committee of sorts. I mean, haven't these people heard of the Travel Channel? It would seem not. I scan the room. It is full of maps and fishing nets cradling plastic lobsters and some seaweed made from old tights. Four middle-aged women and a plump man who looks like Elton John look us up and down.

This is the reception for Day One of our Grand Tour of Reportage around the French Empire.

'Our boss is out,' says Elton, whose real name, we later discover, is Pascal. 'Can we 'elp you?'

Lucien begins to cry. I look wildly around. How could our plans be in such disarray? Gabriel looks at me as if to say 'Told you so'. Honey looks utterly downcast. Is this a classic French moment? I have a suspicion it might well be. When they are lost on the Tube in London, the French are vulnerable and charming. On their own territory they are a bit more hardbitten.

I produce my treasured letter from the Maison de la France, or in other words, the French Tourist Board. This is the only 'official' document that I have managed to secure from a French institution before leaving. It shows our itinerary and thanks the reader, in advance, for assisting us in our *'tâche'*. (I had to look up *tâche*, because I always thought it meant stain. Actually, with the circumflex on the 'a', it means 'work').

Pascal looks at my important document from the Maison de la France, and shrugs his shoulders.

'Alors?' he says. There is a terrifying silence in the tourist office. One of the children drops a backpack.

'At least we have bookings at the Hotel Robert,' I murmur to Pip. The Hotel Robert is the best hotel in Saint Pierre, and is in the Place du General de Gaulle, which apparently looks right onto the harbour and which sounds reassuringly official and proper. I think we are going to have a room, or suite of rooms, with a view of the ocean. Perhaps there will be little chocolates on our pillows, an infinity pool and a nice bar.

'I'll stay here and find out what has become of our, er, filming schedule and all the interviews we are meant to have. Why don't you go and sort out the bookings?' I say to Pip, who looks at me with thinly veiled panic behind his blue eyes.

'Can you?' he whispers. Oh yes, he doesn't speak French. Yet.

'Er, où est le, I mean la, Place du General de Gaulle?' I ask in my best schoolgirl parlance. Pascal shrugs.

'Bien sûr, vous êtes déjà ici.'

Oh, great.

'"We are here already," well, that's jolly convenient,' I translate loudly for the benefit of my family.

'Là,' says Pascal, pointing past a grim-looking bank, towards the looming shape of an undecipherable building. It is undecipherable because the entire Place du General de Gaulle is swathed in a thick, white, wet fog. The fog drapes itself on the square, the adjoining harbour and the Hotel Robert like

a cotton wool pleat. Tall masts from fishing boats randomly appear without any structure beneath them, like the haunted *Flying Dutchman*. A bell from somewhere solemnly tolls the hour.

We leave the tourist office, with promises to return later, and trudge slowly towards the Hotel Robert, lugging our luggage. In our thirteen bags, which are fated to be our dear companions for 64,000 kilometres, are brochures, Doom mosquito repellent, files, Aldrich and Connell, a video camera, a back-up video camera, half of Boots pharmacy, five month's supply of Calpol (Infant and Junior) in sachet form, and two computers. Which means we have hardly any room for clothes. Hence our wholly spartan allowance of five pairs of knickers, two T-shirts, a jumper and a pair of trousers each. I even put my foot down on Gabriel taking his Chelsea football kit, although with the amount of francophone players in the team, I should really have given it pole position in the bag. Anyway, we only have a micro-wardrobe each. And here in Saint P et M, it looks as if we'll be wearing everything at once.

'But we are freezing here, Mummy,' whines Honey.

'I thought you said the French overseas lands were all TROPICAL,' says Gabriel, who has spent the last few weeks poring over our projected route in the Collins Atlas.

'Yes, well most of them ARE. It's just that we've started with the non-tropical version, darling.'

We continue to struggle across the Place du General de Gaulle. I'm suddenly very worried. For the first time in my life, the notion of living alongside the French suddenly seems a wholly terrifying prospect.

CHAPTER TWO

A Rock in the Atlantic

Honey's diary: For breakfast I had a cruisso and jame. I fogot what we had for lunch. Then it was supper time and we had soop (as all ways). We went to an island called Isle aux Marins but the reason why nobody went and lived there was because there was no heating there.

We check in at the Hotel Robert. The Hotel Robert is not the four-star springboard we had joyously envisaged, the well-appointed hostelry from which the first of our documentaries would be produced. A solid, white institution, it faces the harbour with grim permanence. The Hotel Robert is not really a hotel at all. It is an ancient boarding house inhabited by French language students. It stinks of boiled cabbage and the dining room is decorated with a picture of its one celebrity guest, Al Capone, and a grim-looking map entitled 'Naufrages-Shipwrecks'. This shows tragic lists of ship names, revealing when and where exactly along the local coastline each of an estimated 600 shipwrecks have taken place over the last 200 years.

We are led to our 'suite', which bears scant (i.e. no) resemblance to any picture of any of the hotel bedrooms on their website. It is not a series of rooms overlooking the ocean. It is one ground floor room located beneath an outside fire escape that overlooks a benighted stretch of asphalt and a brick wall festooned with an empty washing line. Our room contains the following: a cooker, sink, table and two double beds. There is no cutlery and there are no chairs. There is one electric point.

Madame, who has guided us into this vile, crepuscular place, clasps her hands at the door proudly, almost as if she were the concierge at the Crillon.

'Alors!' she says. 'Le petit déjeuner sera à huit heures du matin.' She then leaves us standing amid our bags – the bags that we packed with such anticipation and excitement, back in what now looks like the civilised world.

I try to make the best of it. Having forced my family out of an entirely enjoyable and benign life, I must now make it seem as if swapping it with existence at the Hotel Robert was a sensible thing to do.

'I thought that you said the French always lived in complete style,' grumbles Pip as we assemble the 'lit pliant' on which one of our shivering children must spend the night. The mattress is musty and damp. I find a large, tough blanket in an ancient wooden armoire, cover the mattress and hope for the best.

I try to work out how something so ghastly could have happened.

'Well, we're a long way from la Métropole,' I say briskly, using Gallic terminology for the mother country. Out here, 10,000 kilometres from Paris in the départements d'outre-mer, there are two words for France. It's known either as la Métropole, as if the country were entirely paved with tarmac, or l'Hexagone, as if it had suddenly transformed itself into a geometric shape.

Anyway, the point stands. We are far from what I fondly like to think of as the most civilised country in Europe.

The *lit pliant* is not being very pliant. We abandon it in pyramidal shape, and venture out into the heart of Saint Pierre.

After about five minutes, we are still wandering past shuttered houses.

'Where are the shops, Mummee?' asks Honey, who has an advanced understanding of how urban centres are organised. 'It's just I can't see any.'

'That's because there are none, darling,' I explain. 'Or at least none like there are at home.'

The entire centre of Saint Pierre is full of brightly coloured wooden houses.

'They are painted all these lovely colours so people can see them through the fog,' I say brightly, as we negotiate swirling clouds of white, which have engulfed Lucien so comprehensively that all I can see is the top of his head. There are no street names and no people. The whole place is empty. One could imagine getting lost in Saint Pierre for a very long time.

We are trying to find a supermarket, since we have been assured that the only restaurant in town serves giant, cheese-covered pizzas for about £15 a head. And we are on a survival budget. We are on a Travel Channel budget, in which living expenses do not feature whatsoever. Indeed, although I am not going to suggest our modest documentaries will rewrite art history, Millard has ended up with exactly the same deal as Paul Gauguin. A single letter of introduction, and no money.

How did he put it, back in 1891? 'Unsalaried.' Quite.

The shops, we discover, are within the houses. There are no shop windows. Just houses in which the ground floor has been given over to a small collection of books, stationery or toys for sale. Outside, the only sign of life appears to be the youth of Saint Pierre doing wheelies up and down the vertiginous streets leading down to the water. There is a square of concrete where older members of the island community play pétanque. There is one cabaret which does Edith Piaf tribute nights, but not in June, apparently. There is one cafe for the population of Saint Pierre, which is 5,509. We venture into it. To their joy, the children discover a giant 3-D puzzle featuring Franklin the green turtle. They colonise a plastic table and, with the ability children have to immerse themselves in the present, immediately start playing.

Pip and I, on the other hand, don't find it so easy.

We drink vast cups of milky coffee and look at each other blankly. We think the same things but we don't say them.

How the hell are we going to survive this trip?

And where the blazes is the supermarket?

Eventually I wrench myself out of unpromising thoughts about returning shamefacedly to Heathrow and ask Madame la Patronne for directions to what I hope will be an Aladdin's cave of comfort and joy.

'*Le supermarché? Là-bas,*' says the lady at the Franklin Cafe, pointing up the road. A calendar behind her advertises French combine harvesters, with a picture of one ploughing a field in the Dordogne. Beside this calendar is a poster for Disneyland Paris. For a small supplement of 200 euros, I notice, one can include a weekend by coach to London. I see a small thumbnail picture of the London Eye. From a wish to keep the general mood buoyant, I decide not to make a point of it.

We wander off up the steep hill, which must have a 1:8 gradient. Eventually we find the *supermarché* of Saint Pierre. Only a pair of shuttered doors indicate that there is a thriving commercial enterprise within. *Enfin*, it is a bit of a treasure trove. Here are the Petits Filous yoghurts, Camembert, semi-skimmed milk, Nesquik chocolate, Hollywood chewing gum, breakfast cereals and Bonne Maman jams that typify the French lifestyle of which I dream. You can even buy Evian, bottled at source, *naturellement*, and shipped to Saint Pierre.

The milk cracks me up, though.

'Look at this,' says Gabriel, waving a carton at me. 'Where does this milk come from then, Mummy? I mean, I thought you said there were no cows here on Saint Pierre, and no farms.'

'I think we are looking at French cows grazing on French fields, *chéri*,' I say.

And, *oui*, on the front of the carton there is a picture of the happy French *campagne* filled with *les vaches*. No matter that Newfoundland is all of 11 kilometres away. The French want to behave as if Saint Pierre et Miquelon are just off the coast of La Rochelle, not an archipelago that shares a time zone with Western Greenland. They don't want to drink Canadian milk. They want to drink French milk, and are willing to pay the price required to ship it over. Why?

'Perhaps it's so they can forget Canada is only next door,' says Gabriel.

Maybe he's right. Blotting out everything from North America might make it shrink in importance. Maybe.

The prices are astonishing. They make us feel like paupers, or people transported 30 years into the future. A carton of milk costs around £4.

We stand with our modestly packed basket behind a woman who is clearly doing the weekly family shop. I notice that her final bill comes to about £400. Pip shakes his head.

'How do they manage here? After all, there's no work around, is there?'

'Shhh,' I say, heaving my basket onto the counter. *'Bonjour,'* I say to the cashier as I unload a tiny packet of pasta, a tiny jar of coffee, a carton of milk, three cans of Campbell's Tomato Soup, some yoghurt and a couple of bottles of red wine. All from *la Métropole*. The bill comes to £40.

We repair to the Hotel Robert and cook dinner.

Only one ring on the oven works, so we have to do things in stages. The pasta is a bit so-so, as the water never really boiled, but the soup hits the spot. Good old Campbell's. Our saviour. We sit on our beds and eat nourishing soup with spoons borrowed from the hotel kitchen. Then we wash the spoons up under the only (cold) tap in the kitchen sink, and eat our Petits

Filous yogurt. After this repast, Pip and I continue making inroads into a bottle of red, while the children try in vain to get an Internet signal on the laptop. Each of us is plugging into our drug of choice, only the wine is more easily accessible than broadband, which has yet to be piped in across the Atlantic.

'But I must Facebook my friends,' wails Gabriel. 'I need to find out how Jack is!' Too bad, *mon chéri*. We are in the back of beyond.

In the end the children give up and go outside, where two boys are kicking a football against a garage. Gabriel and Lucien agree to play with them, even though their only common language is dribbling skills. Honey drifts out alongside them and stands against the brick wall with a little girl called Pascale. They look dreamily at one another, smile, and swap Hello Kitty hair clips. Good, I think. Total immersion. This is why we have come all this way. I look over at Pip and smile. He is busily arranging a baroque assortment of cables, microphones and batteries in his bag. He smiles back.

'All right sweetie?' I say.

'Just doing the checks on the equipment,' he replies buoyantly. 'Can't have things breaking down on our first day, can we?' He is determined not to despair. I love him for it, because I am the same.

Pip and I may have been crazy, planning this adventure, but we are doggedly averse to announcing failure. Through gritted teeth, I think. Through gritted teeth and only if it's the last thing on earth will we admit this trip has failed. We both hate losing.

'Mummeee,' asks Lucien, as he trots back into the room some forty minutes later, 'why is everything here in French?'

'You will know the answer, my sweet,' I say, 'tomorrow.'

That night things are not good.

Our loo decides to regurgitate what looks like the contents of most of the only sewer for Saint Pierre et Miquelon. The archipelago may only have the population of an English village, but there is a lot of *merde* here, I can tell you. And tonight most of it, including industrial quantities of what looks like chewing gum, turns up in our lavatory.

'Well, there's nothing we can do tonight about it, *mes enfants*,' I say brightly.

'We all just need to go to bed.'

I tuck them into their wiry blankets and turn the light off. Pip is already asleep, exhausted by the demands of carrying 50 kilograms of luggage.

I lie on a thick, lumpy and damp mattress trying to work out how we can turn around such a disappointing start into something meaningful. For solace, I switch on a rickety side light, and turn to Aldrich and Connell, my bible.

Saint Pierre et Miquelon, apparently, were 'France's consolation prize for the loss of the Canadian empire of the early modern period'.

This is because in 1763, while negotiating for peace with the British (after losing against the British Navy at Quebec), the French relinquished their chunk of Canada, slightingly described by Voltaire as 'a few acres of snow'.

In return for the whole of Canada, Britain agreed that it would keep away from the French Caribbean 'sugar islands': Saint Domingue (now Haiti), Martinique and Guadeloupe. The French thought this was a fine deal. Indeed, in the late eighteenth century, Saint Domingue was the most profitable spot of land on the planet, because sugar was such a fabulous commodity. Sugar was in global demand. The English, for example, heaped teaspoons full of the stuff in tea, their national drink. They shoved it on their porridge, they made jam and marmalade with it. The French had a national drink already, which was wine. And they didn't eat much porridge. But they had lots of sugar. This was a very profitable place to be. Rather than use it in their domestic market, they proceeded to flog sugar around the world. At that time, it was almost as valuable as bullion.

Goods from the Caribbean (including vanilla, coffee and cotton) were worth nearly half of all France's exports. In those days, to own a sugar colony was tantamount to owning a bank printing money. Furthermore, it puts the trade-off of Canada for two or three sugar islands in perspective. Compared to sugar, the vast snowy terrain of Canada, with its huge lakes, ice-bound terrains, mountains and beautiful forests, was a financial unknown.

So what of Saint Pierre et Miquelon, those two tiny islands in the freezing North Atlantic? Thrown to the French as a sop by *les rosbifs* for giving up on the struggle for the mainland. Anyway, these two weren't always useless. When used for illegal alcoholic imports (during Prohibition), or when the cod fishing was booming, Saint Pierre et Miquelon more than paid their way. Now, however? Aldrich and Connell give it with both barrels: 'Barren and forlorn... places on which all the buildings and facilities had been destroyed or fallen into disrepair.' Well, ten years after these sentences were written, I'll admit I hadn't seen much disrepair. But 'barren and forlorn'? It does sort of sum it up.

I had read about Saint Pierre before, but I never really believed that the French, of all people, were capable of living in a place such as this. I turn my face and discover that I have been resting on a truly horrendous thing, a hard, knuckled affair whose original purpose, that of being a pillow, has been utterly defeated. The sweat of about five hundred visitors has caused its innards to congeal into filthy lumps.

Early the next day, after *petit déjeuner* – namely a greasy croissant and sliver of jam eaten in the main dining room beneath the Shipwreck Map and that sepulchral picture of Al Capone – we tackle Madame about the loo.

'*Le toilette est panne,*' I venture. She ignores my hopeless French and just shrugs her shoulders.

'*Bof.* Toilets break sometimes,' is her assessment of the situation. '*On n'a pas d'ouvrier pour le moment.*'

In other words, go forth and multiply; I don't give a flying French fig about your loo. One thing that has been transported effortlessly from *la Métropole* to this rock is classic French rudeness, I think, swerving back into a righteous Englander for just a tiny moment.

We walk through 'central' Saint Pierre, in other words the Place du General de Gaulle. Charles de Gaulle, who led the Free French during World War Two and subsequently became president, was an overt and energetic supporter of the notion that France should keep its colonial possessions, and visited many of them after 1945. Indeed, he is probably the only other person in history, alongside the Millard family, to do this voluntarily. Even Aldrich and Connell didn't tick off quite as many of the DOM-TOMs as we plan to do.

During the 1944 Brazzaville Conference, which was held to discuss what should happen to all of France's colonies after the war, de Gaulle established the following principle:

'The objectives of the civilising endeavours carried out by France in its colonies exclude any idea of autonomy… even the distant possibility of self-government in the colonies is to be excluded.'

Whereas Britain was gradually relinquishing control of its former colonies around the world, France was gripping on to them tightly. Why? Because of France's 'civilising endeavours'; or its 'mission to civilise'. In the view of the French, or at least, de Gaulle, this was reason enough to deny independence. It backfired completely. The larger French colonies which were kept on board, such as Algeria and Indochina, embarked on a violent struggle for independence in the following years. However, the older, smaller states, the so-called *'vieilles colonies'* which Napoleon once termed 'the confetti of empire', were not so confident about going it alone. They accepted departmental or territorial status and remained fundamentally linked to Paris (ten or eleven tiny enclaves – Polynesia, New Caledonia, La Réunion and a couple of other rocks in the Indian Ocean, two or three islands in the Caribbean, Guyane in South America and Saint Pierre et Miquelon), like a long, long string of onions encircling the globe. Actually, they are each so small, let's call them shallots.

Their new status decreed these places should be clasped even tighter to the bosom of Marianne, symbol of France. Their inhabitants would be French citizens; their official language French, currency French, education French, their legal system, social services, taxes and social services all French. And General de Gaulle visited them, presumably with a spring in his step, having ensured via this policy that not everywhere in the second half of the twentieth century was dancing to the same anglophone beat. Visiting Martinique in March 1964, he could not help himself. *'Mon Dieu, comme vous êtes français!'* (My God, how French you are!) he is said to have cried as he stepped off the plane in Fort de France, the appropriately named capital.

Three years later, in 1967, the presidential plane arrived here in Saint Pierre. It was one of the greatest days in the history of the tiny island.

With this in mind (well at least, in my mind), we all stride through the Place du General de Gaulle, where the bakery makes baguettes with official French flour and the post office sells the beautiful large Saint Pierre et Miquelon stamps beloved by philatelists across the world. In the middle there is a large war memorial, festooned with *tricolores*. It is inscribed with stirring words from General de Gaulle's famous wartime address, delivered on the radio in 1940 in London.

Liberating Saint Pierre from Vichy France via the efforts of a Free French gunboat was one of de Gaulle's first actions, although by doing so, he fatally damaged his relations with President Roosevelt. Roosevelt, apparently, took rather a dim view of the General orchestrating military action on his own behalf. The American secretary of state denounced such 'arbitary action', slightingly referring to the 'so-called Free French' hereafter.

'*Vive La France!*' the memorial triumphantly concludes.

'I think we should shoot this,' says Pip. He puts down the equipment bag and pulls out his camera, putting it on his shoulder in a professional manner. We have only practised with this camera once, a wholly unsuccessful event in our local park during which we managed, briefly, to lose the microphone. Now, 10,000 kilometres across the world, we are doing it for real, appropriately enough at a French national monument. It seems to go all right, although personally I could have done with a slightly bluer sky.

After shooting the monument in various styles, frames and sizes, we walk into the tourist office building.

'*Bonjour,*' says Pascal, who we hope is going to be our ally. Probably our only ally. ''Ow was your night?'

I look at Pip and whisper, 'Do you want to tell him, or shall I?'

Pip leans on Pascal's desk with masculine precision.

'It is dreadful. Pascal, Le Hotel Robert, *c'est terrible*. Cold. Dark. The *toilette est en panne*. We are trying to make a film here about Saint Pierre and we are staying in... *un bordel!*'

I'm glad I gave him that word.

There is silence in the tourist office.

'Mummeee,' whines Lucien. 'I'm bored.'

'Alors,' says Pascal after a few awkward minutes.

'My boss, Madame Florence, she 'as gone away. For a time. We will see about your hotel later. But now I have arranged some interviews for you.'

Oh, yes. Work. 'The mayor, Madame Claireaux, she will be expecting you right now. Then, you will see Annick Girardin, the deputy.'

These two are the most important politicians in Saint Pierre. He's done well.

'We can get the production going,' I say to Pip with excitement. 'This is going to be fantastic!'

We leave the office and trail back up the only main thoroughfare. The sun looks like a creamy disc, only vaguely apparent in the sky.

'Do you realise this fog is so famous it even has its own name?' I ask the children. They are not interested in the history of *'La Brume'* (that's the name); they are too hungry. We have each had just a single croissant for breakfast, after Campbell's Soup the night before.

'Why can't we EAT OUT, Mummy?' whines Honey.

'Because a meal will cost £250, *chérie*. And I don't think there are any decent restaurants here, anyway.' I respond.

'Correction,' says Pip acidly. 'There are no restaurants. Funny, that, since the French actually invented them. Hey ho, things have clearly changed since The General visited.'

At the top of the road, far up on a windswept, desolate and craggy moorland, are two vast television satellite dishes pointing east, towards Paris. I imagine this is so the Saint Pierrais can close their curtains, switch on the TV and watch local French reports on traffic jams in Lyons, or find out whether it's raining or not in Provence. Ah, Provence. Why did we not think about going there for the Travel Channel?

We continue up the hill. I look at Pip, who is grappling with his camera, tripod and bag. He's a compact, co-ordinated man. Yes, he likes cricket and winning at Scrabble, and in terms of male fashion, favours simple styles of knitwear (over scary confections with buttons and tassels). So far, so conventional. But he also loves cooking, parenting and risk-taking. He once grew a beard for a laugh. He is fundamentally decent, honest and loyal. He's also a good few degrees more patient than I am, so when he gets cross, there's usually a pretty good reason. And he's getting cross now. What was it he said about the children learning how to help us?

'Will you PLEASE carry something, Gabriel,' he yells.

'Oh, yeah,' says Gabriel unconvincingly. A giant jeep almost takes his nose off. 'Mind the TRAFFIC!' I yell. 'Remember that the cars are on the other side of the ROAD!'

Eventually we reach the mayoral residence.

On the wall there is a bust of Marianne, and a formal photograph of Nicolas Sarkozy. Dwarfed by the vast *tricolore* which hangs ceremonially beside him, he almost looks as if he is about to bodily wrap himself in the flag.

The mayor of Saint Pierre greets us. She is large and also swathed – not in *le tricolore*, but in a sort of fleecy wrap. Both Pip and I are very nervous; Madame le Mayor represents the first interview in the first of our documentaries.

It is at this juncture that I realise why the BBC travels the world making documentaries with a great team of technicians. After about forty minutes, Pip and I have finally managed to erect the tripod, a light and the camera. We then need to rig up Madame Claireaux for sound. This involves Madame taking nearly all of her voluminous woollen garments off and stripping down to her underwear, so our precious single radio microphone can be attached to her and the battery disguised in a swathe of material.

The children filter off into the lobby, where they are placated by a kindly secretary bearing Bonne Maman biscuits. Once Madame la Mayor is dressed again, we are at last ready to begin.

'Can you believe our plan is to do this *all the way around the world?*' I hiss to Pip.

In the course of the 20-minute interview, Madame le Mayor explains how she truly believes that her little island is a sort of meeting point between France and America, a sort of hand-shaking Gallic springboard for the anglophone world.

Saint Pierre, she tells the Travel Channel (i.e. me and Pip) is all about spreading the mystique that is La Belle France.

'We are, indeed, a bridge between Europe and America,' she says seriously.

'Really? But what about places like, er, New York? Surely New York, the famous melting pot of different races and backgrounds, is more of a bridge between Europe and America?' I stutter in my rubbish French. I'm not sure Madame le Mayor understands the phrase 'Le melting pot'. She shrugs. *'Mais ici, c'est la vraie France.'* Hmm.

At this point, Madame Claireaux decides to focus on things closer to home.

'Are you happy with your hotel, *non?*' she asks, beadily.

A strangled sound comes from behind the tripod.

We leave the mayor and troop off back down the hill to visit Annick Girardin, the deputy. Mademoiselle Girardin travels between Paris and Saint Pierre every fortnight, as if it is 100, not 10,000 km away.

She looks like a little elf, in velvet ankle boots, copious strings of pearls, a fitted white blouse, velvet cuffed shorts and a tank top. She is in a feisty mood. Her dad is the local baker here, and her family have been here for a couple of centuries. She can't envisage a life outside Saint Pierre, and she'll defend it to the hilt, even though she admits that subsidising these two lonely rocks costs the French government 8,000 euros per person, per year. That's a lot of euros; there are only 6,000 people on these rocks, but that makes a whopping bill. Approximately 46 million euros. Every year. Do you think Nicolas Sarkozy enjoys paying this amount of money, I ask her?

'The president and I are not from the same party. I am in the opposition. And I don't agree with his overseas politics. He is less attached to the DOM-TOMs than other presidents, all of them actually, since General de Gaulle. We often hear the phrase that we are like 'spoilt kids' waiting for a handout from Paris. People forget we gave a lot to France over the years. Today President Sarkozy has to understand that we have great advantages for France.'

'What might those be, Mademoiselle Girardin?'

I'm genuinely interested.

'Ah, *oui*, the possibility of oil, you know.' She's right; there is a rumour of oil fields deep under the Atlantic, close to Saint Pierre's territorial waters.

'We are not an expensive liability. But our *raison d'être* is to be French,' says Mlle Girardin stoutly. 'We want to be French, we want to stay French, we want to live in a French way in this archipelago. We defend the *tricolore*!' I fear that Mlle Girardin might start singing 'La Marseillaise' soon.

'We are the world's second maritime power.'

This status is something of which the French are spectacularly proud. If you add up all the watery zones around each of their tiny holdings across the world, France ends up having quite a lot of water. What is the actual advantage of this? More fundamentally, who is the world's first maritime power? Who knows? Yet, again and again we would be confronted with this fact.

'We are very proud of representing France in North America,' continues Mlle Girardin. 'I focus all my energy into defending our position and developing our economy here.'

Indeed, the diminutive Mlle Girardin is personally committed to insisting Saint Pierre et Miquelon get its old fishing areas back off Canada. Thanks to a pulverising deal struck by the exasperated Canadians in 1992, Saint Pierre lost about 85 per cent of its fishing grounds. Its once magnificent fishing fleet was replaced by a handful of tiny tubs, which now cruise around what the French fishermen derisively call *'une baguette'*; a tiny strip of water some 320 kilometres long and 19 kilometres wide.

Mlle Girardin is going to fight for the rights of Saint Pierre. It's not named after the patron saint of fishing for nothing. Tiny Saint Pierre et Miquelon, against the vast Canadian muscle. That's how Mlle Girardin, child of the archipelago, likes it.

'We are discussing it in Paris. France is negotiating a new file with Canada about obtaining a new economical area, near the continental shelf.'

But do they care about you back in Paris? Even if you strike oil?

'In French schools, they don't talk much about the DOM-TOMs. And even less about Saint Pierre et Miquelon,' says Mlle Girardin, suddenly downcast. The National Assembly seems rather far away. 'But we had our part, especially during the two world wars. And we hope to develop tourism,' she says, cheering up by the second. 'People can come here to get married! Saint Pierre is a small paradise with no pollution, no violence and no crime.'

She smiles at us, and twinkles around the giant desk to give us kisses on both cheeks. She loves Saint Pierre, that's for sure, and she loves representing it in *la Métropole*, where she hangs out every fortnight or so with other deputies of the DOM-TOMs who may have blown in from across the world. It is a lonely mission, to be sure, but a mission nonetheless.

We give our *mercis*, and depart, newly invigorated to discover the paradise that lies in Saint Pierre.

Yet the centre of town is strangely empty. I had hoped to pick up some filled baguettes from the Girardin bakery, but it is shut. So are all the other shops.

'Where is everyone?' asks Honey.

I look at my watch. It is one o'clock.

'Having lunch,' I say.

It is cold and misty. We walk past several carcasses of upturned, abandoned fishing vessels, and a signpost with wooden arrows pointing to all the other DOM-TOM capitals; Cayenne, the capital of French Guiana, Fort de France in Martinique and Nouméa in New Caledonia, which is something like 40,000 kilometres away. We are going to all of these places, I think nervously.

'Why don't you do a piece to camera about this?' asks Pip. 'Any thoughts?'

No, apart from the fact I can't envisage we really will get around the world like this. Suddenly, the whole enterprise seems too unwieldy, too unlikely and too unpromising. I doubt whether we can really pull it off. These, of course, are not views that I wish to share with the Travel Channel, let alone with my spouse and filming companion. So, focus on the moment.

'This is boring!' yells Lucien.

'I'm hungry!' echoes Honey.

'I'm freezing!' shouts Gabriel.

I could echo all of the above comments, and add a few more. I'm wet and cold, my hair is lank, I am exhausted with working out how to do the subjunctive, and I don't want to do a piece to camera.

Yet this is why we are here. So I have to.

'This,' I say, leaning into the wind, which hits my face like a wet salmon, 'is Saint Pierre's famous wooden signpost to the French world. I am here to learn...'

Viewers of the Travel Channel never do learn what I am here to learn, as at this point the tripod falls over.

We're running hopelessly late, so we abandon the signpost and continue to the FrancoForum, a damp showcase for the eternal glory of French culture. This is where the bourgeoisie from Nova Scotia come to learn how to speak perfect French.

The FrancoForum is a huge, shiny building with a vast atrium. When we arrive, the head teacher Joseph Busan and his sidekick Jean-Paul are just getting going with forty Canadian adolescents from Villanova Junior High, Nova Scotia.

We push open the doors to discover Monsieur Busan, who must be in his late fifties, in a smart suit and tie, jumping around on tiptoe, pointing in the air like John Travolta and loudly exhorting his students to sing a French nursery song with him. We stare at the goings-on, taking it all in.

'Well, this is quite exciting,' I say finally to my family.

Gabriel and Honey stare at him. They have never seen a middle-aged figure of authority like Monsieur Busan behave in such an extraordinary manner.

'*C'est le bâbord*,' yells Joseph Busan, to half of the class. (It's the port side.)

'*Qu'on chante, qu'on chante!*' (Who are singing, who are singing.)

'*C'est le bâbord, qui chante le plus fort.*' (It's the port side, who are singing the loudest.)

Jean-Paul then gets going with the other half, exhorting them to sing it his way.

'*C'est le tribord*,' he screams, '*qu'on chante, qu'on chante!*'

And so on and so forth, with each teacher exhorting his side to be the *bâbord* (port) or *tribord* (starboard) of the song.

Jean-Paul hits upon the notion of going up the stairs in the atrium and shouting down to his minions from the balcony.

The pupils are very excited, yelling and waving back to him.

Our children stand quietly with their backs to the wall, watching the sight of about forty Canadians yelling their heads off. Pip films the entire scene, and then turns the camera on his singularly unimpressed children.

'Will you say *bonjour*?' I ask Lucien, hopefully.

'No! HATE FRENCH!' he yells.

After the song climaxes with Jean-Paul almost self-immolating with excitement on the roof, everyone calms down and starts their next duty, namely filling out questionnaires about their experiences. I take the opportunity to chat to a couple of Villanova students about whether they have enjoyed their trip to Saint Pierre.

'Well, how did you get on?' I ask one girl.

'Good.'

'Is it what you expected?'

'Nope.'

'What did you expect?'

'I didn't think everyone would be so French.'

'Has it improved your French, then?'

'Nope.'

I decide to abandon the interview.

'We offer a real service 'ere,' says Joseph Busan afterwards. 'Canadian children can come 'ere and see that real French life goes on. And it's much easier than going all the way to Paris, *non*?' Hmm.

Except that Paris is Paris, and Saint Pierre is Saint Pierre.

After the FrancoForum experience, we pick up some baguettes, only the filled ones have all gone, because they are only made for lunch. And the croissants are only made for breakfast. So we get some cakes from the Giardin bakery, which are warm and iced and utterly delicious. After this repast, we go for a swim in the lovely warm public swimming baths. We seem to be the only people in the entire establishment.

'This is how I imagine people in Soviet Russia might have felt,' muses Pip. 'You know, giant state-funded institutions and not much official work going on.'

I nod to him, holding Lucien up under his arms.

'Kick! Kick!' I say encouragingly.

'I mean, we are the only people in this entire pool, probably in the entire sports centre. It's extraordinary. Bet it's not like this over the water in Newfoundland.'

'Race you, Daddy,' shouts Honey. They all swim off, Honey almost totally submerged in her excitement and anxiety to get to the other side first.

After drying and changing in spectacularly luxurious changing rooms with boiling hot showers, we walk back to the hotel.

'Can I have a go with the camera?' says Gabriel.

'No, no, you'll only break it,' says Pip loudly.

'Well, can I do some presenting then?'

Oh, go on.

'Welcome to Saint Pierre,' says Gabriel, sauntering towards the camera, hand casually jammed in his jeans pocket. 'It's practically deserted here,' he says, gesturing to the pier and the choppy water. 'It's pretty expensive too because they don't grow stuff themselves here and have to import it all from France. And everyone is highly overpaid.' Whoops. 'And the hotel is OK-ish.'

'OK, cut.'

The hotel is absolutely not OK-ish. When we return, walking gingerly past the washing line to our room, we discover the toilette is still very much *en panne*.

Mildewed turds float in the bowl.

'Yuk! Eeeeggh!' shouts Gabriel, shooting out of the bathroom.

'Aaaagh!' choruses Honey. 'I am NOT going in there, no way never.'

'Can I see?!' shouts Lucien, whose fascination with bodily products has not diminished over the Atlantic. 'I wanna see!'

'Right,' says Pip. We all leave the room and march off back to the tourist office, which is clearly becoming something of a comfort blanket to us.

In the office a DVD of *Ice Age 3* has miraculously appeared. The children sit down and watch it, lapping it up with the enthusiasm with which Victorian urchins might have faced a bowl of stew.

The head of the tourist board, Madame Florence, has just returned from a trip to Bordeaux. Madame Florence is blonde and doe-eyed and clad in a beautiful woollen dress which I warrant did not come from a shop in Saint Pierre, but somewhere on the Boulevard Saint Michel in Paris.

'*Chère* Madame,' begins Pip to Madame Florence. This is it. The big speech. 'Our project is a prestigious and informative one. We are paying for accommodation which is expensive, dirty, cramped and frankly sub-standard.'

Mme Florence opens her eyes very wide and beckons us into her private office.

'*Eh, bien*. You will have a new hotel in the morning,' says Madame Florence. 'And today, I have prepared a trip for you to L'Île aux Marins.'

Well, that's unexpected.

'I understand your feelings,' says Madame Florence mournfully. Even more unexpected. 'I am, I am from Provence.' She shrugs simply, gazing out at the rolling fog. It's time to leave, before Madame Florence gets any more doleful.

'Come on, children,' I say brightly to my three offspring.

'We're off to, er, a little island. It'll be fun!'

Eventually, Pip and I succeed in hauling them away from *Ice Age*, out of the tourist office and down to the dock, where we clamber aboard a small ferry bound for L'Île aux Marins, or Sailors' Island. This is where the entire population of Saint Pierre used to live some 200 years ago.

We chug out of the harbour of Saint Pierre. The ocean is choppy. The boat bounces along determinedly to L'Île aux Marins, which looms up ominously in front of us through banks of cloud. It's not raining but the air is so wet our faces are damp and our hair sticks down on our foreheads.

We arrive, clamber out of the ferry and start to walk down a short, stone pier which leads to a couple of houses.

'There is no electricity here, and no running water,' says our guide. 'But people love to come here in the summer months.'

'Why?' asks Gabriel.

'Because they like to get away from busy life in Saint Pierre, I think.'

This silences him.

'Makes the Hotel Robert look positively baronial,' mutters Pip as we stand in the biting wind and look across the island silently at one of the tiny clapboard turquoise houses.

Beyond the wooden houses is a small stone church, with a squat steeple. Several graves in the graveyard are decorated with small shields of *bleu, blanc, rouge*. These *tricolores* pay homage to locals who died on the Western Front in World War One. We push open the heavy oak door of the church, which immediately slams shut behind us with a wild gust of wind.

Apparently the entire population of Saint Pierre comes here once a year for a Thanksgiving ceremony. Beyond that, the church is usually empty.

About ten minutes' walk towards the wild rocky shore there is a giant, rusting carcass of a vast cargo ship, the *Transpacific*, which foundered here about thirty years ago. Marooned on the huge boulders, surrounded by slippery seaweed, it seems to exist now almost as a symbol of the hazards surrounding this tiny outcrop of humanity.

Actually, the *Transpacific*'s calamity was not too tragic. It came to grief on the island without any loss of life. Furthermore, it was full of brand-new, ride-on lawnmowers and jukeboxes, most of which ended up the next week in the houses on Saint Pierre.

'Er, would you mind taking the children off?' I ask the guide. 'We need to do a bit of filming.'

We have made the somewhat obvious discovery that children and television-making are hopelessly incompatible. Every time Pip turns the camera on and I begin to wield the microphone, the children start shouting 'This is boring, boring, boring.' And we are just two days in.

'They don't even know what boring MEANS,' I say to Pip. Then I turn on the children. 'You lot, you are so lucky to be brought here!'

At this point I focus on what I am saying, and look around. Small huts battened down against the ferocious wind. White-topped waves coming off the ocean. Fishermen chugging off across the sea to find diminished stocks of cod. Fog everywhere. We are all in dirty clothes because I can't wash anything, and I can't wash anything because I can't dry anything.

'The children probably find it hard to see how lucky they are,' I admit to Pip as the guide trudges off with them to visit a nineteenth-century schoolroom whose star exhibit is an entire dinner service from the *Titanic* (it sank quite near here). They battle away behind her, tiny figures in their bright John Lewis cagoules, bent double into the relentless wind.

Pip is fighting to put the tripod up in what appears to be nearing a gale force wind. 'But we are lucky, aren't we?' I shout over to him. 'Imagine, we could be in London right now!'

He gives me a steady look. Actually, I would give anything to be in London right now. Even if I was doing something horrendously dull, like getting a parking ticket or standing in an endless queue at The Carphone Warehouse.

'I want to go home. I'm sorry, but I do,' I murmur.

'Just do the piece to camera, could you?'

That night we settle down to a supper of bread and soup. Even though L'Île aux Marins has given us a chill which is bone-marrow deep, there is contentment in the hot bowls. Our shared privation means everyone has stopped arguing. It has even dawned on my bickering children that the one thing we must do in this cold, foggy outpost is pull together.

After supper we play a French CD with basic words on, and follow it with a series of little French booklets that I have brought from England. Then we have a quick blast of singing 'C'est le bâbord!' which makes us all laugh, even Lucien.

At this point I express a secretly held ambition that I might send one, or possibly all, of them to the French Lycée in London.

'You are sad, Mummy,' says Honey.

CHAPTER THREE

A Slightly Bigger, Emptier Rock in the Atlantic

Honey's diary: *We woke up and strate away we got dressed! Because we were going on a ferry and we didn't want to miss it. I ran ahead and got two panners chocolas. And one cruisso. Then we walked to the ferry and hoped on. Then a nice lady picked us up and we put our lagage in the back of the car and the hotel was really nice.*

If you thought Saint Pierre was bleak and unforgiving, try a sojourn in Miquelon, population 300.

Miquelon is separated from Saint Pierre by a treacherous 6-kilometre strait, known locally by fishermen as 'The Mouth of Hell'. I'm not making this up.

It's like its sister island, only more so. The shops are in people's garages. There are no cafes. There are no trees. There is no nightlife, cinema or arts centre. Saint Pierre, with its arts centre, showing a programme of exclusively French films and music, is positively bohemian compared to Miquelon. We have been told this by a Canadian film crew we chanced upon during one of our meagre Hotel Robert breakfasts. When we told them we were off to Miquelon, they rolled their eyes meaningfully and laughed ominously.

These are of course not facts we will reveal to the children. *Pas devant les enfants*, as far as the supposedly grim nature of Miquelon is concerned. Onwards and upwards is the spirit of the Enterprise Millard.

'We are off to another hotel, guys!' I say, as we pack up the folding bed and I give Gabriel the large, clunky cutlery on which a shine has long been absent. 'Take these back to the hotel kitchen,' I command.

I pile up the four chipped plates and two mugs which have been our dining ware for the last five days, and stack them neatly under the sink. To this I add our battery of cooking utensils; the single wooden spoon and two saucepans. I think of my flash German kitchen in London, with its big stone-topped island, my Le Creuset casseroles, perfect cutlery, and fashionable crockery. I think about my kitchen quite dispassionately, though; I'm not remotely homesick for it. Now that we are packing up and going somewhere else, I'm excited again. Anyway, something about the process of packing all my possessions up into cases has taken away any sense of emotional ownership. I don't really understand how this has happened, but it has.

I take down my personal washing line from the bathroom and fold up all the dry, clean clothes from it. Then I scout underneath the beds, trying not to notice the volumes of dry, grey dust that lie there like a forbidding snowdrift. I put any dirty clothes into a little red drawstring receptacle, which in another life was a sports bag from Hanover Primary School. This bag is a very comforting thing. Practical, light, always able to take a little more without complaining, it is fast becoming my favourite travel companion.

We close the little door and step into the asphalt courtyard.

Astonishingly, the wet fog has lifted. The sky is as blue as a delphinium and there is no wind. Honey runs ahead to get our breakfast, which I tell Madame we must eat out of napkins, while hurrying for the ferry. Alas, we cannot stay to enjoy them in the Al Capone dining room.

I pop into the main reception to pay the bill. To the end, Madame has been a sniping misery, counting out greasy croissants with her gnarled fingers and making sure nobody had extra helpings of jam. She sniffs at me as she pushes a bill for nearly a thousand euros across the counter.

Never mind, we are off and almost running across the square and lining up to get onto the spanking new ferry. Like its new airport, the white, shiny catamaran was a present to Saint Pierre, a bone tossed by Paris to keep the islanders happy.

Madame Florence is out on the quayside to wave us goodbye. All coiffure and décolletage, she bids us a mournful bon voyage, sighing in a sort of Chekhovian manner about when she will see Provence again.

On the way to Miquelon and the Mouth of Hell we go past a large, low, green landmass. This, we learn, is Newfoundland, some 11 kilometres off.

'Hello,' says Gabriel to the camera. 'It's me again. We are leaving Saint Pierre at quite some speed, actually. And this large island over here is Newfoundland.'

Our guide is a white-bearded Frenchman called Roger Etchberry, who is a nature expert and speaks perfect English with a hilarious Canadian twang. A devotee of amateur dramatics, he has been in several plays by Noël Coward.

'He looks like one of the seven dwarves,' murmurs Pip. 'I wonder whether he'll tell us the grotesque secret behind life in Saint Pierre et Miquelon.'

'Is there one?' I ask him.

'Of course. There must be. It's far too like *The Wicker Man*,' he says, referring to the cult British horror movie set on a spooky Scottish island far from the mainland. 'Roger would make a feasible Christopher Lee,' he whispers, 'Madame Florence would be Britt Ekland, banging on the walls of the tourist office.' He pauses ominously. 'Our own roles, my sweet, are obvious.'

I giggle, envisaging myself as one of the twisted islanders – and him, of course, as the upstanding detective played by Edward Woodward. He has a point.

'Tell me, Roger,' I ask, 'who lives in Newfoundland these days?'

'Gee, nobody,' twangs Roger. 'At least, nobody *these days*. Since the cod ran out there was no work for the Newfies, the people from Newfoundland. The bottom fell out of the property market and there were no jobs. So they've all gone back to the mainland.'

Some even took their whole house with them, carting it away on a truck for a brighter future elsewhere in Nova Scotia, leaving Newfoundland full of ghost towns peppering an empty landscape.

Of course, the same could have happened to Saint Pierre. Economically speaking, it would have been cheaper for the French state to have paid for every single resident of Saint Pierre et Miquelon to up sticks and move to Quebec. But France, it seems, is more sentimental than Canada and is determined to prop up its sole holding in North America for as much, and as long, as it takes.

This is why the French cruise around Saint Pierre in shiny 4x4 jeeps, while over the water, Newfoundland seems devoid of life. We sail past its empty shoreline, a jovial crowd of people in fashionable knitwear drinking black coffee, reading *Le Monde* and indulging in *bavardage*, chatter. Under their chunky sweaters I bet all the men are wearing Petit Bateau underwear and the women Huit lingerie.

Roger excitedly breaks off my reverie, grabbing my arm, binoculars at the ready.

'*Les baleines*! Humpback whales!' he calls.

There is a small commotion in the ferry as everyone scurries to the windows to watch the massive, sleek backs of two whales that seem to be following our boat.

'Honestly, we could be just off the coast of La Rochelle,' I say dreamily to Pip. 'Only we are just down from the Labrador Sea! Isn't it magical?!'

He is ignoring me. Seconds later I realise why.

Gabriel has just vomited on the floor, bringing a new meaning to the Mouth of Hell.

'Eeeeugh, urgh, urgh,' shouts Honey.

'That is quite unecessary, Honey,' I hiss. 'Be quiet. Go and look at the whales while I clear this up, and go and sit with Roger. He might let you play with his binoculars.'

'Binoculars!' shouts Lucien, charging over to Roger who looks absolutely horrified that his precious Nikon 10x32 HGs might be subject to the attentions of a four-year-old.

After a rather messy few minutes, we reassemble in some sort of order, just before the boat cruises imperiously into the tiny harbour of Miquelon, where a couple of dozen houses cling onto a long, thin finger of land. It's foggy, of course. We can just discern a clutch of people standing on the jetty excitedly saluting our arrival. According to Roger, there are more seals on Miquelon than there are people.

The curving bay is the island's only hospitable harbour. It resembles the famous Croisette in Cannes – in shape only. It has a grey shingle beach. The green mountains on either side of the bay are without trees. The place is wind-whipped and exudes a nature of dogged survival, rather than an Arcadian getaway. This latter, however, is what Roger would have us believe it is.

'Oh, plenty of people from Saint Pierre come here for holidays,' insists Roger. 'They have country homes on Langlade, which is connected to Miquelon by an isthsmus. But on Langlade there is no electricity or running water. Everyone camps there.'

Why is it called Langlade?

'I think it is a corruption of L'Île à l'Anglais, you know,' says Roger. 'Englishman's Island. Maybe a whole colony of English came there about two hundred years ago. That might be why it's so desolate and unluxurious now, ha ha ha.' Indeed, the sole inhabitant of Langlade, Charles Lafitte, died in July 2006.

'I feel like we've had our camping experience already, in the Hotel Robert,' I mutter to Pip. 'I'm looking forward to experiencing a hot bath and a working loo. Let alone some proper food.'

I smile politely at Roger. The children strap on their allotted backpacks and line up beside the starboard exit. Gabriel, white-faced but perky, is in a completely new outfit. Everything he was wearing prior to the travel sickness episode has been crammed into the Hanover Primary School sports bag. I tell you, it's a godsend.

'Allons-y,' cries Roger, stepping jauntily off the boat. 'Here is Patricia!'

A large woman standing beside a jeep greets us with a shy smile. This is Patricia, manager of Miquelon's only hotel. She is in her mid thirties, with long hair scraped back into a bunch.

She was born and bred on Saint Pierre, and made the journey over to Miquelon with her husband when the hotel job came up. She seems quite excited to greet us, and makes this clear by clasping us individually to her not insubstantial bosom.

We all pile our stuff into the back, and jump in. Minutes later we are driving past a row of clapboard wooden houses with steep roofs, all painted in bright colours. There is only one row of houses in the town, which snakes along past the bay like a bright ribbon. There is a distinct feeling of frontier country in Miquelon. We could almost be in a covered wagon rather than a canvas-covered jeep. We shoot past a couple of people jogging down the road. Apparently long-distance running is big on Miquelon.

'Because it's all they have to do here,' murmurs my husband.

'Will you SHUT UP!' I hiss.

'There's a big race every summer,' adds Roger, blandly. 'Le Miquelon Vingt-Cinq. Actually, it's on next weekend.'

'That's a shame as we'll be in Martinique by then,' says Pip briskly. Wow. Martinique. With palm trees and sunshine. I can't comprehend such a thing.

I almost don't quite believe we will ever get away.

'Maybe Miquelon's charm is that of a remote Scottish island,' I cheerily say to the camera. 'Which makes it either gloriously empty or morbidly quiet, depending on your viewpoint.'

We arrive at the hotel. It's more of a pub with a clutch of tiny rooms scattered in a horseshoe shape around a blasted field. At the end of the field, there is a dog kennel, and a dog. It leaps, barking, at the end of a long, thin chain.

'Everyone has dogs here,' explains Roger, who was born on Miquelon. 'They go hunting with them on Langlade in the fall.'

All other times, the dogs are kept chained up, it seems.

An array of dried-up dog turds scattered pathetically around the kennel testify to the fact that it is never walked. *'Bien,'* says Patricia, looking at us with not unfriendly fascination, once we have dumped our bags and are recovering from the journey with coffee in the bar. The children are greedily drinking chocolate Nesquik, and beaming. It would seem we are the only guests. French television blares from a screen on the wall, informing us that it is sunny in Bordeaux. This place is crazy.

'Would you like your children to go to school?' asks Patricia.

'What, now?'

She nods her head, clearly rather pleased that her initiative has paid off.

I smile at Pip as if to say 'You see, our children are having an Extraordinary Experience.'

There is a honk from the road outside, and a bright yellow bus pulls up. A kindly looking man gets out. This is Jean-Louis Gazel, the schoolmaster of L'École Les Quatre-Temps, the local primary.

'Alors,' says M Gazel as he enters the pub. 'I can have your children, *non*?'

'Right, you two,' I say to Gabriel and Honey. 'You are going to school today.'

They are much too startled to say anything as they put down their mugs of chocolate and trot off after M Gazel with a sort of shocked obedience.

The bus roars away. 'Where, er, where is the school?' I ask Patricia. About a hundred yards away, it seems. And there is a total of thirty-two pupils. In the entire school.

'What sort of things do they learn at school?' I ask Patricia, thinking perhaps that an island so close to Canada must somehow take a bit of North American influence in there somewhere. In this, I am entirely wrong. Patricia informs me with pleasure that all lessons follow the state French curriculum, including of course the first lesson, obligatory in all French schools, which kicks off with the questionable but iconic phrase *'nos ancêtres les Gaulois'*.

'Nos ancêtres les Gaulois' is such a famous statement that there is even a restaurant named after it in Paris. In NALG, Paris, you pay 30 euros to get hunks of meat, cheese and bread on wooden trenchers, which you then wash down with goblets of red wine. I once went there with my sister. After a stomach-busting meal we were followed into the Ladies by a Frenchman who had clearly taken the title of the restaurant as a personal challenge, and who was hell-bent on removing our garments, possibly to propagate the *'ancêtres'* of the future.

I remember him yelling 'I love you!', with the qualification 'I am French!', while hammering on the door of the toilet. We crouched inside, giggling helplessly. My sister left Paris the next morning, her wildest imaginings about the immoral French reconfirmed forever.

Not that there's much immorality going on in Miquelon. Patricia wanders around the bar, picking up cutlery and polishing it. She took over the hotel a year ago after leaving Saint Pierre, where she has lived all her life.

Eventually, we trail off to our room where I exhume the fetid contents of the Hanover Primary bag and wash them in the basin. Then I sit down and write a caustic blog about how grim Saint Pierre is. I will later discover this was a silly thing to do. They may be isolated here in the Atlantic but the Saint Pierrais are certainly not technologically backward.

Of course, I don't think about this. I'm still being a bit loftily concerned with the business of ensuring our trip goes As Planned. Certainly, our first documentary is not going as I had expected. We are not being fussed over, or made to feel important. We are treated as we come across – an English family with dirty children who only cheer up when they are watching American movies. Equally, Pip and I cannot possibly resemble a top-class media outfit. I'm still wearing the clothes I arrived in. My hair is matted. My teeth are dirty. I'm starving. I hated Saint Pierre with a visceral venom largely because I was disappointed in it. It was cold and wet, and nobody was expecting us. This is obviously not the fault of Saint Pierre, but I take it out in the blog. How very foolish of me. Yet there is no time to consider my actions, since I'm disturbed by a knock. It's Patricia, shyly smiling around the door.

'Shall we go?' she says. 'This is an important week in Miquelon. I want to show you the dried fish.'

We gather all our stuff and walk off up the road after her, me, Pip and Lucien. The sun, amazingly enough, is shining. There are white crests on the ocean and the wind is fresh. It's a bit like wandering around a Scottish moor on a lovely summer's morning.

In the drive, Roger Etchberry waves au revoir to us. 'I'm off to inspect a colony of sphinx moths,' he announces.

'Welcome to the Natural History Unit,' mutters Pip.

'Don't be disrespectful,' I say. 'Roger seems very knowledgable and at least his English is brilliant.' Yes, Roger is a rather capable English speaker, thanks to the fact that, as he revealed to us, he once had a Canadian mistress.

Roger's love life is proving more valuable than we had previously thought. It is fantastic to be able to speak my natal tongue with one of our interviewees. My head aches with trying to speak French all day. I'm great when I have to say things such as 'I am fascinated in the history of the *départements d'outre-mer*' because that is part of my official script, which I have learned by rote. But the unofficial stuff is so difficult.

Things like 'Please will you mend this loo', or 'I am so terribly sorry but my son has a gastric problem' reduce me to pre-GCSE level flailing in French, or DE (Desperate English), which I feel is rude. I hate to admit this, but Roger, with his English, is something of a lifebelt to me in the vast, formal ocean of *la francophonie*.

Pip, Lucien, Patricia and I pass by a large industrial unit with a metal roller blind pulled up. Patricia gestures to it. '*La boulangerie*. This is where the bread is baked and distributed. Opposite it,' Patricia gestures again, '*Notre église*.' We inspect a small, simple white church, outside of which there is a flagpole bearing *le tricolore* and the war memorial. Bread, Church and Nationalism; it's a triumvirate we will find propagated in various versions across the Gallic world.

'*La Commune de Miquelon à ses Enfants Morts Pour La Patrie 1914–1918*,' proclaims the grey obelisk, which is adorned with fresh flowers. There are five names engraved on it. One is for Georges Louis Girardin, who must be the great-great uncle, or great-grandfather of Annick, the deputy.

We carry on walking through the main, indeed, the only village on Miquelon. Patricia suddenly leads us down a little alley past one of the coloured houses, where she brings us out into a garden on which has been erected a series of long, low wooden frames covered with mesh. These mesh frames are about 6-foot square and are supported by trestle tables. Small, grey glittering things lie on the mesh in neatly serried ranks.

'*Eh, du capelin*,' says Patricia, and rushes up to them with almost the same fervour as a woman in London or Paris might rush up to a table of shoes at a Chanel sale.

We are looking at literally thousands of tiny dried silvery fish. Women keep on arriving and selecting vast quantities of them, which they count out and clasp in their fists in groups of thirteen. Why thirteen is unclear. Something to do with French rugby? Something religious? Who knows. Every so often an elderly man takes a newly emptied mesh frame and moves it over to the open boot of a car, where he takes more fish out of a bucket and lines them up carefully on its horizontal surface. Then he returns the filled frame to the trestle table.

This scene has been going on for years on Miquelon; I have a book featuring vintage black and white photographs taken by a Docteur Louis Thomas in 1914 showing the capelin being dried on the same style frames and picked over by locals in exactly the same way. The only difference between the two scenes is that the women in the photos are wearing long skirts and bonnets. In all other ways, the passage of time has been frozen.

Lucien is fascinated by this. He stands by the fish, counting them, touching them gently and feeling their dry, shiny scales. The fish have been lined up head to tail in perfect order by the elderly man.

'Where do all these fish come from?' I ask Patricia.

'They come up nearly onto the beach. And we collect them,' she tells me. It is all rather biblical, the miraculous draught of fishes, and happens every June on Miquelon. After the high tide you simply walk down onto the shingle shores and pick up hundreds of little fish in specially designed triangular nets. The fish simply ask to be taken away, flopping in the foam. Then you put them on a mesh frame and dry them. The capelin harvest is probably the nearest Miquelon comes to a seasonal attraction. It's certainly part of the heritage of the island.

Patricia pays for five bags of thirteen little fish, and turns to me formally, as if to announce the next chapter of our time on Miquelon. She's sorted out our two elder children, she's got her fish and now she's going to help us with our programme. I'm so grateful.

'We will now go to Le Ferme d'Ouest,' says Patricia.

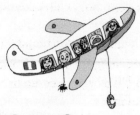

CHAPTER FOUR

Pâté de Foie Gras

Honey's diary: Me and Daddy went out to the beach and threw stone's in the water. And then we went inside and Gabriel went on Daddy's computer and I did my dirry. And Daddy just lad around.

Le Ferme d'Ouest lies down a long, long road which starts opposite the Maxotel. It appears to be the only fully working business on Miquelon, bar capelin selling and the tiny bakery. I know its name sounds like something out of the Laura Ingalls Wilder American classic *Little House on the Prarie*, but instead of the heroic Pa, with his mustang pair and long beard, here is Thierry Gautier, a charming thirty-something in a Paris Saint Germain baseball hat and shorts.

Thierry used to be an accountant on Saint Pierre before deciding to devote his life to upholding the French tradition of duck farming.

Thierry's farm consists of a white factory and a huge field fenced off with chicken wire. In this field roam five large alpacas, and around their legs waddle about five hundred lovely fat white ducks. We may be within spitting distance of the Land of the Free, but this is the Land of the Force-fed.

After customary cheek-kissing, and that interesting moment when a French person senses a) deep relief you are going to speak their own language to them, followed by b) urgent alarm that your French is rather rubbish, Thierry and I take a wander around the farm.

Pip is filming the goings-on. Lucien has been allowed to go into the field and is walking around Jemima Puddle-Duck and her friends that have just ten days left on this earth. These ducks have been fed in the French way, in other words they have been through the dubious system of *'le gavage'*, where food is put into metal funnels inserted into the beak of the duck. After this, they are now to be killed in the French way, after which they will be eaten in the French way. In France.

'Yes, they are all doomed,' says Thierry philosophically.

Which is maybe just as well, I think.

'Bien, on fait le gavage ici, n'est-ce pas?' I ask Thierry, which is really quite polite although M Gautier and I know full well it means 'Admit it, you heartless Gallic farmer, you do that horrendous thing which the rest of the Western world has long since abolished, namely force-feeding your ducks, *non?*'

'Ah, oui,' responds Thierry, whose farm churns out thousands of pots of foie gras and *rillettes de canard* every year. He confirms that most of it is flogged back to *la Métropole*. Yes. The French, who produce it on an industrial scale, pay to have the Miquelon variety shipped 10,000 kilometres to their tables. Apparently having a pot of foie gras de Miquelon at your dinner party gives you a certain cachet.

'There is someone who comes from the Dordogne every year to check we do it properly and observe the rules,' says Thierry, who was paid by the French government to abandon his accountancy practice and retrain as a farmer.

'I went to France to learn how to do it properly. Then I came back here and the government helped me build this farm.'

'Do you get the ducks from the French mainland, too?'

'*Non, non.* We get them as little ducklings from Canada.' (Clearly it's life on the Ferme d'Ouest which gives them their Gallic taste.That, and the traditional herbs used.)

The ducks amble around Lucien in the field. They make little quacking noises as they dip their beaks into the drops of water coming from a dripping tap. They seem to be very docile, probably because they are very fat. Lucien is very happy, playing quietly with them. He makes little clicking noises to them, as he walks around them and they walk around him. It's probably the first time on our trip that he's been away from airports, suitcases, collapsing beds and his parents urging him to hurry up because they have to go and speak an unintelligible language while interviewing a politician. No wonder he seems content.

Thierry looks fondly at his ducks. What about the alpacas, then? 'Oh, I get them sheared,' he explains readily. 'The wool goes to France and is knitted. Then it comes back here and we make it into alpaca hats. Then we sell them online back to people in France.'

'You must be joking!'

Of course, Frenchmen never joke. '*Mais non,*' shrugs Thierry. 'This is how we make things work here.'

There is an awkward silence, filled by Lucien. Although he was born in central London, under the shadow of the BT Tower, he has something of a fixation about farms.

'Does this man have a real farm with a farmhouse, Mummeee?' he queries.

'Sure, we have a real farmhouse,' smiles Thierry. 'And I have a field beside the farmhouse, with sheep. You will come over and see it sometime? You will come to see us in our country house on the isthmus near Langlade, *non*?'

He goes into a back-room of the industrial building, and reappears with two lobsters, which he insists we accept as a gift. Then he sends us on our way.

When we get back we give the lobsters to Patricia, who tells us she will cook them for us tonight.

'*Merci Patricia, merci,*' I say. She really is a kind woman.

Honey and Gabriel are waiting for us in the bar, drinking mugs of Nesquik.

'How was school, guys?' I ask them.

'OK,' they chorus.

'Did you do *"Nos ancêtres les Gaulois"*?'

'No.'

'What, then?'

'Mr Gazel got a big globe out and showed the class where London is,' says Gabriel. 'Then he spent ages showing us where all the DOM-TOMs around the world are,' chimes Honey.

'Did you tell him you were going to visit them all?'

'Yes.'

'What did he say?'

'He laughed,' says Gabriel. 'Why?'

That makes me laugh.

Former adversaries in the middle of the family, Honey and Gabriel, the two 'inner' children, have formed a close alliance since we left London. Without their friends, their school, their older sister or any of the formal structure to their lives, they have developed a symbiotic relationship with one another. I think it's a sort of survival technique.

Now we are are faced with amusing ourselves for what feels like several hours. I'm prepared, however. If you are envisaging a journey to somewhere like Miquelon – or, frankly, any long-haul journey – with young children, you need the following things:

Cheap notepads and Biros – Cost almost nothing, come in batches of three and provide hours of disposable fun. Hangman, Boxes, Battleships and Consequences come into their own at these moments.

Zoos – I draw the residents of an entire zoo, one animal per page. Then I draw food. The children spend hours, literally hours, feeding one page to another page.

Blanket – Gabriel has brought his baby comforter, a yellow aerated blanket from London with him. It is invaluable. It doubles up as a towel and is perfect for making dens.

Books – Each child has only five. All paperback.

But what about another section: **Gadgets (Nintendo DS and the like)?** No way. My view on battery-run gadgets and long haul is to leave them at home. They will only run out of power, having caused horrendous arguments and a couple of punch-ups between your kids, or you and your kids. Or you and your partner. They also have the subsidary effect of making other travellers hate you, because they tend to wreck the journeys of anyone near you, as well. I speak here as the wretched parent who has had to watch her offspring fight and bicker over a Nintendo DS. Eventually I was so fed up I gave the device to Cancer Research.

After the children have played with their paper animals and fed them paper food in the den, it's time for lobster. Which is good, because by then I am longing for a glass of red wine. It's not that I'm a compulsive boozer. It's just that after a day of washing unspeakable clothes in a tiny basin, trying to speak French, working out what to film and filming it, red wine looks like not just a great idea, but the only idea.

The Miquelon way of cooking lobster is not quite our way. They basically bung it on the barbeque until it's black, then tear it apart. Oh, well. When in Rome, etc. We take over a table in the hotel restaurant. We are still the only guests. The television is still letting us know about the travel problems in Lyons, where there appears to be a broken-down traffic light. The lobster is good, in a rather intrepid way. At least, Pip and I think so. The children pick about at it. Outside, the dog wags its tail, hoping someone is going to release it. (We stay in Miquelon for three days, during which time I never once saw that dog off its lead.)

The next day we are all quite hungry. We creep out of our lodgings in the early morning and walk along the main road to find anything resembling a grocer's. Eventually we discover a house which has a basement doubling up as a shop, and invest in a large carton of Rice Krispies and some milk from Normandy. We return to the hotel and pour the cereal into the only available containers in our room, namely a couple of mugs. The children gulp it down, sitting in their den.

At 11 a.m. Roger arrives and takes us all in his jeep to visit Thierry on the isthmus. It feels as if we are going to pay a call on an old friend, such is the intense experience of being on an island with a population of 300. We pile into the jeep and drive along the bumpy road. At a certain point, we can see the isthmus stretching out before us, and Langlade a grey-green mountainous region behind. There are beautiful curves of shingled beach, and the ocean is blue.

On one curve of the road, Roger suddenly stops the jeep.

'Look out there,' he says in his funny Canadian drawl. And there we see it. A giant, speckled leopard seal, basking on the rock. What a magical sight.

'Can't see, can't see,' yells Lucien.

Roger patiently hands over his binoculars. He's clearly decided that we are all right.

'Close one eye and look through the other.'

'It's all gone black! Can't see, can't see!'

'Keep closing one eye. Point the binoculars up a bit. Do you have the rock?'

'Yes.'

'Go to the left.'

'What's left?'

'Towards your mama. See him?'

'No. Oh, oh! Yes! Yes!'

'Can I see, can I see?' yells Honey, realising she's missing out on a better option.

'We have to get on,' I murmur.

'Why?' says Roger, handing Honey a spare pair of binoculars that he happens to have in his knapsack. Although he has no children, he has a calming effect on them, possibly because he shares their sense of awe with regard to nature. The other possibility is because when they get too noisy for him, he simply shouts at them to 'SHURRUP!', which has a spectacularly instantaneous quelling effect.

'Thierry will be in his farm all day. There's nothing else here on Miquelon. Now, have you got the rock in view?'

In the end we spend about an hour looking at the seal, lying fatly on the rock, oblivious to us, with the ocean lapping below and the birds flying above.

Thierry, his wife and their sheepdog are at the door of his farmhouse, ready to greet us. Thierry's farm sits on the grassy finger of the isthmus between Miquelon and Langlade. Here he keeps sheep, hardy and hairy and used to being beaten up by the never-ending Atlantic wind. In their cosy farmhouse, which is constructed on stilts, Madame Gautier serves coffee and biscuits, while the children pat the dog. The dog, a long-legged beige hound, rolls over, loving the attention. The Gautiers have one child, a daughter who lives on Saint Pierre and comes over every other weekend with her children.

'*Voilà!*' says Madame, ushering Honey and Lucien to the deck outside where there is a plastic farm and some small plastic animals. They immediately crouch down beside the little plastic toys and start playing. Thierry, Pip and Gabriel march off to the tractor, which Thierry uses to round up his sheep. He is moving them from one giant, wild piece of land onto another. Thierry's farm, which seems to stretch as far as the eye can see but has no obvious sense of border or regulation, is a completely different breed of enterprise from the farms with their immaculate fenced-off fields in northern France that one glimpses from the Eurostar. And this wilderness is certainly nothing like the combed, wealthy order of the Bordeaux vineyards.

Miquelon, where the cold wind shivers through rippling miles of long grass, where clouds of tiny birds fly up as you walk and flocks of sheep are dwarfed under giant skies, certainly offers a notion of airy openness I have never seen in mainland France. Maybe this is the point of the French *outre-mer*. Perhaps this is why France clings onto this tiny residue of its former empire. Perhaps it enables the French to continue living contentedly in their ordered, bureauocratic country, because they know that just over the Atlantic there is a wild domain, an expanse of freedom and space.

Of course, that might all be absolute nonsense.

I convey these thoughts to Roger. He looks at me kindly.

'For most people in France, we are a far-off dream. They think we are either in the Caribbean or up in the Arctic. A few make their way here to see the nature, to experience life without roads, life in the boreal forest, on an island where there are more seals than people. But most people in France have no idea where we are.'

We carry on walking through the long grass. It's so quiet that I can still hear the voices of Lucien and Honey, half a kilometre away, playing intently with the toy farm animals under the beady eye of Madame Gautier.

'It certainly feels a long way from the Champs Élysées,' I say to Roger, who laughs knowingly. 'Not really. Because we are heavily subsidised, of course.'

From a long, long way away we can hear Thierry whistle to his dog.

We return to the farmhouse and reluctantly pile back into Roger's jeep. He sets off bumping back along the only road in the island, listening to a radio station. Suddenly he pulls over.

'Mon dieu!' he exclaims. 'Billy Jean' is playing on the radio. After a few minutes it's clear what has happened.

'Michael Jackson seems to have... died,' I say to the rest of the group in the car.

'Poor old Wacko Jacko,' says Pip.

Somehow it feels utterly right to have such an unlikely newsflash in the midst of what is a rather surreal landscape.

We sit in the bar all night eating savoury crepes, which are rubbery and very salty, indeed almost inedible, and watching old videos of Michael Jackson dancing.

The next day we take our leave of the hotel. Patricia gives us little wrapped-up presents, brooches of the archipelago. I thank her for her kindness and solicitude. She shrugs and waves us goodbye. Roger escorts us to the ferry. He is preparing for a group of visiting Parisian nature nuts keen to see the sphagnum moss in Miquelon's boreal forest. 'We have three-fifths of the sphagnum moss species found in North America!' he tells me. 'Thirty species out of fifty. The Indians used it for babies. To absorb liquid, you know. As nappies.'

We all stand at the window of the catamaran, waving goodbye as the only town in Miquelon disappears into a monochrome curve of grey shingle and grey mountain. Twenty minutes later, we approach Saint Pierre, which looks like a veritable urban hive of activity by comparison. As the catamaran docks at the quay, we spot Pascal from the tourist board. He has news for me.

'You are required to do a television interview this evening, can you do it?'

'Let me check my diary,' I joke, before remembering that my jokes have little currency here.

'Sure,' says Pascal.

'Why am I to be interviewed?' I ask.

'You are probably the first English visitors to visit Saint Pierre for twenty years. And people have been reading your blogs, you know.'

Oh, dear.

We walk slowly through the Place du General de Gaulle. Even though we have only been away for three days it feels, almost, like we are coming home.

We are staying at a new hotel, the Hotel Iris. To the children's joy, it is opposite the Franklin Cafe. So we dump the thirteen bags, then return to the Franklin Cafe and have brightly coloured milkshakes and weak coffee, as we did last week. Michael Jackson music is playing from the radio. The children play with the Franklin puzzle. We have laid down habits almost immediately, I realise, even though they are as footprints in wet sand.

After a few sessions with Franklin, we repair to the hotel, which is a lot more civilised than the Hotel Robert. Here, where we find an invitation for lunch from the director of the Cultural Centre, Yannick Arozzamena.

M Arozzamena comes from a long line of Arozzamenas in Saint Pierre. He does the Miquelon Vingt-Cinq Kilometres every year. He believes in the DOM-TOMs and he believes in France and its mission to civilise. He has programmed the Cultural Centre as if it was the last civilising outpost before the hooligan shores of North America. The place is full of Juliette Gréco posters, references to Jacques Brel and clips of the latest Éric Rohmer movie.

We are to go to his house, where Yannick repairs every midday for lunch (there is an obligatory two-hour lunch break here, as in the mother country). His house is beside Saint Pierre's only cabaret (still closed) overlooking the harbour (still foggy). Yannick is small and spry, his trim frame no doubt fortified by the vast amounts of soy milk which he drinks. There are lace curtains in the windows and flowers by the sink. The furniture is homely, wooden and very French. At least, I recognise it as being European rather than American; antiques rather than giant sofas, wood rather than plastic. On the wall, there is a calendar of famous French monuments. The photograph for June is the Mont Saint Michel in Britanny.

Madame Arozzamena has prepared us a delicious lunch of vegetables and pasta. The children play with the family cat and settle down immediately into the comfort of being in a normal domestic situation.

Sitting at the kitchen table, Yannick explains how he plans the programme for the Cultural Centre. 'We are Bretons,

Normands, Basques, here.' A 4x4 Chevy whistles past the window. Yannick grins.

'*Alors*, we have the American cars here, of course, and the way our houses are built is North American. But the culture here, it has to be French. It has to be. And we only show French movies here, because people, you know, they are not going to come out of their houses for American blockbusters. Last March we had a French singer who came all the way from Paris.' M Arozzamena sighs. 'She succeeded in shifting 800 people, which is a lot for Saint Pierre.'

Yannick opens a bottle of Perrier, before telling me to my surprise that he is actually planning to leave Saint Pierre, home of his forefathers.

'I was born here, as you know,' he says slowly. 'But my wife,' he says, gesturing to Madame, who smiles sweetly at him, 'was born in the *Métropole*. And we've been here for about thirteen years. My daughter is about to go to university in the *Métropole*, so I am tempted to experience life in France.'

This is one of the idiosyncracies about the whole set-up; out here, French children are offered tertiary education back on the mothership. Quite apart from the dislocation they must feel, coming from the other side of the world hoping to fit in with their peers from the metropole, what trauma must that provide for their parents left many thousands of kilometres away?

But what is the alternative? Going to Quebec or Newfoundland would mean they would have to go as foreign students, with the attendant cost implications. Plus, they would have to be able to speak English effortlessly. Unsurprisingly, most choose to stay within a Gallic orbit.

'France is trying to improve our lifestyle here, by introducing big building projects, but...' Yannick says, looking at our politely enquiring faces, '... the 1970s were the rich years here. There were a few more restaurants and cafes, animated life and... Saint Pierre had a soul. We are doing well here, it's true, but we get a lot of help from the French government. There is no real economy here to give us... a future, and the young generation a desire to stay here.' I understand what he's saying, but I feel almost sorry for Saint Pierre et Miquelon. I mean, I would never opt to call this my home but I am beginning to feel something of a bizarre fondness for the wet, foggy place.

We have a lovely meal, and chat about the half marathon on Miquelon. Yannick explains that he's about to do the Ironman in Switzerland. He's run around these islands for so many years, it seems, he needs new horizons. Humanity cannot be sustained on *grands projets* alone.

It's time to go to the television station. We take our leave of the Arrozzamenas, kissing them both on both cheeks. Eating normal food in a normal kitchen has been astonishingly emotionally filling. I hadn't realised how quickly we would need such sustenance.

'Awww must we go Mummee?' says Honey. She has loved sitting in a normal living room and eating lunch in a kitchen, not a half-empty hotel.

'Come on,' I say. 'We have to go to a television station now. That's exciting, isn't it?'

Gabriel walks ahead with Pip. I put both hands out and clasp the small soft hands of Honey and Lucien which unhesitatingly fall into my palms.

Everyone trudges up the grindingly steep hill towards Réseau France Outre-Mer, or RFO, the state-funded TV station. We wave to a fisherman we vaguely know on the other side of the road. We walk past the old men playing pétanque on the concrete rectangle. We walk past the wall for Basque football, which I notice is covered with rude graffitti about Carla Bruni. Eventually we arrive at RFO.

An awful lot of people, probably about 200, work at RFO in Saint Pierre. I go into Make-up where I meet a charming woman from Martinique. 'Well, I could have gone to *la Métropole*, of course. But the money is much better here, *quoi*?'

I like the way she peppers her sentences with *'quoi'*, and decide to try doing it myself. Only I suspect I won't be able to without sounding like a complete idiot, rather than sounding like (say) Jane Birkin. Whom I quite envy.

The theme tune for the show rings out as I am brought into the studio. This is the nightly news magazine show, which is broadcast solely to the two islands. All this, for an audience of several thousand. It would probably be cheaper to film it on DVD and post the programme individually to each household, I think. But this is France and these are French citizens and as such they have the right to a live nightly news programme. That's how it is.

I sit beside the presenter, who introduces the programme. It's completely nerve-wracking being interviewed in French, and I only hope we can stick to the script, which goes along the existential lines of:

'Why are you here?'

To which the answer is a very unprofound 'Because it's so interesting.'

The interview begins.

'Why are you here, *alors*?' says my interlocutor.

'*Alors*, because it is so interesting,' I start, before explaining that as a former imperial power who gave up with the Union Jack overseas aeons ago, we English are fascinated to see how (and why) the French are still out there waving the *bleu, blanche, rouge*.

'But that makes us the second maritime power,' chirrups the presenter. Aha! That old fact.

'Indeed,' I continue. 'And that is very interesting.'

The children wait outside under a monitor positioned high on a wall, where they can watch their mother broadcasting to the French overseas territories. They have about as much interest in this as they have in the fact that I once passed my Cycling Proficiency Test, in other words none whatsoever.

Pip loyally attempts to film my efforts at being interviewed live in French on our small portable camera. It's not easy. He has to cope with a cacophony of noise, screams and the occasional hand of a child caught in mid leap as it slaps the screen. Back in the studio, I think I'm doing quite well. I even say *'quoi'* a few times. Pip, of course, knows nothing of this, as he is trying to film alongside performing extreme crowd control. The children are simply leaping around the room, like soaring trouts, while Pip attempts to interest them in the monitor. Pip starts swearing in strangled fury. Meanwhile, I am telling the presenter how lovely Saint Pierre is, how we are so excited to be here, and so on, *'quoi'*.

Why do I not tell the truth? That I find Saint Pierre depressing and cold, functional rather than elegant, and hostile rather than unusual? The truth is that I've started to forget about The Plan which was hatched back in another world, the London world, and enjoy just getting on with our trip, as we find it. I find I'm calming down somewhat on my early assessment of Saint Pierre et Miquelon, and am happy to be quietly enthusiastic about these islands. It's easier, anyway, to say that the DOM-TOMs are *'très intéressants'* and keep smiling. And they are not only interesting, but a lot less barren and hostile than they first appeared.

Unfortunately, this does not fool the beady Saint Pierrais who have been enraged by my earlier online criticisms.

When we return to the house, I take the rash step of seeing what's been logged online.

'Well, why did she not say all those things on air that she said in her blog?' went one email.

'Yeah, about the loo blowing up and the rudeness of the people in Saint Pierre!'

'Yeah, and the fact it's always foggy here. We KNOW it's foggy here. That's what we like about Saint Pierre!'

'Yeah, well have you googled her?' went a fourth. 'You'll find out she's almost like a reporter for a British newspaper known as *The Sun*!'

I'm flattered. Of course, nobody will confront me face to face, but it's reassuring to know in a way that the Saint Pierrais are prickly and smart.

The children are still on a high and will not go to sleep. After a few sessions with the paper animals, and a bit of good-natured shouting, I eventually turn all the lights off and sit in their bedroom in the pitch-black darkness. The occasional car drives by in the street below the window. There is no other noise. There are not many birds in Saint Pierre, because there are no trees, and I certainly doubt whether there are any owls. I give each child a kiss. They didn't want to come and they certainly did not opt to come to gloomy old Saint Pierre.

I'm pleased to be here, however. At the risk of sounding perverse, I'm grateful that I know Saint Pierre et Miquelon exist, and that we have explored them. I'll certainly never forget them.

Rather than being cold, this hotel is perishingly hot, making condensation pour down the window panes. Every time I open a window, however, a bitter chill scythes through the room. Eventually Pip and I go to bed, where we again encounter the special phenomenon of the DOM-TOM pillow.

'Never mind, *chérie*,' whispers my dear husband. 'In two days' time, we'll be in Martinique.'

Eventually I fall asleep and dream about Aldrich and Connell visiting Saint Pierre and being interviewed on the local TV show.

CHAPTER 5

Long Haul *Avec les Enfants*

Honey's diary: *On Friday we woke up at four in the morning and got dressed. We new what to wear because the day before we chose our clothes. I was really tired. And a person had all our stuff on a speshle trolley. And we all hoped on that trolley. And Daddy said no no no and was cross.*

We have left the wet, clingy fog of Saint Pierre et Miquelon far, far behind. I'll never wear all that winter stuff again. Weak joy. Bikini time, here we come. Well, maybe not bikini time. But swimsuit time, certainly. Because we are off to our next destination, the home of sugar, rum and bananas. Martinique.

We have to go to Canada in order to travel down to the French Caribbean. Then we have to go to New York. Then we have to go to Puerto Rico. Finally, we will arrive at Fort de France, Martinique. Of course, we could have done all this far more easily on an Air France local shuttle, but that would have required a BBC budget.

I did contact the Air France press people to request a lovely free travel pass for all six of us to go around all the DOM-TOMs (Air France almost achieves a shuttle service, so regular are the routes). Having picked themselves off the floor after laughing hysterically for about eight minutes, the press people told us that the answer to my request was, *naturellement*, 'Non'. Anyway, we would have had to keep repairing to Paris and starting out from there, which would have been crazy. And so, we are doing the journey on le bargain basement.

This means we have to hop back into the anglophone world for a few hours, travel several thousand kilometres, and then return into the zone of the *tricolore*. Not ideal, but there's no choice, and popping back into a place where English is spoken as a matter of course happens to delight the children.

We are in Halifax, Nova Scotia. It is not even early morning; it's the night before. At FOUR in the morning, we are dressed and in the lobby of The Lord Nelson Hotel, Halifax, ready to leave. There are Canadians carousing in the street from revelries that started the previous evening, and stars are still in the sky.

I have sore eyes, unbrushed hair and a face still bearing pillow creases.

Beside me is a small mountain. Our thirteen bags. Each bag has been packed, unpacked and repacked so many times that I know where every pair of knickers, sock and fleece is. My hands are decorated with a small array of quietly bleeding, minute cracks, because I have done so much handwashing of clothes.

Pip and I start heaving the luggage onto a large, brass luggage trolley in the lobby.

'Look, Mummy, we can all get on alongside the luggage, AND get the trolley moving,' yells one of our delightful children. Within seconds, they have all swarmed aboard.

The hotel staff smile tensely, clearly wishing for dawn to break and the English to disappear.

'Get OFF that trolley,' bellows Pip.

'Ha ha ha,' sing the children, as the trolley starts to roll away.

'Look here,' shouts Pip. 'Get off that trolley, or, or…' He runs out of inspiration. The children push the trolley and disappear down the hall.

'If you break your leg, that will be it!' I yell after them. 'We'll be on the next flight home.'

'Yay!' they all scream in unison.

Of course, going home to London, Facebook and English culture is exactly what they want. Indeed, is French culture so ineffably superior to our culture at home? I had always assumed it to be, but maybe I've just been subject to the French propaganda which insists that its wine, cheese, perfume, cinema and general know-how in bed are vastly better than anything offered by the poor old United Kingdom. Since we have been away, a warts-and-all investigation of overseas France has revealed quite a few warts, probably more than I expected to find. The social structure is certainly very different from ours. But is it better? Take the crisis in cod fishing. Is it wiser to take the social subsidies and carry on living in Saint Pierre, not doing very much, than to live like those over the water in Newfoundland, for example, who have had to leave and seek work in mainland Canada, taking their houses with them? Two radically different answers to the same problem. While I'm musing on this fascinating diversion in the politics of the capitalist West, all sorts of activity is going on in the lobby.

Gabriel takes a potentially ill-advised leap from the luggage trolley and leaves it spinning away down the hall with Lucien and Honey clinging to it. He wanders over to the front door and peers through.

'Isn't that the bus over there, Mummy?' he says casually.

Oh, God. Our bus to the airport appears to have stopped beside a large statue of Sir Walter Scott, about 200 metres away.

'Honey! Lucien!' I yell. We tear our bags off the trolley and charge off to the bus.

'Goodbye, y'all,' shout the hotel staff, with undisguised relief.

We clamber on board the bus and set off for the airport, bus trundling, all good, all good.

'Did you pack the toothbrushes?' I ask Pip. He looks at me blankly.

'I just look after the filming stuff,' he says.

Oh, great. Two weeks into our trip and we have lost all six toothbrushes.

'Not including my Hannah Montana one?' wails Honey.

'We will have to buy some more while we are still in an English-speaking country,' I continue, envisaging with trepidation the commercial transaction this will require when back in La Belle France. 'I am NOT paying fifty euros for six toothbrushes!'

As we roll through the sleeping city, I inspect my children. Gabriel's face is deathly white.

We stop at the Plaza Hotel to pick up some more early birds.

'Come with me,' says Pip grimly, taking Gabriel outside where dawn is breaking over Halifax.

Gabriel comprehensively throws up all over a park bench.

'That looks like a posh hotel,' observes Honey, when we are all back on the bus and moving slowly in the approximate direction of the airport.

'How many stars did it have?' asks Lucien.

'Five,' says Honey pointedly.

'Why didn't we stay there, Mummy?'

'Because we stayed in our lovely hotel, darling,' I say testily. 'And anyway, we hardly stayed there.'

Getting up at 3.45 is not my idea of how to use a hotel properly. Using a hotel properly, in my book, involves shared baths, hot sex and breakfast in bed. None of which were on offer at The Lord Nelson Hotel, Halifax.

'I'm so sorry, I should have given you my sickness tablets,' says a young woman in a ponytail. 'I have some here for my son Scott.'

She is meeting her six-year-old son off a flight from Vancouver, where he lives with his dad, some 32,000 kilometres away. 'We are separated, you see. So we have to share Scott across Canada…'

I suddenly realise how lucky we are to be doing this trip together.

I leave Halifax with a sort of fond yearning for Saint Pierre et Miquelon. Yes, it was a crazy place, but with their authentic French bread, French culture and French language schools, the islanders were all at least united around a common cause. Maybe the fog was the common cause, actually. It was certainly the common cause behind all those shipwrecks.

Two hours later, we land at JFK airport in New York and transfer to our plane bound for the Caribbean. At which point, Lucien decides to lie on the floor of Terminal 1 Departures and indulge in a full-blown, five-star luxury tantrum. The sort that involves throwing back the head, arching the back and drumming the feet, prostrate on the floor and yelling extremely loudly. People are looking at me sternly as if I am the reason for all this yelling. I smile broadly and try to gather him up into a big hug. Lucien immediately does his rigid stick insect impression.

Of course, Lucien can hardly be blamed. It's only 9 a.m. and we are already in New York, with two more flights ahead of us. And he has been separated from his beloved Trunki, a small pull-along suitcase shaped like a tiger. Lucien likes having his Trunki to sit on; it's part of his airport experience. And each new experience must go the same way as the one before.

Only this time we chose to do things differently and put the Trunki in the hold.

'Oh, put the Trunki in the hold,' I muttered to Pip, when we arrived at JFK and transferred. 'It's just one less thing to forget.'

'Just popping Trunki in the hold, Lu-Lu,' says Pip brightly. In it goes.

The hold, as far as Lucien is concerned, is his version of the Mouth of Hell.

'Gee, what is that noise?' says a burly uniformed customs man whose badge says his name is Fletcher. Lucien goes on and on yelling.

'What's the noise, bud?' Fletcher repeats to Lucien.

'Is that your first name, or your surname?' I ask politely.

Fletcher gives me a wary look. 'Surname.'

'Thanks for that. Look, Lucien, Mr Fletcher is going to be VERY cross if you don't calm down. Mr Fletcher is... Mr Fletcher is...'

I turn away, convulsed for some reason with laughter about how I am going to weave the irritation of Mr Fletcher into a threat which will frighten Lucien into reasonable behaviour. The fact he has the same name as Ronnie Barker's character in *Porridge* only makes it funnier.

'You know you are late, ma'am,' says Mr Fletcher. 'Let me help you with those,' he says, gesturing to the three separate customs sheets which have to be done for each of us, even though we are only on American land for about three hours.

We all start filling in endless forms.

'Want Tru-uunn-ki,' sobs Lucien. 'Lucien wants Tru-un-ki!'

'Look,' says Honey, who has a Trunki (shaped like a cow) of her own. 'My Trunki is in the hold.' She folds her arms and fixes him with one of her smug faces. 'And I don't mind a bit. Do I, Mummy?'

'Buddy, you'd better quieten up now,' says Mr Fletcher testily.

I mumble something inaudible, continue form-filling and try to distract Lucien with an offer. This has to be carefully monitored, however. Offer too little, and the tantrum continues. Offer something stupidly generous, and the tantrum will be instantly switched off, with the screamer suddenly calming down and choosing something for $35.

This is indeed what comes to pass.

Eventually, after all the forms are filled and we are allowed through, Lucien ends up with a fire engine plus figures, which has apparently been produced by toymakers within the New York City Fire Department.

He spreads the toys out on the carpet in Departures and plays with them contentedly for an hour.

'Now, I call that money well spent,' says Pip.

We walk past a fast-food place with a huge advertising board in the window. It reads 'The Passenger Next To You Will Have Food'.

'My God!' says Pip, snorting with laughter. 'Do you see that? Sort of anxiety creation about someone eating beside you on the flight while you won't be able to, having not been clever enough to think about stocking up with food. No wonder all Americans are so fat.'

'Like you, Daddy,' says Gabriel.

'Look here,' I say, 'your father is making an interesting anthropological observation. Do NOT say he's fat. He is not fat.'

'Shut up you,' says Lucien.

I look despairingly at Pip. 'If they were French children, they'd never be allowed to get away with that,' I say. Apparently the average French parent is far stricter with their children about things like bad language.

'Mmmm,' says Pip, still laughing about the food poster.

We eventually board our flight to somewhere in the Caribbean, along with hundreds of Americans including a couple and their tiny, crated white dog ('She's called Precious,' they tell us proudly). True to the poster, most of the people beside us do indeed have food.

Lucien pays close attention to the packaging of his fire engine. To my horror, he has spotted a potential further purchase advertised on the back wrapper.

'Can I have this whole fire station, Mummee?' he asks.

I look at it vaguely. 'No. It can only be bought in New York, and it costs sixty dollars.'

Lucien is, however, not so easily dismissed.

'Can I, Mummee, can I, can I?' he goes on, and on. Three hours later, we are still on the flight to the Caribbean and he is still asking for the fire station.

'Do you want to keep your fire engine?' I threaten. 'Because you might well lose it if you keep going on like this, you know.'

'Can I have the fire station, Mummee?' asks Lucien again.

Honestly.

I glance over at Pip, who is in pole position. That is to say, he is ensconced between the two older children, both of whom are reading books and therefore are letting him pursue a dalliance between the *International Herald Tribune*, a film by Nick Hornby and occasional sleeps. I feel a sense of injustice start to engage with my arteries.

I look at Honey, who is diligently writing in her diary. She does this every day with a variety of coloured felt-tips. She is taking this journey very seriously. 'How do you spell Miquelon, Mummy?' she queries.

Eventually Lucien wears himself out with fire station longing, and falls asleep. I read 'I'm the Greatest', a Michael Rosen poem, to Honey. Gabriel is playing Tetris on the seat-back screen, and Pip is reading the paper. It's perfect.

The trouble is that when something is just perfect, it isn't perfect for very long. I'm sitting there with Lucien asleep on my knee, reading Michael Rosen poems to Honey. Everything is wonderful and I am congratulating myself on getting the family out on our dream trip. Then I start worrying about how we will cope in Martinique, with the prices for everything.

'Yes, but the great thing about having a whole day in the air is that we don't have to PAY for any food,' whispers Pip to me. He's got a point. Flying all day will save us about £100.

All of which is great, unless you are travelling with the fussiest children on the planet.

'But I don't eat airplane food, Mummy,' says Gabriel, ever so nicely.

'Nobody does,' chimes in Honey.

As the French stewardess bends over us with something in a plastic dish, I spell the situation out to my spoilt children.

'We do, and you will. I am not letting all this food go to waste and then spending hundreds of euros buying you food at the next airport. Really, I'm not.'

'Well, I'm not eating it.'

'You are,' I say. Putting the slumbering Lucien down I lean over to show Gabriel and Honey that they are going to eat, they will eat, and what's more, they will ENJOY eating. Fellow passengers look at me askance, hoping perhaps the glamorous stewardess will reappear and bind my wrists to the chair.

'Eat this food!' I shout at Gabriel, waving a fork in his face.

'Don't want to!'

'Eat it!'

'No!'

I produce a bread roll and push it towards him.

'Eat this, then. Eat it!'

'No!'

I toy with the idea of force-feeding my lovely nine-year-old son, who has eyelashes like spider's legs and periwinkle-blue eyes. I decide I cannot.

'Can I have the fire station, Mummeee?' says a small voice behind me.

I admit defeat. I wrap up a fish stew and two cheese rolls and put them in my bag. Someone will eat them later. Probably me.

At this juncture, Honey is whining about the whereabouts of her copy of *'Oui! On Fait du Coloriage!'* Pip is, of course, asleep.

Why do it? Why fly with kids? Oh yes. My own 'It's Now Or Never' plan. That's what brought us here.

When we finally arrive in Martinique, three planes and some 19,000 kilometres later, I discover that American Airlines has lost my bag containing all my clothes.

I have started to write every flight we take down in a special Flight Notebook, with distance, flight number and key events. This is because I know I will never attempt a journey like this again.

So, for example:

June 13 – AA 4773, JFK–Halifax, 960 kilometres.
'Arrived in rain under a low red moon. No food.'
July 1 – AA 5020 San Juan–Fort de France, 480 kilometres.
'My bag is lost. Still, we had ham sandwiches.'

Funny how many times I mention food in the log. I now realise how prescient is the 'The Person Beside You Will Have Food' poster. On-flight nutrition has become extraordinarily important to us already, and not just because it is free on the plane. It's the automatic quality of it. When the trolley arrives, the next hour is taken care of. 'Chicken or beef?' has become a quasi-Pavlovian signal for me to relax. It signifies that someone else is in control. Pip and I have to be in control of so much – the children, the tickets, passports, luggage, all the filming, arranging interviews, marshalling our way through French red tape, even down to remembering to pack the washing line – that the simple event of someone giving us food on a tray is sheer heaven. The next morning, under the radiant heat of a Caribbean sun, I discover two squashed cheese sandwiches and the fish stew in my bag. I eat a sandwich, and throw away the fish stew. Then I eat the other sandwich. I conclude that the children were quite right to reject them.

Martinique

Dominica channel

Dominica channel

North Atlantic Ocean

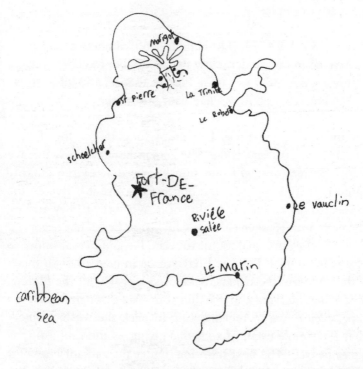

margot

st pierre

La Trinité

Le Robert

schoelcher

★ Fort-De-France

Le vauclin

Riviére salée

LE Marin

caribbean sea

Saint Lucia channel

CHAPTER SIX

A Spoonful of Sugar
in Martinique

Honey's diary: *I got a new snorkler and Gabriel a new float which was much bigger than Lucien's float but Mummy wouldn't let him swim in the sea with it. We noiticed some crabs we saw about ten when we were walking on the beach.*

My suitcase has not yet arrived. Hence at the moment I'm wearing Gabriel's gym kit. To be honest, I hope my bag never arrives. The further we get from home, the faster shrinks my concern about clothes. I have no meetings to go to or lunches with important employers or would-be employers, so I don't need to worry about impressing anyone with my fashion sense. Plus, I brought such a minute selection that I had no choice of what to wear anyway.

The only dull point in all of this is that the fashionable French, usually several notches above me in style anyway, are in a different stratosphere here in Martinique.

'Er, je porte le costume de sport de mon fils,' I explain casually at breakfast to a French banker. The banker is leaning up against a wall beside the swimming pool, stylishly glancing over a copy of *Le Monde* and clad only in bathing suit and glasses. The trunks in question are long and light blue, with a print of promenading camels. There is a large linked watch on his wrist and a gold chain around his neck. These pieces of jewellery are not flashy, but carefully chosen. They adorn a classic French masculine body; small in stature, lean in proportion, hairy enough to be manly, but by no means covered with something which you would call a pelt. He is a banker. Yes, in France even those with the most mundane of jobs are things of beauty.

Although we are discussing the fiscal problems currently facing France and her overseas territories, I feel the need to tell him why I am standing there in a PE kit consisting of a white M&S T-shirt and a pair of boy's Nike shorts. Whereas this sort of information might have excited an Englishman beyond compare, I don't think it impresses my French banker too much.

As we progress in our conversation, I am dimly aware of some people shouting above me from a balcony. They sound like they are yelling in English. I squint up and identify Pip, who is screaming at me to get upstairs as we have a film to make, don't you know.

'*Désolée,*' I whisper to the banker. I feel like saying '*quoi*' a few times, but don't dare.

The banker smiles politely as I move off.

'Sorry, I was just talking to a very *French* banker,' I say to Pip, laughing, when I get to the bedroom. My husband merely raises one eyebrow. He knows full well my penchant for the Gallic touch, and tolerates it with amusement. If my Francophile nature wound him up too much, there is no way he would have agreed to this crazy trip in the first place.

A Channel 4 producer, who made a series about adults choosing to have a Gap Moment, told me: 'People think they go away to renew their lives and relationships. What happens, we found, is that going away only magnifies various elements of their lives and relationships.'

I'd say his observations are quite near the truth. Take Pip. Here in Martinique, where it's about 80 degrees every day, and sunny, he has taken to wearing a panama, which he feels gives him directorial authority. Being British he has of course teamed it with shorts and long white tennis socks, which makes him look more like Alan Parker than Stephen Spielberg. He is very much the director, anyway. And his inclination to be a teensy bit bossy has been upped to EXTREME level in the process of having to come out here and direct six documentaries.

'No, don't say it like that. Say it like this. Again. Again,' he is inclined to say when we are doing pieces to camera. He will crouch down beside the camera, with his chin in his hand and a despairing look on his face. It is as if he is thinking 'Why the hell have I been lumbered with this amateur?'

I admit that it's weird, being directed by your husband. I'm not sure he means it when he says 'That'll do for me', and calls 'Cut!' Is he happy? Does he think I look OK? Does he think I'm analysing the situation properly, interviewing people adequately and generally doing an excellent job? I can't tell.

So we just plough on, recording interviews with people, doing shots of the car driving past, shots of the landscape, shots of the children and pieces to camera about how life is lived.

In Martinique, there's so much more to shoot compared to the desolate moors of Saint Pierre, and Miquelon's moonscape. It's a dry and sunny visual smorgasbord by comparison.

Even the motorways are interesting. Renaults, Peugeots and Citroëns shoot along the roads, which every so often bear a giant plaque that reads: 'Funded by the EUROPEAN COMMUNITY'.

'That's you and me, sweetheart,' says Pip grimly.

Behind the EU plaque and the blue flag with its yellow stars, there are hills packed with small, chaotic-looking houses with corrugated iron rooftops bearing crazily angled satellite dishes, and tattered window frames out of which are strung loaded washing lines, along roads entitled Boulevard Général de Gaulle and Avenue Victor Hugo. There's also an Avenue de Paris, as if the pavements themselves are yearning to get closer to the French core. Past the urban areas, French commerce strides across the landscape; Galeries Lafayette, Maersk shipping and Mr Bricolage all have vast out-of-town establishments here. We love Mr Bricolage, the DIY chain. Behind these great *hypermarchés*, the far off hills are dominated by the emerald splashes of the sugar fields. Mile after mile of sugar canes. Then mile after mile of banana plantations, with the fruits hanging to ripen secure from the birds in their blue mesh bags beneath the trees.

'They aren't trees, actually,' says Gabriel. 'They are herbs.'

'What?' I yell. I am so far in the back of the car that I'm actually in the dog cage. This arrangement is because Gabriel will be sick if he's in the back seat, so he has to sit up beside Pip in the front. The back seat has been taken up by Lucien and Honey. Then there's our guide, Laurent, who sits beside Lucien and Honey. All of which means that I'm right in the boot, sitting in the cage alongside a giant bottle of water and the camera equipment. I'm not very happy about this. I sit here for hours, grumbling that I can't see anything and hey, am I not the presenter of these damn programmes?!

'How can I do reportage from the boot of a car?' I demand, rhetorically.

Nobody takes any notice. Nobody can hear me. Eventually I switch off from the family and mainline a bit of Aldrich and Connell, but reading makes me feel sick so I end up just looking out at the banana plantations and counting the number of branches of Mr Bricolage that I can spot. At one point we go past a small bay where I see a boat with a giant green Mr Bricolage sail. Pretty strange boat, however. Eight or ten youths seem to be hanging off it on long horizontal logs.

'What's THAT?' I shout to Laurent.

'It is the *yole* sailing. It is our speciality here in Martinique.'

'Bet it's great for your core,' I shout, watching the men balance expertly over the waves as they shoot along the bay. I have never heard of these boats before, but in English, a *yole* might be known as a skiff.

'*Quoi?*' yells Laurent.

'Never mind.'

After an hour or so of this, we swoop down off the motorway and arrive at Saint Pierre, historic capital of Martinique.

Laurent, a patient man who has been loaned to us by the tourist board for the week, guides us downtown to the beach where we find a suitably historic-looking spot beside the open-air market to do some filming.

'Can we go and buy something?' say the children.

'Yes, go and buy a pineapple,' I say, giving Gabriel a euro. 'In French.' They trot off happily with Laurent alongside them.

By the time they return, pineapple successfully acquired, Gabriel beaming triumphantly, I'm all wired and microphoned up with the battery pack in my underwear. There is a lovely wooden pier decorated with old iron railings right beside the market. It looks like something out of an advert for Bacardi rum.

'Go up the pier and walk down towards me,' orders Pip. 'Everyone! Action!'

'Compared to other Caribbean islands, Martinique seems delightfully uncommercial,' I commence, holding Lucien and Honey's hands, walking down the pier.

I'm meant to be carefree, maternal, Francophile, welcoming, holding the hands of my children, encouraging viewers of the Travel Channel onto a journey with us. That's the idea.

'If this, the main waterfront of the old capital...' I continue in Whickerish earnest mode.

This is when Honey decides to launch herself in front of the camera, yelling. 'Yada, yada, yada. I'm BORED!'

'Cut. Go again!' commands Pip.

'Please darling, please behave nicely,' I beg my daughter.

'Compared to other Caribbean islands, Martinique seems delightfully...' This time, it's Lucien. He is wearing a striped sunsuit and looks like something out of *Death in Venice*.

'Mummy,' he queries quietly, 'can I hold your other hand?'

'Cut!' bellows Pip. 'Again!'

'Compared to other Caribbean islands, Martin... Gabriel!! WILL YOU STOP BARGING HONEY!' I shout, turning on my heel and marching back up off the pier while contemplating pushing one of my offspring into the turquoise Caribbean sea beneath us.

'This is impossible!' I yell to Pip. 'I'll do it on my own!'

'No, no, please, we'll be good, please do it again with us,' chime the children as one.

'All right. We will all RUN towards Daddy. Then I will speak. That's ME speaking. Not YOU. You have to be SILENT. Got it?'

We run towards the camera like a joyous family in an Andrex advert, or something out of *The Sound of Music*. I lose a shoe. Then the battery for my microphone falls out of the back of my knickers, although it is still suspended by a single wire from the microphone. As I run it dangles rather dangerously between my bare legs. I ignore it.

'Compared to other Caribbean islands, Martinique seems delightfully uncommercial,' I say, doggedly, for what seems like the fourteenth time. 'If this, the main waterfront in the old capital, was in Antigua or Barbados...' I'm gabbling, because I'm so anxious to get it correct.

'... it's completely laid-back and rather deserted. One of the reasons for this is that Martinique [gulp for air] is a fully fledged department of France.' Cut.

'That's good,' says Herr Director.

'Yay!' shout the children, and rush off.

The microphone unplugs itself and the battery falls down onto the pier. I grab it milliseconds before it disappears through the wooden slats and into the Caribbean Sea.

'That was lucky,' says Herr Director.

'How many spare battery packs have we got?'

'None.'

I wander back to get my shoe, and then down off the pier to the esplanade to find Gabriel in deep conversation with an aged crone who appears to be gutting fish into a bucket.

'Mummy!'

'What?' I say tensely, while smiling briefly at the crone.

'This is Nicolas Anelka's old nanny!'

I look at the crone. She grins back with a toothless smile. No, honestly. She has no teeth. She carries on washing fish.

'*Bonjour madame, enchantée,*' I say.

Could she really have been the nanny of the millionaire Chelsea striker? His wet nurse perhaps? The whole idea is surreal.

I'm pretty doubtful, but Gabriel, who, as fortune would have it, is wearing a Chelsea T-shirt, nods his head and is as pleased as punch. He points to a man on a bike wearing a bright orange shirt with 'Digital' emblazoned across his paunch. The man on the bike grins and points a stubby finger at the crone.

'*La nounou de Nicolas Anelka. Oui!*'

'I think he paid for a stadium just up the road. Can we go there, Mummy?'

'Er, maybe. Hmm. I think it's lunchtime. I mean, really. *Au revoir, monsieur, madame.*'

It's very hot. The sun is beating down on the wooden promenade by the seafront. The open-air market has filled up spectacularly with a vast noisy crowd of people buying fish, cheese, fruit and spices from temporary stalls that throng the hall. To our fog-accustomed eyes, this market is extraordinary. Its style, smell, noise and colour is on another planet from the morbid, darkened, desolate basement supermarkets in the houses of Saint Pierre et Miquelon.

The spices are piled high in little transparent bags with yellow labels. They have a huge variety; *Poivre, Poivre Blanc, Poivre Vert, Poivre Rouge, Piment, 5 Baies*, and something called *Girofle*. Behind them are hundreds of home-decanted bottles with bright pink handwritten labels; vinegar, oil, honey, hot sauce and chilli. The pineapples, mangoes, bananas, guavas and limes are packed into wooden crates or pyramids so high that they occasionally fall off the trestles. Flowers spill over the pomegranates. Bolts of brightly coloured waxed cotton are stacked high beneath clothes rails on which hang pink and purple lacy prom dresses and little cotton plaid skirts fringed with broderie anglaise. Wooden knick-knacks crowd around teetering piles of electronic equipment, live crabs in tanks, candles, alarm clocks, nests of mixing bowls, knives and colourful plastic toys.

Bare-chested men are decapitating tuna, severing squid, splicing the woody stalks of giant lilies and chopping up coconuts, all with giant machetes. You can buy crescents of the sweet coconut flesh, or simply stuff a straw into a coconut and drink the milk.

'Yes please,' says Gabriel, when offered one.

He takes one gulp, and then politely smiles at the man who offered it to him and hands it over to me while making a face.

'You have to finish it, Mummy. It's disgusting.'

Up a set of wrought-iron stairs is the upper floor, which is packed with bars and restaurants. A giant scarf reading 'Olympique de Marseille' dangles across one of the bars – this is the big team around here. Yes, it is 10,000 kilometres away in the south of France, but never mind. The world of football is small. I mean, Nicolas Anelka's nanny is gutting fish down there.

'Alors,' says Laurent. 'This Saint Pierre was known as Le Petit Paris. Before the volcano it was very beautiful. Beautiful and rich.'

Indeed, by all accounts Saint Pierre, which crouches beneath the vast volcano of Mount Pelée, was very elegant, with its raised pavements, wrought-iron balconies and lush palms beside the colonial buildings, and a vast cathedral dedicated to the patron saint of fishing. But on Sunday 8 May 1902, everyone in the city was at church and Mount Pelée erupted. Thirty thousand people were killed: the entire population of the city, bar one person. In four minutes, the whole city was buried.

'Who was the one person?' asks Gabriel.

'Cyparis. He was a prisoner. He was already entombed, you see, in an underground cell.'

Being the only survivor of the Mount Pelée eruption was something of a stroke of luck for Cyparis, who was released, since there was no one alive to look after him in prison, and who went on to become something of a minor celebrity in the Barnum & Bailey Circus.

Poor old Saint Pierre, however, never really recovered. It lost its capital status (the capital was moved to Fort de France) and its cathedral.

We leave the market and poke around the giant stones, which are all that's left of the cathedral. It's very hot.

'Could we go through this again, Laurent?' says Pip. He beckons me over.

'Get him to explain what happened in the cathedral.'

We start filming again.

'So, this day in 1902 was a pretty bad one for Saint Pierre, wasn't it?' I say by way of introduction.

'Cut!' shouts Pip. He beckons me over again.

'Just ask him what happened in the cathedral!'

'Right, Laurent, where are we now?'

'Cut!' shouts Pip again.

All right, all right.

'Laurent, what happened in the cathedral?'

Television. It's paying our way around the French world but, honestly, it's a medium for dummies.

After Take 8 of 'Laurent, what happened in the cathedral?', I am pouring with sweat, red in the face and frankly wishing I had never sold this silly idea to the Travel Channel in the first place. We drive up to a spot where a large white and turquoise statue of the Madonna looks over the city.

'She was meant to protect Saint Pierre,' says Laurent mournfully. 'Only she didn't. At least she wasn't devastated by the eruption.'

That's 30,000 people dead; one large statue of the Virgin intact. That's religion for you.

'*Bonjour!*' somebody shouts over to us. We all turn round. It's the man with the orange Digital T-shirt and the bike. He must have followed us all the way up the hill.

'Let me guide you back down!' he yells, hurling his bike into a magnolia bush.

Pip and I immediately click into British mode – in other words, being rather unfriendly.

'No, thanks very much,' we chorus.

Our guide looks at us, astonished.

'But this is Jean. He is local to Saint Pierre. He will help us.'

Oh, all right then. We all climb back in the car. Jean and his very large belly are firmly ensconced in the front. The children are round-eyed in the back.

Jean laughs a lot as we bounce back down the hill, and points out a long, white building.

'The hospital. Behind that we call this the Stairway to Heaven and *les maisons closes*.'

'What's that?' I whisper to Laurent.

'The brothels, of course. No Frenchman, wherever he is in the world, would ever be without them.'

Later that night we return to Saint Pierre in a tropical thunderstorm. Pip has taken it upon himself that we should hear and record some Creole music and by chance there's a local Creole star, Victor O, playing in the Bar Fish Bo Kay (which means 'Fish At Home' in Creole). The thunderstorm is at full pelt. This is no passing shower, but tropical rain, with large, heavy, splashing raindrops that really mean business. The water itself is as hot as a tepid shower. We park the car by the market and run towards Fish Bo Kay. Everyone is wearing sandals and T-shirts. It takes about two seconds before we are fundamentally drenched. Pip has had to use his coat to protect the camera. I am carrying the tripod.

We flash by houses whose front doors are open, leading right into their living rooms. Anyone can see that the rooms are rudimentary. Lit by neon, some are furnished with only a table, chairs and a fridge. Some have a little shop in the front, or a counter selling things like French ice cream. Televisions flicker showing local French news (i.e. not local at all) and *'la météo'* (the weather) 10,000 kilometres away.

We arrive at Fish Bo Kay.

'Bon soir, bon soir,' says Victor O's brother, who runs the bar.

Victor O is just doing a sound check. He waves at us and raises his eyebrows at the sight of us, an English family soaked to the bone, carrying television recording equipment. We sit down on white plastic chairs under a canopy. Rain drums above our heads. Victor O's brother pulls up a table, which he sets with baskets of spanking fresh fried fish. It is delicious. Even Lucien breaks his monastic routine of breakfast cereal or egg mayonnaise and tries some.

On the tables are bottles of Saint Émilion. The classy red wine is not half as expensive as it would be in England, because there is a special exclusion tax allowing French citizens the world over to drink French wine cheaply. So a bottle of Saint Émilion, which might cost around £20 in England, costs about €4 in Martinique.

Eventually, we have a moment with Victor O.

He comes over, laughing. They like him in Martinique, because he is a local boy made good. They like him in France, because he doesn't represent the awkward squad of political malcontents who are cross about being dependent on France.

He has white musicians in his band, too.

'Do you feel French or Caribbean?' I ask him.

'*Mais*, French, *bien sûr*. I am French, of course. I have no problem with that,' he laughs. 'My music is more folk and acoustic than zouk,' he says, referring to the famous Caribbean pop style. 'It's a new way to see Caribbean French music.'

'Caribbean, *le petit pays*,' he sings, strumming his guitar.

Lucien strums alongside him in a sort of air-guitar style.

I look over at Pip, who is filming us all. He's smiling, we are all smiling.

'You look so beautiful, darling,' he whispers.

'Say it in French,' I laugh.

'*Tu es rayonnante, ma chérie.*'

We are still wet, but the crispy fish and the red Bordeaux wine is warming our bellies. Victor O is singing, locals have arrived and people are dancing. It's still raining outside, and the tide is lapping against the beach about ten metres away. Lights twinkle in the port of Saint Pierre.

When we leave, splashing through the puddles on the street to find our car, we can see very distant lights from the next island along, St Lucia. But you can't get there very easily. You need a visa. The rest of the Caribbean might be geographical neighbours, but they are foreign to the French departments of Martinique and Guadeloupe. Let the rest of the Caribbean go its way; we will look to Paris.

Returning to our hotel, we drive past a high white wall.

'Look!' shouts Gabriel, who now considers himself something of a Victor O groupie.

He's spotted a huge poster for Victor's latest album.

I'm looking at something else.

A big sprayed-on circle, in which has been scrawled the following words in huge red capitals:

'BEKE RACISTE; LA FRANCE, COMPLICIT.'

Most of the sentence needs no translation; the *'beke'*, however, is a special Martiniquais term. These are the direct descendants of French slave owners. They still hold most of the power on the island, and are deeply resented.

We are about to meet the awkward squad.

CHAPTER SEVEN

A Rum Deal

Honey's diary: *We went to this place where there was a pond and it probably had leches in it and other biting thing's. We came to a Rum Fatury a trying Rum place as well as a buying Rum place and Mummy tried a spisy one. I smelled it and it mad my eyes sting.*

'All right, children, we are off to a rum factory.'

Cue general groans from the junior assemblage, who correctly identify this as a Filming Day, and are therefore preparing to be as irritating as possible, and tell us how bored they are, all day. Cue furious reaction from parents: *don't you realise how lucky you are, you could be sitting behind desks at school, you will probably never come here again,* and so on.

This has been the routine so far. How did I think it would go, when we were back in London? 'The children will play around our feet, learning snippets of French, etc.' Yes, well.

'Actually, I might come back here again,' says Gabriel calmly. 'I really have no idea what trips I am going to plan when I am an adult. Yet.'

I react badly to this sort of indifferent confidence, and launch forth with another tirade.

He smiles at me knowingly.

'The trouble is that you haven't had your coffee yet, Mummy, have you?'

No, of course I haven't. Because we haven't yet gone down to the breakfast buffet. We are staying in the Hotel La Batalière. It is light years away from anything we have so far experienced. Slightly seventies in style, with camel-coloured swishy curtains and huge crystal chandeliers, it is very laid-back. It does not have the array of goodies which most large hotels in the Caribbean bring out for the tourists. There is no programme for residents offering rum punch nights, aerobics, fancy dress parades or quizzes. There is no kids' club. There is no all-day dining or midnight feasting. The hotel is for French businessmen and Air France hostesses. Anyway, the breakfast buffet is terrific. Where would we be without it? The buffet not only gives us breakfast, it looks after us all day. This is because we steal outrageously from it.

Our system is thus: I prowl around, getting bowls of cereal, pilfering some cheese, a bit of bread, and put six eggs on to boil. Then I return to the breakfast table.

'Cereal, children?'

This is the preordained moment for Pip to go and get salami, more bread and a bit of butter. And some fruit. Oh, and some yoghurts. He then starts making up the sandwiches under the white table cloth, while we all eat vast amounts of cereal and croissant. After a decent interval, I go and grab the eggs, which by now are hard-boiled.

Meanwhile, Pip deposits the swag, namely sandwiches, hard-boiled eggs, yoghurt and fruit, plus a few pieces of cutlery, into a bag which we have from The Lord Nelson Hotel back in Halifax.

'Have you filled the Lord Nelson bag?' becomes a password for 'Is lunch sorted?'

We have to do all this without being rumbled by the staff.

After the breakfast buffet has worked its magic, and the Lord Nelson bag is full of lunch, we return to our room and prepare to leave.

'Wot?' says Honey. 'Why? Why can't we stay here playing shops?'

All of Honey's little treasures – her pencils, the *Oui! On Fait du Coloriage* book, and some key icons (a teddy, a torch, a tiny beaded purse and a shell) – are spread out neatly on a bedside table. The table represents a miniature version of Galeries Lafayette. Lucien has been press-ganged into being the only customer.

Gabriel is watching French traffic reports, discovering how busy the circulation is in Lyons this morning.

'Come on, you lot,' I squawk. 'We have to go to a rum distillery!' This is met by zero response. 'Well, you know, we might catch the Tour de Martinique.'

'Okaaay,' the children chorus, lumbering to their feet like one reluctant being.

The Tour de Martinique goes around the island like a mini sort of Tour de France.

Laurent says it might hold us up on our way to the rum factory, and twenty minutes later, on a hairpin bend somewhere in the middle of the island, this indeed comes to pass.

'Must we stay here on this corner, Laurent?' I ask him as I unpick myself from the boot of the car. Cheering crowds are standing by the road, whistling. Laurent takes no notice of me, but gestures up the road.

Suddenly, to the bleeps of hundreds of klaxons, come the leaders: six or seven bicycles whizzing around the corner, ridden by whippet-thin men in bright Lycra suits. After five minutes come two hundred more, followed by a huge entourage of support vehicles which reveal, on huge rooftop billboards, that they are sponsored by Danone, RFO television, Perrier and Renault.

'Film it! Film it!' shout the children, and we do. It's great. It's impossible not to get whipped up by the excitement, the speed, the colour. Everyone associates the Caribbean with cricket, but of course nobody plays cricket here. It is just as much of a colonial import as cycling races are. It's simply that one is a British imposition, the other French.

Just as quickly as they appear, the entire party vanishes. Back in the car, the children clamour to see the footage, and we rewind the tape. What a stupid mistake that was. When we arrive at the rum factory, we forget we had done this, and record over everything. All our footage of the Tour de Martinique is lost, the images only a memory.

The Clément Distillery is one of a handful of rum factories left in Martinique. A by-product from sugar, rum was discovered rather useful in World War One, as it was doled out as 'grog' to the hapless troops in the trenches. It then became frightfully fashionable and promoted by the likes of Josephine Baker in Paris, as a bit of 'tropicana' in the *quartiers*.

The reason we are interested in the Clément Distillery is because it was the only such distillery to be founded by a black man, and as such, was rather an anomaly in Martinique, where the white *'beke'* – or French slave owners – had complete power on the island. According to some, their descendants still have the whip hand.

The *beke* own 80 per cent of the industry, the shops, the hotels and the garages, while the Creole majority who live on the island must be satisfied by working for the descendents of people who used to oversee their forebears labouring on the vast sugar plantations which once dominated the island.

Of course at the Clément Distillery, where the rum matures in oak barrels under the tranquil strains of piped-in Debussy, the unhappy history of Martinique is rather played down. Instead, the distillery promotes the fact that it also has a giant arboretum with thirty or forty different species of palm tree growing beside a large lake. There is also a rather outrageous contemporary art gallery exhibiting paintings showing audacious interpretations of sexual congress.

So I'm rigged up with my microphone and battery pack, and start wandering around the place, doing several pieces to camera about rum, palms and the history of Martinique. Crouched behind the tripod, Pip appears contented, for once. Laurent is getting the children to find, and eat, industrial quantities of mango. At this point Honey decides to go for a swim. In the lake.

'I only wanted to get my foot wet,' she says afterwards, when I am desperately searching for dry clothes suitable for a six-year-old child, and trying not to think what might have happened had not Laurent suddenly spotted our daughter struggling up to her waist in a large, muddy lake, yelling to be pulled out.

My father's words as we parted echo again in my head. 'Just remember. Keep the children safe. That's the only thing.'

'And we didn't!' I shout at Pip underneath the giant, slim trunk of an historic palm. 'Honey wandered into a lake! She nearly drowned!'

'You nearly drowned!' I shout at Honey. I quickly take off her soaking clothes and put her into a long Clément Distillery T-shirt.

'I was just trying to measure the depth of the lake,' she replies, examining her small, thin, dripping leg.

'Mummeee?'

'What?' I gasp.

'Do you think I might have leeches? Gabriel thinks these brown things might be leeches.'

Indeed, on my daughter's calves there are brown blobs that look like splashes of mud, only they will not be washed away so easily.

'Yes, they are leeches,' I say, almost pleased that my child can now witness the folly of her ways, in the relatively benign form of blood-sucking annelids. I can't face touching them and I know Honey will put up a struggle if I try.

'Laurent, could you…?'

Laurent patiently puts down his bag of mangoes and expertly dismisses the leeches with a flick of a broad thumbnail. A tiny trickle of blood runs out from each place on her leg. Honey is too amazed to cry, or even give him a kick, both of which she would have certainly done to her mother had I been in charge of leech removal.

Our assistant at the Clément Distillery, who has clearly replaced her assessment of us as a smart media outfit with one of us as a chaotic family who have no idea how to look after their children, invites us to go for *la dégustation*. This is a very good idea. We spend the next forty minutes trying out a range of fabulously flavoured rums, which have clearly benefited hugely from having been matured to French classical music. Not in Gabriel's opinion.

'This is nasty!' he splutters, after I have allowed him to have a tiny taste.

Eventually, the director decides we have filmed enough on the subject of making rum, and we pile everything back in the car. When we arrive at the hotel, hot and tired, there is only one thing to do, which is to have a refreshing swim in the Batalière's deep, round and unpeopled swimming pool. Air France hostesses clearly don't like getting their hair wet.

I never see more than about two people, other than us, in the pool during our entire stay.

Anyway, we have bought the children new masks and snorkels at the local supermarket, and they are keen to try them out.

'Ha ha, I've got your snorkel,' shouts Gabriel, dancing around by the deep end of the pool.

'Will you just behave?' I ask him. 'We've already had one incident today. Can everyone just calm down and do some nice swimming?'

I'm in the shallow end trying to get Lucien to push himself off from the wall and swim into my arms.

'He's my youngest child and I WILL teach him how to swim,' I had announced on the way to Martinique. For some reason, I consider this part of dutiful parenting, probably because I feel rather guilty about not teaching the others.

From the deep end, a wail goes up. Gabriel has tossed Honey's snorkel into the pool, and it is now gently sitting on the bottom, 5 metres down.

'I'll go and get it,' I say bravely, carrying Lucien out.

'You all sit down here on this towel. Look after Lucien.'

I stride up to the edge of the pool like a modern-day Wonder Woman. That's the idea, anyway. Then I dive in. Blimey, 5 metres is a long way down. I can see the snorkel, but I just can't reach it. I start to panic about running out of air, and resurface, spluttering.

'I'll try it again.' I don't want to seem weedy before my children. I have this airy-fairy notion that I might inspire my offspring that, yes, modern-day woman can have it all. In other words, she can knock off a bit of journalism about palm trees in the morning, and dive 5 metres in the evening, while being a calm, level-headed and glamorous parent. I dive in again.

Again, the snorkel lies temptingly just out of reach. Again, I panic about not having enough breath.

'It's just as well you're not going for the free-diving championships,' snorts Pip, who has joined the children on the lounger.

'Look, help is at hand!'

Humiliatingly, Gabriel has spotted a long pole with a net on the end of it. He pushes the offending snorkel along to the shallow end where I can collect it by simply bending down.

As I get out, I discover I am unable to hear anything.

I shake my head, and poke my ears.

'You should never put anything smaller than your elbow into your ear,' advises Gabriel. He sounds like he is speaking at the far end of a long Hoover tube.

'Will you be quiet,' I snap at him. 'I'm only like this because of your idiocy.'

I march, still dripping, over to the reception desk.

'Je n'entends rien!' ('I can't hear a thing!') I say to the receptionist in a panic. Imagine spending the rest of the trip like this, is all I can think. My French is bad enough as it is, meaning that I can only grasp about 50 per cent of what people say to me anyway.

'I can't go around the world like this!' I yell at Pip.

'Er, j'ai besoin d'un medicin,' ('Look, I need a doctor') I say in a slightly more reasonable tone to the receptionist.

'Pas de soucis,' ('No worries') she trills, dialling a Special Number.

I turn triumphantly around to the children, who are watching the proceedings in hushed concern. 'This is why we are going around the French world, rather than any other world. Well, this is one of the reasons why. Because it is civilised. And they have doctors here.'

One hour later there's a rat-a-tat-tat on my bedroom door. Indeed, it is a French doctor, with his bag and instead of a hat, a comedy haircut. I greet him and courteously invite him in to inspect my ears.

'Where are you from?' I ask.

'Alors, Bordeaux!'

Tempted by the 30 per cent pay increase you get in Martinique, *n'est-ce pas*? No wonder the Air France flights out here are packed full of smartly suited professionals.

He looks at my ear while I gaze, fascinated, at his crazy coiffure. It's a sort of mad explosion of curls, somewhat like the hairdo belonging to American philosopher Malcolm Gladwell. He gives me a prescription for a variety of complicated ear solutions and a bill for 200 euros.

Gosh, that's quite a lot of money. We walk out together, the doctor and I, to a cashpoint where I hand over the notes and he gives me a receipt, written of course in that looping style all French people seemingly learn from birth.

When I get back to the hotel room I discover the children watching a Jacques Tati film.

One of the ideas behind the French Empire was that it would not only bring riches and luxuries to France, but in return, it would spread French culture; turning non-Europeans into French people and creating versions of *la Métropole* across the world – education, administration, the legal system; it would all radiate out from Paris. That was the idea, at least. This political theory, known as assimilation, sounds noble and worthy, but it's not. 'The policy was manifestly unworkable, and simultaneously both naively utopian, sexist and racist,' write Aldrich and Connell in a book which, it's safe to say, has probably not been read all that much by the French diaspora, since it is in English. This is not to say that the French can't read books in English, of course.

It's just that I suspect critical judgement by outsiders of the political set-up is not welcomed. When we return to England, I will write a rather questioning piece for *The Sunday Times* about the cost and future of the DOM-TOMs, and receive a most aggrieved email from the cultural attaché of the French Embassy in London. Get on with your world and we'll get on with ours, seems to be the over-riding attitude.

The British were no saints when they had their empire, but they were rather more pragmatic about the notion of turning people in the colonies into versions of themselves. The French didn't think this way. They considered that everyone should take part in singing 'La Marseillaise' and practising *liberté*, *égalité* and *fraternité*. This, according to Eliacin Luro, the first director of the École Nationale de la France d'Outre Mer in the nineteenth century, was how it was done:

'One must not go too quickly... one must understand, penetrate the civilisation of the conquered, know their language... then little by little, patiently direct their steps, modify their pace.'

The problem is that in some ways, the deal looks rather appealing. When Martinique, led by the charismatic Aimé Césaire, was granted departmental status, having to speak the language, play the ball games and read *Le Monde* seemed like a small price to pay for all the benefits involved in being run directly from Paris. Indeed, Césaire pushed for it.

But it's difficult being fully French in the Caribbean. Foggy Saint Pierre et Miquelon is one thing; it is rather European in its outlook, and there was no indigenous population to win over. This is not the case with Martinique. It is a beautiful, lush, fertile island and being annexed onto Europe doesn't necessarily sit well amid the banana groves.

Not everyone on the island wants to have their hearts and minds attached to *le tricolore*. Césaire, of course, understood this too, and always insisted that Martinique's influences came as much from Africa as from France. As we drive around, we spot plenty of houses flying the red, green and black flag of Independent Martinique. The *indépendantistes* (in other words, the political faction agitating for total independence and separation from the metropole) would like to wash the French Touch away for ever, and venture out into a brave new world without the presence of universal benefits, health care, *nos ancêtres les Gaulois*, and Mr Bricolage.

One of the key issues on the island is the legacy of slavery. When the island was originally discovered, it was a valuable prize. Abundantly fertile, with its volcanic soil and a perfect climate, it was an ideal place to farm luxuries such as sugar, coffee and spices. The issue of labour was unproblematic, too, since Martinique's position in the Caribbean meant it could benefit from the slave trade, in which Europeans took Africans by boat across the Atlantic, forced them to work in the Caribbean and exported the valuable goods they produced back to Europe. The French first arrived in 1635, and had to work hard to stay in charge, particularly against the British. Eventually, the British grabbed the island in 1762. But one year later, there was the Canadian carve-up between France and Britain, so France was allowed to keep Martinique, along with Guadeloupe and Saint Domingue.

In 1789, the French Revolution threw everything into chaos, however, and a few years later a chap called Jean Baptiste Dubuc effectively gave the island back to the Brits. The crucial effect of this was that the practice of slavery was continued in Martinique's sugar plantations. (France abolished slavery in all its colonies in 1794, but the British did not abolish slavery until 1807.) From this point, the island was handed back and forth between the two countries and somehow the slave issue was forgotten about. It wasn't officially abolished in Martinique until 1848, some fifty years later than in the rest of France.

And according to some, the odour of slavery still hangs over the beautiful Île des Fleurs.

'There's nowhere more disgusting than Martinique,' spits Caroline Popovitch.

Caroline is British, married a Frenchman, lives in Guadeloupe and profiles the yachts belonging to millionaires for a luxury magazine. She's thin, tanned and a class warrior.

We are sitting (Caroline and I) outside on the terrace beside the deserted bar in the hotel. Pip is filming our encounter. The children are upstairs watching French cartoons on the television. I left them sitting in the room, resigned despair etched on their faces.

'I can't wait until I get home and see *Chuggington* again,' said Lucien sadly, as he settled down to view a Gallic cartoon about a donkey.

Chatting to Caroline, I still have my head on one side, but every so often her voice comes in loud and clear, before disappearing back into a rumble down a long tube. My ears are getting better.

'There is not an easy relationship here with France,' she continues. 'We are very good consumers here, you know. Did you know we are the department that consumes the most champagne? Out of all the departments in all of France! We buy Renaults and Peugeots and we buy lots of air tickets. And we are very good taxpayers, I might add.'

A beautiful white yacht sails past behind her. 'Because of the distances, because of the whole history of slavery, because of what they consider to be a lack of sensitivity by France, there are problems. The society here is feudal, because of the *beke*,' Caroline says, with venom. 'They still own everything on the island.'

There are only 1,000 *beke* on the island, yet they own over half of Martinique's wealth. Apparently the term comes from the word 'beak', as if they fed their slaves with their beaks, like parent birds feeding utterly dependent chicks. The *beke*, it seems, have the island somewhat as a personal cash cow and tropical playground.

They have their own special ghetto, an area called Le François, where they have their mansions, hotels, parties and their own marriages. And when they can't find another *beke* to marry, they import someone of their class and race from France.

'They have maintained all their old privileges,' says Caroline. 'And they still think they have the island to themselves. Martinique has never got slavery out of its system. It's like an abscess here that never burst. The trouble is that Martinique never had a revolution. Hey, Pascale,' she says, swinging off her chair and greeting a Martiniquais woman who walks over and sits down with us. This is Pascale Lavernaine, a local TV reporter.

'Just filling in Rosie about the *beke*,' says Caroline, rolling her eyes dramatically and sipping a Diet Coke. 'They have this way of living which... raises a lot of questions.'

Pascale nods her head. 'They inherited their power and money from the slave trade, and when slavery was over, they went into other areas of the economy. We needed Papa Césaire,' she says quietly, referring to the celebrated poet, intellectual and politician, Aimé Césaire.

Césaire reminded the black Martiniquais that they were as much African as they were French. Deputy to the National Assembly and mayor of Fort de France since 1944, he was crucial in Martinique's status as an official department, yet advocated autonomous rule for the island. He died in 2008.

'We miss him a lot. Every day he was among us.' She pauses, and looks up at the whirring ceiling fans. 'He wasn't some sort of... abstract personality, some celebrity that we couldn't reach. I interviewed him many times. He was going to his office until the very last weeks of his life.' There are giant posters of Césaire across town. In the airport, alongside the brass clocks which tell travellers what the time is in Paris, giant billboards quote his poetry, which he always wrote in French.

'Yes, well, he wasn't going to write in Creole, was he?' says Caroline with a grin.

To communicate internationally in Martiniquais Creole would lead into something of an intellectual cul-de-sac, as it is not a globally understood language. This is what happened to Creole-speaking Haiti, and Martinique certainly has no intention of following the fortunes of that island, which broke away from France during Napoleon's rule. There are some advantages in being forced to learn French.

Yet the island seems to be caught in an uneasy stranglehold. It's a bit like seeing the traditional *yole* boat being blown along forcefully by the Mr Bricolage sail.

'I think we should definitely go and do some interviews in Le François,' I say to Pip. 'Why don't we go to the *beke* hotel out there?'

He nods. First, however, we have to go the other way.

The Slave Colony, or La Savane des Esclaves, is a very sober affair. Built by local historian Gilbert Larose, this purports to show how the slaves lived, once they were emancipated in 1848 and escaped from the plantation bunkhouses to their own social structure. It seems that the liberated slaves constructed huts from banana leaves and stems halfway up a hill. We meet Larose at the entrance, and he takes us to the building where the slaves would have had meetings and communal meals.

It's pretty hot in La Savane des Esclaves. I mean, it feels like we are on the surface of Venus. I'm trying to chat to Larose in a meaningful way, but my face is puce with heat, and sweat is simply cascading down my legs. I estimate there are about twenty mosquitoes on my arms and legs at any one time. Small squeaks from the children indicate they are suffering likewise.

'We have to get this done fast,' says Pip grimly. 'And I have to interview him in the light, not the shade. Can we please move to a sunnier spot?'

We move from the surface of Venus to the surface of Mercury.

'I'm hoping to get people here to do sleepovers,' Larose confides in me.

'What, tourists?'

'*Mais oui*. Eco-tourists.'

You'd have to be a pretty ardent eco-tourist to weather a night in La Savane des Esclaves, frankly. Moreover, Larose is struggling against the system. The Martinique Tourism Authority is not about to put the slave colony high up on its list of must-sees, although it is a remarkable reconstruction.

'Madame la Grandmaison has yet to visit us,' admits Larose, referring to the head of the tourist board. He shows me an authentic kitchen (lots of earthenware bowls) and a bedroom with a sacking mattress on the bed.

'Looks about as comfortable as the Hotel Robert,' mutters Pip, who has yet to fully forgive Saint Pierre et Miquelon for being so hideous.

'Now we absolutely have to go,' he whispers to me. 'The children are about to pass out.'

We take our leave of the beaming Monsieur Lerose. 'Come back and taste some of our ground manioc!' he pleads. 'We pound it with the coconut stem!'

Instead, gasping, sweating and bitten, we go to a cafe by the seaside where a waiter from Le Mans serves us with the sort of barely disguised indifference which you might have thought was peculiar only to waiters in Paris.

Pip takes a call from the people at the *beke* hotel. We are not welcome there, it seems. There is nobody available for interview, and if we want to do some filming there, we must rent a room for that purpose, at a cost of about 300 euros for a day.

On Laurent's advice we go to a chocolate factory the next morning. This is one of the local points of interest. It is a noisy metal box full of heat and oil. The people here have moulded and wrapped dark chocolate for over twenty years.

'Oh, great!' says Gabriel over the roar of the presses. 'We did this as a project at school, we called it From Bean to Bar.'

'Any Big Thoughts?' shouts Pip. Oh, God.

'Well, other than the fact our child is seeing a project he has done at school Come Alive, no,' I yell back at him.

'Take me to the loo, Mummy!' says Lucien, correctly divining that I am about to start doing a piece to camera.

And yet however much I rail at Pip for directing me at every opportunity, and however often I shout at the children, we have got to make this work. There is no question about what if? We have to come back with six documentaries, which can be filled with whatever we think will help the viewer analyse what makes this weird empire tick, and capture its essence. No matter what.

Pip decides, probably correctly,that the factory is too loud to do any sensible work at all. We explain this to Laurent, who very sweetly offers to take us to the beach. The beach is fabulous, in a way that only Caribbean beaches can be; a Bounty-bar advert come alive, with swaying palm trees and platinum sand and turquoise water. We run in and out of the water, laughing. It's all right, everything is going to be all right. I think about this that evening as we sit on our beds eating pizza from a nearby mobile takeaway. It's a rather good bonding experience, and anyway, we can't afford anything else.

CHAPTER EIGHT

An Unforgettable Night

Honey's diary: *I learnt how to take malaria tablets. You get a drink. Befor that you put the malaria tablets in the back of your mouth and get the drink gulp gulp gulp.*

At least when the darkness falls in Martinique it's still safe to walk up the road and buy a pizza from a mobile pizza place. Or get some cash from the cashpoint for the doctor who has sorted your ear out. And there is no malaria or yellow fever. Tap water is drinkable. There are clean, safe beaches on which concrete rectangles for the evening game of pétanque have been built. The insects are reasonably sized.

None of the above is true in French Guiana, or as the French call it, Guyane.

Apart from the pétanque, that is. Pétanque is played throughout the French empire, even in Guyane, which is without doubt the most obscure and savage diamond in the glittering holdings of *la République française*.

Guyane is a sliver of South America perched above Brazil. It was grabbed by the French at some point in the seventeenth

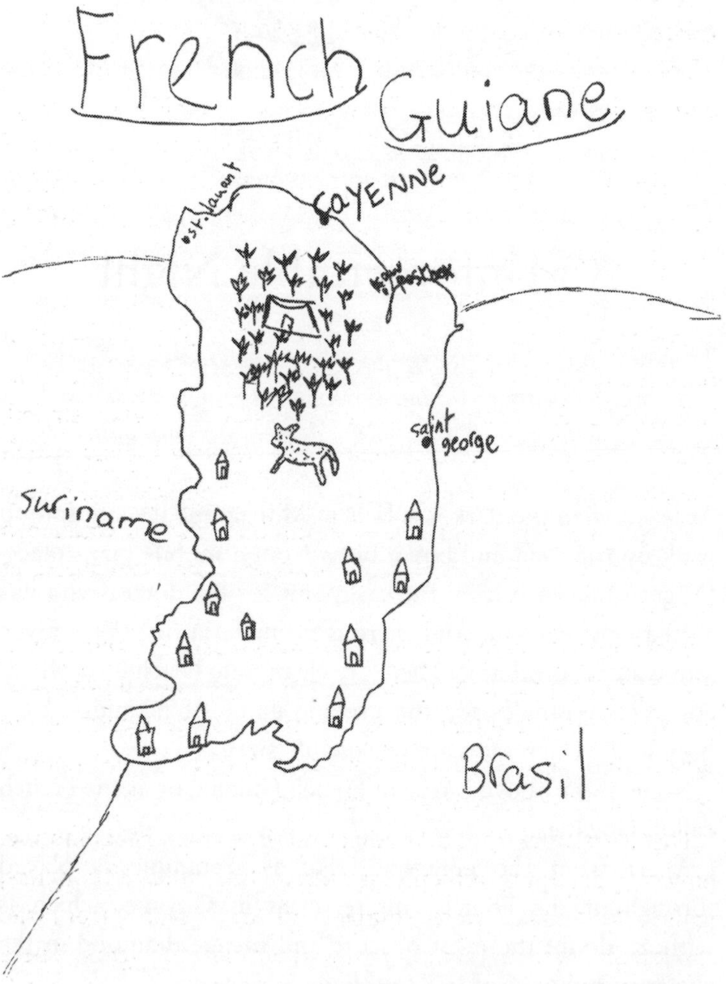

French Guiane

st-laurent
CAYENNE
saint george
Suriname
Brasil

century in the mad search for the legendary city of gold, El Dorado, which was said to lie somewhere in the equally legendary range of the Tumuc-Humac Mountains, a plateau which leads down into the Amazon basin.

The Dutch and the British were both chasing the same notional booty. Only several hundred years after Walter Raleigh turned up, it gradually became clear that clambering around the Tumuc-Humacs trying to spot El Dorado was probably not worth it. The dripping, boundless rainforest was full of lots of things; spiders, a thousand different mammals, three thousand species of tree, and nasty diseases. What it was not full of, however, was easily accessible gold. The governments of Britain and Holland eventually pushed off, leaving a residue of still hopeful prospectors in their wake. But the French stayed, finding themselves saddled with a bug-infested colony which was too treacherous to be mined, its land too wet and jungly to be planted with sugar, like Martinique, and its water too full of alluvial soil to be fished effectively, like Saint Pierre et Miquelon.

So what to do with Guyane? The French chose to reinvent it. Firstly, they turned it into a huge depot for unwanted prisoners. More recently they have tried to shake off the legacy of the prison, and turn Guyane into a haven for eco-tourism and a centre for hi-tech adventures into space.

The despairing sound of shackled feet and the guillotine, however, are quite difficult to erase. Thousands of convicts, male and female, were shipped off to Guyane from the end of the eighteenth century for the next 150 years. These included the innocent French officer Alfred Dreyfus, whose life imprisonment for espionage caused an international scandal in the late nineteenth century, and Henri 'Papillon' Charrière, whose adventures were turned into the best-selling book and eponymous Hollywood movie. You could be packed off to Guyane for common or garden crimes, revolutionary crimes, political crimes; you could even be sent for pinching an apple on the streets of Paris. It was known as 'Green Hell'. Why? Because being sent to Guyane was tantamount to a death sentence.

Of the thousands who were shipped out there, most died of a noxious combination of malaria, yellow fever or starvation. Even if you survived the horrendous conditions of the infamous prison known as Le Bagne, you would probably perish under the strain of having to work an equal number of years in hard labour, which was the legal requirement by the French state.

Le Bagne and its hellish conditions might explain why the French turned Guyane into a fully fledged department, and hung onto it with such determination. Assuaging the stain of Guyane's shameful past might have been the catalyst for France to pour millions of euros into the Ariane space station, a commercial venture to send satellites into space which is co-funded with the EU. It might also have been the prompt for France to look after Guyane's millions of square kilometres of virgin rainforest responsibly, promoting eco-tourism and turning the forest into national parks. Only 250,000 people live in Guyane, a space one sixth the size of France, and not many French people visit it. But the over-riding sensation is that France belatedly wants to do the right thing in this uncelebrated corner of its empire.

We are on Air France flight no. 3970, travelling 1,400 kilometres from Martinique to Guyane and enjoying a perfect *petit déjeuner* served to us by an outrageously glamorous stewardess.

'More stewed apple!' shouts Lucien, glorying in the only clearly recognisable food he has seen since leaving England, bar Campbell's Soup.

'More stewed apple!' Our hostess, whose blue eyeliner matches her perfectly fitted suit, reappears with a tray and a smile and obliges his wish.

When his malaria tablet is produced from my special Malaria Pill Pouch and turns up on his tray, however, things are not so happy.

'No! No!' he yells. 'No pills!'

'Put it on the back of your tongue, like a really big, big boy,' I beg him. He clamps his lips tight, meaning I am forced to prise his rose-coloured mouth open like someone forcing a bit into the mouth of a particularly stubborn Shetland pony.

The pill goes in. I clamp his jaws tightly shut.

Lucien struggles in his seat, making mechanical-sounding wails. Bright yellow fluid runs out of the corners of his mouth; the custard-coloured tablet is melting in his saliva, but he refuses to swallow it. People in seats around me start turning to have a look at this cruel mother and her poor little son. In vain, I push the fluid back through his lips. The volume of yelling increases, forcefully and exponentially.

'Do you want to be bitten by a mosquito? Do you?' I shout. 'And possibly die?'

He looks at me through tear-soaked lashes and continues to yell.

The immaculate stewardesses closes the curtain through to First.

'Look, Lucien, it's easy!' says Gabriel, showing off as he takes his.

'You see?' I shout. 'You see? Gabriel has to have TWO tablets. And now he is going to have... another stewed apple!'

It is the perfect bribe. I signal frantically to the stewardess to come back, and provide us with an entire tray of stewed apple. Eventually Lucien takes his tablet, amid much stewed apple and more weeping. I fret that he has not ingested anything like the necessary quantity.

'My father will kill me if I bring back the kids with bloody malaria,' I say to Pip, who rolls his eyes and continues reading *Ulysses*, because he never got past page 345 when he was a student.

'If four months of long-haul flights aren't enough for me to conquer this bloody book, I don't know what will be,' he grumbles.

I breathe deeply, take pleasure in a tepid cup of coffee, and look out of the window.

We are 9,000 metres above the rainforest, and the trees go on and on like a misty, emerald carpet, right up to the horizon without stopping. A giant brown river winds its curves through the green like a muddy snake. There appear to be no roads, cities, indeed no single sign of human habitation.

Eventually we start our descent into Cayenne. It feels like we are flying through a bright green duvet.

'Mummee,' says Honey quietly. 'Will there be insects here?'

I choose not to answer this.

'This place is going to be a challenge,' I murmur to Pip.

As we arrive at Cayenne airport and produce our Yellow Fever Certificates, which are obligatory, the air is shaking with wet heat. Through the voluminous greenery beside the airport can be spotted the unmistakable sign of a bright green Mr Bricolage building. And through the pouring rain the *tricolore* is flying triumphantly on the small white airport building. *Bien sûr*, we are still in France.

Regina, the mother of Noemie, our wonderful French assistant in London, is here to greet us along with her younger daughter. Her husband Herve is a gendarme working in the DOM-TOMs; they're coming to the end of a three-year stint in

Cayenne. Regina is motherly and French, with properly coiffed hair, a flowery dress and pearl earrings. Herve is broad and capable looking, with epaulettes and a pistol swinging from his official leather belt.

We are enfolded into the generous embrace of a real French family who know our names and are excited to see us. The warmth and emotion of being met at the airport by people we know, even by proxy, is overwhelming. Regina is crying, and I probably would be too if I wasn't so hot.

'Alors,' says Regina, 'bienvenue à Cayenne!'

Under a canopy of giant trees, storm clouds and vultures, we splash out to the car park through gusts of tepid water. The rain appears to be multi-directional, rather than falling from the sky as it might do at home.

Regina drives us to the Motel Beauregard – which for some reason is universally known as the Cric-Crac – on roads which are solid, tarmacked and furnished with signs bearing the familiar font of French motorway signage. Superficially at least, the capital of Guyane appears as a civilised Gallic outpost. We are not staying in a hotel, because there aren't any. Actually, there is a Hotel Mercure and a solitary Best Western in the centre of town, but on Trip Advisor a recent guest wrote that when he arrived at the Best Western, all his luggage was stolen, thirty minutes after check-in. So we aren't going there. We've been advised to steer clear of the Mercure as well, because it's in the same location.

The Cric-Crac is a guarded motel used by French business people who are in Cayenne for work. Nobody visits Guayne for fun, it seems.

We arrive at an unassuming assemblage of bungalows clustered around a central building. There is a small concrete-lined pool enlivened by a single slide.

I push open the main door, which has a sticker saying *'Bienvenue en France'*, and a cockerel in the colours of the *tricolore*. We stagger in with our thirteen bags.

Inside, a large television is tuned to RF1, where a besuited newsreader is going through the French news. I'm immune by now to the way the French are content to watch reports on events 10,000 kilometres away, but it still makes me smile.

The children jump up and down beside the reception counter.

'Where's our house, where's our house?! Where's our hutch?!'

We are not staying in rooms, but our own little bungalow.

Contrary to the promise of the sticker on her door, the owner of the Cric-Crac is not overtly welcoming. Madame Briand must be in her sixties, with blonde coiffed hair and a smart sundress. Her face is leathery and not given to smiling too much. She slings a key at us, informs us our bungalow is still being cleaned, and retreats into a back room with a Gitanes between her fingers.

We wait for half an hour in the restaurant, drinking Coke. The restaurant is decorated with a frieze showing how French prisoners who stupidly tried to escape from Le Bagne were tortured and guillotined before the gaze of their compatriots. Honestly, what is it about French dining rooms? What with the maps of shipwrecks in the restaurant of the Hotel Robert, and now this, I conclude that the French, or at least their interior designers, must be guided by some sort of macabre 'life in death' philosophy, that you must be reminded of your mortality while you eat.

Needless to say, our children are riveted by this gory fresco.

'Come on, you lot,' I say brightly, picking up a menu for diversion. There appears to be a whole section on wild animals that you can have roasted and served up for your delectation.

'Look, you can even have guinea pig here.'

'Wot, as a pet?' says Lucien. 'Great! I love guinea pigs.'

'Not quite what Mummy meant,' says Pip brightly, pushing Lucien in the small of the back. 'Come on, come on. I think our bungalow will be ready now.'

The forest looms up on the other side of the wall which encompasses the motel compound. Giant palm trees, lianas, towering mahoganies, tamarinds, pineapple trees, mangoes and unidentifiable plants with vast leaves and towering trunks dwarf the buildings. If the plants themselves cannot reach out and touch us, the creatures of the rainforest can. Rather large, vivid lizards stalk the terraces. Chunky centipedes march along the railings. On the roof of one bungalow, a toucan stiffly bounces. It hops with bright blue legs and is burdened with a multicoloured beak of impossible dimensions. The glory of seeing this extraordinary bird slightly diminishes the fact that our living conditions are somewhat basic. Our lodgings are akin to a barrack. There are two bedrooms. I recognise the pillows; they are the Saint Pierre et Miquelon familiars, hard, sweat-encrusted rectangles from which any softness was squeezed many years ago. There is a lino-floored sitting room illuminated by neon and furnished with two chairs and a spare bed. A kitchen with a single cold water tap, and a fridge. A dining table and five chairs are outside on the terrace. The departing flash of a green tail around the corner and the looming jungle indicates that the presence of one or more large insects in our house is highly likely.

On cue, Honey starts wailing from the bathroom.

'Aaaaghhh!!! Mummeee!!!'

I find her beside a cockroach as long as a cigarette, but three times as wide, in the corridor. Oh, God. Well, it's what Croc shoes are made for, I think as we watch Pip manfully dismembering it with one. A creamy substance pours out from the bisected body of the cockroach.

'Look! Cockroach blood!' shouts Lucien.

'Well, at least we're going to have a nice night out tonight,' says Pip.

Indeed. We are going out with Regina and Herve for supper at the home of the chief of police.

'What are we going to eat for supper, Mummee?' says Lucien.

'Oh, I don't know, darling,' I say brightly. 'Something delicious.'

We unpack our neatly folded clothes and put them away in the usual routine. This now takes us about eight minutes.

'Right, everyone,' says Pip. 'Regina and Herve are meeting us by the security gate in about two minutes, so let's get going.' We lock the doors, but take all our camera gear and passports with us just in case.

I can't wait for supper. Is not French food altogether delicious? And are we not in a department of France? Yes, the institutional food we have experienced so far in the DOM-TOMs has not been great, but we have spotted traces of superior French cuisine around the place. Particularly on the few occasions we've eaten with people at their homes. Surely now that we have been befriended by Regina and Herve, all will be plain sailing into the safe berth of French country cooking.

Sadly, at this point I do not realise that of course, here in savage, wild Guyane, French country cooking cannot help but be somewhat altered.

When we arrive at the house of Jules, the chief of police, there is a lot of laughter. The chief of police is a huge black man sporting an immaculate suit and Christian Dior sunglasses. He roars a greeting, half encouragement, half amazement. I suspect we are the first English people he has ever encountered on his home turf. He enfolds us in a bearhug. Staggering from his embrace, I walk through the kitchen, which is decorated entirely by full-length posters of topless women in thongs.

'Bien sûr, on dois avoir du rhum!' ('Of course, we've got to have rum!') booms the chief of police, bearing a bottle of the stuff in a giant paw.

'Allez! On va à la cabane!' (Let's go to the summer house!')

The *'cabane'* is a small shady pavilion in the garden, where a giant swimming pool takes up what would have been the lawn. At the *cabane*, other guests are already sitting at a round table; Regina and Herve, who is still in uniform, two other policemen, a jolly chap called Richard, who is also a gendarme, and an ageing but still reasonably sexy Frenchman called Jean-Lou. Jean-Lou has a beautiful Guadeloupian woman on his arm. And when I say beautiful, I mean beautiful. Tiny waist, impossibly perfect breasts, long legs, plaited hair, face like a doll, laugh like a tinkling bell. She laughs and kisses me on both cheeks, at which gesture Regina raises her eyebrows disdainfully.

The rum is handed around, and Coke for the children, who are immediately thrilled and suggest jumping in the pool.

'Er, not just now, guys,' I say, steering them back into the house.

'Come with me, Rosie,' laughs Richard. *'Je vais vous montrer le dîner.'* ('I'll show you supper.') As well as being Herve and Jules' best mate, Richard is a high-up in the gendarmerie, something of a gastronome, and is in charge of tonight's supper. What will it be? I wonder. We repair to the kitchen.

I gasp in horror. Richard is holding up two iguana.

These striped lizards are about a foot long. They have a ruff of frilled skin around their heads. They have long, long tails. They have prickly spines delineating their skeletal spines. They have enormous claws. They look like nothing you would ever dream of putting in your mouth. They are also very, very dead.

'Shot them this morning, in honour of your presence,' says Richard.

'Where?' I manage to whisper.

'Oh, just around the corner, close to my house.' Richard leans forward. He is still holding them. I can hardly bear it.

'They are female, which you know is the great speciality. Because they still have eggs inside them, and that is delicious. Eating the unborn eggs, *ah oui*.' He gestures to a stainless steel basin where what look like twenty or so small ping-pong balls are floating in diluted blood. Iguana eggs.

'Great, I'm hungry already,' I say weakly, shepherding the children towards the television where a French evangelist is enthusiastically broadcasting from a christening.

'Oh yuck!' shouts Honey. 'I am NOT eating that!'

I push her hurriedly away. For once, I agree with her. Guinea pig, by contrast, is looking like a much more palatable choice. Sadly, it's not on the menu here.

Behind me in the kitchen, Richard has started to prepare the iguana. He is chopping them up with a giant blade. Lucien is standing beside him, curls damp with sweat, eyes bright with curiosity over the edge of the counter. Richard is not skinning the bright, bloody iguana meat. He is just expertly cubing it. He will then casserole the chunks of meat, plus eggs, with herbs and spices for about two hours.

'Let's go back to the, er, *cabane*,' I suggest to the children.

We walk slowly back to the *cabane* where the champagne and 50 per cent proof rum is flowing.

After about ten minutes, Richard joins us.

We sit for about an hour and a half, drinking steadily. I am trying the 'one glass soft, one glass hard' technique, but as soon as we have satisfied the chief of police that we have tasted one type of rum, another turns up. I figure that he might be kindly trying to anesthetise our tastebuds with rum before the Dish of the Day arrives.

The children are quietly doing *'Oui! On Fait du Coloriage!'* at a table beside us. Darkness falls like a shutter and the jungle seems to burst into noise, clicking and whirring with thousands of unseen living things. It is still terrifically warm and moist. Indeed, the sensation reminds me somewhat of sitting in that sauna underneath the Islington Angel, except when I look up, I see thousands of equatorial stars, not the timber slats of a ceiling in N1.

Honey asks if she might go to the toilet.

'But of course!' says Regina. 'I'll take her. You stay talking to Jean-Lou,' she says.

They are away for about ten minutes.

Suddenly, there is a commotion outside, back up at the house. The chief of police runs across to the building, followed by Richard. There are raised voices and lights go on across the garden. Honey comes walking carefully back to us.

'There was a burglar,' she says quietly.

'What happened, what's going on?' I ask.

'I think I scared away a burglar.'

What?

The situation appears to have been thus. While a total of five gendarmes, plus the chief of police, were drinking champers and rum in the *cabane*, an opportunistic thief ventured onto the terrace of the chief of police's home. At which point a small English girl, aged six, arrived on the terrace. He was in search of things to steal; she in search of a lavatory. Had Honey, plus chaperone, not made an appearance at that precise moment, there is no question that the thief would have gone into the sitting room. Presumably he would have pinched the first thing he found to hand; our bags, which we had left on the sofa, with our passports, money, travel documents, plus our camera gear. It appears the would-be thief took one look at Honey and scarpered on his bike.

'I feel as if I'm going to have a heart attack,' I say to Pip. 'Imagine!'

'I'm imagining, I'm imagining,' he says, with feeling.

To our amazement the chief of police finds the whole episode absolutely hilarious.

While Pip and I are recovering, he is roaring with laughter, cracking open another bottle of rum and plucking a papaya from a nearby bush, almost simultaneously.

'Well, we do call Honey the Force of Nature,' I say to him.

At this juncture, Richard brings out the casserole. Supper, after this exciting and unplanned interlude, is ready.

'Pa pa pa pa!' sing the French around the table, to herald the arrival of the iguana.

Of course, as we have come all the way from England, we are the first to be served. The casserole lid is opened, delivering clouds of pungent steam and a deep smell of ginger with tones of cloves. The meat is put on my plate, along with some rice.

'I've left the heads out,' says Richard, grinning. *Merci*. I'm grateful for small mercies.

I pick at a piece of meat very carefully, trying to slide it away from the striped skin which appears to have been cooked alongside it. A claw floats on my plate.

'Iguana egg?' says Richard, proffering a gelatinous white orb on a spoon. I feel as if I am going to fall underneath the table.

'*Er, non merci,*' I squeak.

Everyone watches as I put a minute piece of iguana into my mouth. I feel like someone on a TV reality show, and grimace my pleasure.

'Mmm, delicious,' I say, hoping I don't have a frill between my teeth.

I notice that the Guadeloupian beauty is tucking into her portion of iguana with unalloyed gusto. She's even eating the eggs.

'Oh, Mummy, please say you hate it,' says Honey, laughing.

After her triumph with the burglar, she's having the time of her life. Gone is the lost look, the clinging to my legs, the whining about wanting to have something English to eat, do or watch. Suddenly, the possibility that our adventure could be just that is very real for Honey.

I manage to ingest a polite amount of iguana casserole. Of which all I can say is thank God for cloves and cinnamon, whose strong presence half obliterated the reality of what else was on my plate.

CHAPTER NINE

Devil's Island

Honey's diary: *The stormyist day of my life. We wer freezing we hated it so much it was so stormy. When we got on this little boat a splash came over and because we wer at the back we got the splash and all our stuff was soaking including my hat.*

The next morning, we eat the chief of police's fresh papaya, plate after plate, on our terrace for breakfast. It is fresh, tender, perfumed and utterly delicious.

'Tastes of sick,' comments Pip. We ignore him.

The children slept well, even though there was a large green lizard crouching on their bedroom wall all night. As the sun burns down and the jungle looms up, emerald, beside us, I feel pathetically grateful to still be in one piece. We haven't had our passports stolen, we haven't been bitten by a giant insect and I haven't fallen ill thanks to iguana munching.

I force everyone to take their malaria tablets. We mask the bitterness with gulps of UHT milk and bites of *pain au chocolat*. Lucien only feels obliged to make a modicum of fuss.

Well, it's progress. A car honks its horn outside. It's Regina and Herve, who are taking us on a tour of Cayenne. 'You will need to go with me,' Herve had said last night, patting his holster in a friendly manner. 'I will take my gun.' This makes me feel extremely comfortable. Guyane is clearly one of those places in which you should expect the unexpected.

'He might be a gendarme, but he certainly takes no prisoners when driving,' mutters Pip as we cruise into Cayenne at top speed. At one point we pass a sign to something called BS147.

'What's that?' I ask from the back of the car.

'The favela. Or one of them,' says Herve, who is occasionally called upon to patrol it. The favela is where thousands of Brazilian émigrés live, with no legal electricity, no schooling and no real rule of law. Attracted by the salaries, decent roads, jobs and civilised infrastructure of Guyane, Brazilians pour over the right-hand border while Surinamese pour over the left-hand border. If the French pulled out, Guyane would be pulled apart, some say, by its neighbours.

On the main route into Cayenne, rickety shops selling piles of fruit are interspersed with vaguely respectable supermarkets, whose Asian signs indicate they are run by settlers from Laos. Having ceased sending convicts to die in Guyane, in the 1970s the French government devised the Plan Vert (Green Plan) which was supposed to encourage farming and forestry, and which involved the migration of about 30,000 people to populate this empty corner of South America. They were mostly French citizens and Hmong refugees from Laos. It wasn't a huge success. The Hmongs had little or no French, and the French themselves, it seems, weren't overtly interested in decamping to a rainforest wilderness. Quite quickly, most of them went back to France. Many of the Hmongs followed them. Those who stayed seem to have cornered the market in small, exuberant, neon-lit grocery shops.

We continue down a street which appears to specialise in stuffed tarantulas. The windows are crammed with giant, black arachnids. They are displayed on squares of polystyrene and are simply vast.

'Can I have a spider? Please! Oh, please can I have a spider?!' begs Gabriel. 'They live in burrows, not webs! They jump out on birds and small mammals! They are awesome!'

'Herve, where are we right now?' I ask. 'Just in case we... need to come back and buy a spider.'

'*Eh bien*, it is the Avenue du Général de Gaulle,' he replies.

I look up to see the de Gaulle name proudly resting above a neon sign for a sex shop. The General must take a pretty dim view of Cayenne, I think.

'Please can I have a spider?!'

We park up beside a large canal.

'Herve bought me one last year for my birthday,' sighs Regina, getting out of the car. It's as if she is talking about a bottle of Chanel No. 5. 'It was lovely.' She has clearly recovered her composure from last night.

'That woman!' she says, referring to the Guadeloupian beauty who ate all the iguana eggs. 'So rude! When you left, they all stopped talking French and started talking Creole. When they know that we can't understand it.'

Indeed, Guyane is one *département d'outre-mer* where the embrace of la France seems less comfortably assured than it is in some of the others. The force from *la Métropole* is certainly present, but it appears to be more as a veneer than a fundamental.

Indeed, the sense of the French way of life is probably strongest in Cayenne's central square. We walk through it, taking in the momumental buildings. Amid the swaying palm trees, here are the staunch pillars of the French institution. The *hôtel de ville*. The *palais de justice*. The *cathédrale*. The *bibliothèque*. the *école central*. All, incidentally, built by convicts at a time when the French empire grew to a size of around 80 million square kilometres and encompassed some 50 million people. Marianne smiles alongside the *tricolore*, which flies beside a European Union flag. If you ignored the tarantulas, the donkeys and the hammering heat, you could almost be in Nice. Almost.

Just behind the square we come across a life-size bronze statue commemorating Victor Schoelcher, the French abolitionist who devoted his life to banishing the slave trade, particularly in the French West Indies. He died in 1893 and is buried in the Pantheon in Paris. This statue was erected three years later.

Victor Schoelcher is depicted in smart, knife-creased trousers, laced boots and a frock coat buttoned up to the cravat at his neck. His hair is properly styled; his sideburns groomed. He is elegant, cultured, educated, esteemed. Gesturing towards the light of emancipation with one arm, his other arm rests lightly around the shoulder of a young black man whose disengaged shackles indicate that he has just been liberated. In contrast to the voguish Schoelcher, the noble savage is practically naked. He clasps his hands over his breast, looking up at his saviour with eternal gratitude, while Shoelcher indicates the glory of the free future that could be his.

Beneath the pair is inscribed *'Liberté, Égalité, Fraternité'*. On a purely narrative level, Schoelcher is welcoming an African archetype to a future free from slavery. On another, he is pointing out what it is to be French. America might well consider itself to be the Land of the Free; but the French have copyright on the Enlightenment. General de Gaulle put it thus: 'It is France, the nation designated by its immortal genius, whose initiatives are steadily raising men toward the summits of dignity and brotherhood.'

My ruminations on French enlightenment are rudely interrupted by my young charges, to whom I am comprehensively shackled.

'This is boring!'

'We're HOT!'

'Please can I have a spider?'

We collapse into the welcoming dark shade of the neighbouring Marché Victor Schoelcher, where despite its name the French Touch is almost completely absent. There are giant fruits, songbirds in cages, tables groaning with haberdashery, people pushing sacks of flour in wheelbarrows into darkened scented halls full of spice, candles, orchids, live fish and *pains aux chocolats* sold by the dozen. We gratefully drink iced Coke in a bar and dream of air conditioning.

It's been great, but as the day goes on, it all starts to disintegrate. We are hot and tired. The children are hungry. I am nervously anticipating an evening of cockroach avoidance. Pip is slightly anxious about driving to Devil's Island, where we are scheduled to go tomorrow. Regina and Herve have assured us the trip will be worth it, but now we have arrived at the Cric-Crac, and nobody has been murdered so far, I'm keen to stay in it. I'll admit it, I feel safe walking around in the company of a gendarme and staying in a place which has a 24-hour guard on patrol. We watch Regina and Herve drive away with a sentiment akin to despair.

Gabriel teases Lucien, who starts crying. We are meant to be filming but it is impossible with all this wailing and shouting.

'Let's have some soup,' I say desperately. 'I think everyone needs feeding.'

So we open up a tin of Campbell's. Honey, usually so fastidious about her food, spills it all down her white T-shirt. And I only have cold water and travel soap with which to clean it. Hot, hungry and anxious, I lose my temper completely and rage around the terrace.

'How can we travel effectively if you are spilling your food over everything, and just not being careful?' I yell. I know, she is only six and I am being unreasonable, and thus will not be reasoned with. Lucien continues to yell.

'We need to do a piece to camera,' says Monsieur le Directeur.

'What! Are you stark staring mad? What am I going to say? I don't know what to say!' The noise continues behind me.

'Will you lot Shut the Hell Up!' I shout and lash out at the nearest person. It happens to be Lucien. This is the first time in his life that I have ever struck him. He shouts with surprised pain and anger, and bursts into tears. I am consumed with shame and despair and sit, sobbing at the table on which there is a lone, wooden crocodile.

After a while I calm down and pick up the crocodile.

Then I go to the main restaurant and there, beneath the frescoes of hapless *bagnards* (convicts) being guillotined, I email my eldest daughter Phoebe, who has been at school in London all this long time.

I've missed her so much. And I feel worried about her arrival in a week's time. It's not that I doubt Sarah and David have been caring for her, as I know they have. It's more that what we have been experiencing here has been so intense I'm not sure how she will manage, joining the group. She has been commenting on our blogs with short, prickly observations such as 'Cool. Not.' They are very revealing.

'Tomorrow we are going to Devil's Island, darling. Not that we are staying there. It was a dreadful prison. We're staying on the next door island in an auberge, which sounds much nicer.'

Yet again I am undone by the French way of describing things. My problem is that I have invested the word auberge with a huge amount of Francophile romance, conjuring up softly tinted pictures involving bottles of wine in straw caskets, soft brioches warm from the oven, garlic, thousand thread count linen sheets, lavender and so on.

'L'Auberge des Îles du Salut on L'Île Royale. It sounds lovely, doesn't it?' I say excitedly to Pip the next morning, as we put our computers and the majority of our clothes, books and papers in a locked security cupboard, and head for a more luxurious spell. We're coming back here in two days' time. We drive from the Cric-Crac through a wet weather moment which feels as if gallons of water are being fired at us from a nearby water cannon. In other words, it's pouring.

'I imagine it will be a charming Provençal cottage with delicious food and proper linen on the beds. And great wine. Of course, the Îles du Salut are now a major tourist attraction,' I say. 'I'm sure that they won't give us any more iguana. I mean, they have to attract proper tourists.'

'Yeah. Probably the only decent place in Guyane worth staying in,' says Pip.

By eleven o'clock we are boarding the glitzy Catamaran *Tropique Alizes*, bound for the Îles du Salut and two nights in the auberge.

The Îles du Salut in the Atlantic Ocean are made up of the Île Royale, Île Saint Joseph, and the Île du Diable, or Devil's Island. About 16 kilomteres in very deep water off the coast of Guyane, they are wholly surrounded by needle-sharp rocks, dangerous currents and other unwelcome natural phenomena, like sharks. A perfect location for a prison. They were used by the French for prisoners perceived to be the most dangerous. Furthermore, they are out of the reach of mosquitoes. So once you were sent there, you stayed there. Even disease couldn't touch you. You stayed and stayed, mouldering in the tropical Atlantic, for ever. Napoleon III considered the conditions in Guyane were so atrocious that in 1869 he stopped using it for the majority of prisoners; a decision reversed after his demise by the Third Republic.

This is what Albert Londres, the pioneering French journalist who revealed the horrors of the French penal system to the world had to say about the Îles du Salut:

'I ask that these isles be debaptised, for they are not the Isles of Salvation, but the Isles of Punishment.'

All of this has changed. Regina and Herve can hardly recommend them highly enough. The tourist blurb provided sounds similarly enthusiastic: 'For you and your fellow travellers, visiting the Îles du Salut is a quite pleasant, civilised excursion into a lovely tropical island resort. The prisoners would have wanted to escape from this place that invites you to stay.'

We cannot wait to get there. We are on a civilised boat trip, with free biscuits and a morning aperitif.

'Why can't we dock at Devil's Island?' says Gabriel, who thinks the place sounds like something from a Disney film. In fact, he's heard all about *Papillon* the movie, with Steve McQueen and Dustin Hoffman, who end up being incarcerated on it.

'Oh, because it's too rocky and dangerous.'

Devil's Island itself is off limits to the casual tourist. Nobody can visit the shack in which Captain Alfred Dreyfus was incarcerated for life. This is probably just as well. The Dreyfus Affair, as it became known across the world, is a particularly horrifying story. In French cultural terms, its legacy is the counterpoint to that claimed by Victor Schoelcher, and it is fascinating that Guyane bears the imprint of both figures.

In 1894, Captain Alfred Dreyfus, a Jewish officer in the French army, was framed for an act of treachery. A cleaning lady in the German embassy in Paris found a torn-up letter in a waste bin, containing military secrets; Dreyfus was accused of writing it. He was found guilty of spying, convicted of treason and condemned to life imprisonment in Guyane, even though political prisoners were usually sent to New Caledonia, which was considered a better option. He was humiliated in public, his epaulettes ripped from his shoulders and his sabre stamped on and smashed. Life imprisonment in Guyane; it was even worse than facing the guillotine, and gave voice to the hideous anti-Semitic factions in the French establishment. Captain Dreyfus was not allowed to embrace his wife Lucie farewell, nor was she allowed to tell him where he was going. After a six-week Atlantic crossing, he arrived at the Îles du Salut and was unceremoniously dumped on Devil's Island.

After a few months in a solitary but habitable cell, things got much worse. He was moved to a palisade, from where he could only see the sky. He spent his days in solitary confinement; at night-time, he was manacled by silent guards to his bed, his leg irons connected to a long horizontal bar. He was condemned never to hear a human voice. His time there was described by a contemporary writer as a 'true excursion into hell'. Nearly all his teeth fell out, and he almost lost the ability to speak. Pathetic pieces of paper still exist, showing little imaginary drawings and snippets of algebra, which presumably saved him from going mad. If his guards so much as saw a sail on the horizon, they would hold a gun to his head, fearing his rescue.

Dreyfus was held on Devil's Island for four years. He was then brought back to France, and acquitted, but then retried, and found guilty again. By this stage his plight had drawn the attention of the world; a mass rally of supporters in Hyde Park attracted 50,000. Eventually Dreyfus was pardoned in 1899. Astonishingly, for an innocent man who had received so much suffering at the hands of the Establishment, he went on to fight for France in World War One (and survived).

Odile, Captain of the *Tropique Alizes*, hands out pictures of Dreyfus' shack alongside the morning aperitif. Sub-Jacques-Brel-style music noodles around as we sip sparkling wine and Odile chats informally about the lovely place in which we are going to stay.

'Oh, *oui*, there will be plenty of guests staying in the auberge,' cries Odile as we dock at the Île Royale after an entirely benign half-hour voyage. '*Alors*, it is just up this steep slope. In case you need to come back to the ship, we will be leaving for the mainland in one hour.'

We start ascending the slope. Small peccaries, hairy fat pigs, trot about. There are palms everywhere, and big, splashy, green plants in which sit turquoise macaws with bright red, long tails. After a while, we suddenly come out into a clearing. The auberge is before us. It is a long, low, grey building, with open corridors linking a series of identical small rooms. It is clearly not a bespoke hotel or B&B. These buildings were obviously once part of the prison. There is a huge, overgrown empty water tank in front of the Auberge. In it are some large, sharp rocks on which are crouching several iguana. On top of the tank bounces a toucan. Some derelict buildings can be seen in the background, behind the mango trees.

There are some places in the world where there is a clear atmosphere, a sensation of human experience which cannot be ignored. Delphi, in Greece, is one such place. The Île Royale is another. It is not a benign feeling, however, as it is in Delphi. It is a very forbidding, malevolent feeling, a feeling of human misery.

There are no doves over the gables or roses over the door of the auberge.

'This doesn't look like a proper French auberge,' I say.

'When will your ridiculous romance about France ever die and be replaced by a willingness to understand reality?' says Pip, somewhat irritated.

We walk in and meet the manageress, who looks like a distant relation of Madame Defarge, the macabre woman knitting at the guillotine in Dickens' *A Tale of Two Cities*.

In a triumph of unsuitability, she is called Angel.

'We live in a place called Angel, in London!' I say, idiotically.

Angel delivers a grunt, tosses a greasy grey lock of hair and gives a sort of shrug of recognition by way of acknowledging this geographical coincidence.

We put our bags in the lobby, in which a few bored-looking tourists are sitting around reading *Le Monde*. A small dog runs up to one of our backpacks and cocks its leg on it.

'Do you mind?!' I yell at its owner, as dog urine splashes over my bag.

'*Désolé*,' says the owner.

We are all starving. We spot a food counter in the lobby, at which we order five baguettes filled with cheese. This is all that is on offer. My formerly fussy children have no qualms in devouring these straight away. The bill comes to around £20.

'Put it on the room,' I command.

Madame Angel gives us a giant key and gestures to where our rooms are to be.

'They are in Block D,' she says ominously. 'But I must tell you there is no air conditioning.'

'Can we go to a room with air conditioning?'

'*Non*,' says Madame Angel.

'Come on,' says Pip tensely.

We gather up all our stuff, including my backpack, now damp with dog urine, and walk hesitantly towards Block D.

'Are you thinking what I am thinking?' I ask Pip.

'What, that this is going to be a prison cell?'

I can't speak.

'I think it probably is,' he murmurs.

We arrive at Block D and unlock the first of our two reserved rooms at the auberge. Then we unlock the next room. Each room has a ceiling fan, and three beds. Each bed is furnished with a nylon sheet. The only window in each room is a barred aperture above the door. The overriding feeling is one of doom.

We go outside, slightly stunned. A macaw hops in the coarse grass in front of us. Opposite, a large French family is sitting on some plastic chairs outside their room. They have brought a picnic and are all sitting around cracking open plastic bottles of wine and laughing.

How can they be like that, I think. There is another empty and rampantly overgrown block crouching ominously behind Block D.

'Probably for people on life sentences,' says Gabriel, hopefully.

I look at Pip. I think about the manacled prisoners ending their lives here in solitary, slowly going mad as the shark-infested Atlantic boiled on the rocks outside. A palpable sensation of cruelty hangs in the air.

Pip looks at me. It is so hot. We are booked in here for two nights. The boat, in the meantime, is leaving in about half an hour.

We are going to say what the prisoners never could.

'Let's get out of here.'

'The boat will be going back in about thirty minutes. Let's try and catch it back to the mainland.'

'And stay where?'

'Let's go back to the Cric-Crac.'

The very name sounds like a haven of refuge, not what it is, namely a cockroach-infested motel whose restaurant serves bush meat and is decorated with pictures of people being guillotined.

'Children,' I say calmly. 'We are leaving now. Gabriel, can you please go and give the key back to Madame. Just leave it on the front desk.'

He looks at me trustingly.

'Why? Why can't you?'

'Just do this for me, now.'

I know it's bad, but it will give me a small sense of satisfaction to leave without paying.

'Are we leaving without paying the bill? Is that what you call doing a runner?' asks Honey, thrilled.

'Er, yes,' I admit. Never done before, probably will never again. But here normal rules do not apply.

'Does that mean we are escaping from the Îles du Salut?' says Gabriel slowly.

'Yes, yes I suppose it does.'

'Awesome. Only THREE people in the world have ever done that before!' He grins and runs off with the key.

'See you just down the path where it leads to the Prison Museum,' I call.

While he goes to the auberge, Pip and I, with Lucien and Honey in tow, go and wander around the Prison Museum, which is filled with things like shackles, old prison uniforms and piteous letters from the condemned.

After five or six minutes, there is no sign of Gabriel.

'Where is Gabriel?' I say. 'He knew he had to meet us here.'

'He'll turn up,' says Pip.

Five minutes later, there is still no Gabriel.

'What if he's fallen in that tank?'

'Which tank?'

'That huge bloody giant tank! The one which is covered with iguana!' How could I have been so stupid to have left our son on his own up there, just for the sake of a silly bill?

'I'm going back to the auberge,' I say, anxiety filling my stomach.

I run back up the hill, where the tropical flowers and brilliantly coloured birds simply cannot dispel the feeling that this place is haunted. I run into the auberge, which smells of boiled cabbage. Lunch is clearly on its way. No Gabriel. I run back to Block D. The French family are still having their picnic and laughing. Maybe they don't sense the spookiness of this island. How they can sit around, eating crisps and drinking Evian is beyond me, but perhaps they just accept their past.

Perhaps we are interlopers here, looking upon the grievous history of this prison island with a foreigner's sensibility. I don't care. We are leaving, but not without our son.

I start shouting his name.

I start to run back down the hill to the museum.

Finally, I see him, a small, vulnerable figure, crying by a mango tree. It seems he just lost his bearings and, understandably, started to panic.

I enfold him in my arms and, not for the first time, wonder at the sense of this mad trip.

'Come on, darling. Let's go and meet Daddy at the museum. I'll show you some leg irons.'

He manages a weak grin.

Five minutes later we're on the lonely little jetty, awaiting the arrival of the *Tropique Alizes* which has been 'cruising' around the other islands in the archipelago. I imagine newly arrived, disorientated prisoners being pushed, stumbling up the stony path, looking back at the distant shadow of the mainland.

Suddenly Gabriel, who has quite recovered his composure, cries out. 'Look! Look! Down in the water! A turtle!'

We follow his pointing finger and there, swimming in the deep green ocean, is a large sea turtle. It puts a pointed snout out and opens its mouth to take a breath, and then dives back beneath the waves.

'Well, that's made us all feel a bit better,' says Pip. 'Good old nature.'

At this juncture the *Tropique Alizes* turns up. Odile raises an eyebrow at us when we all clamber back on board, but she is more concerned with looking up at the sky and organising her crew to batten down the hatches. We set sail back to the mainland, at which point the most savage storm I have ever encountered in my life breaks over our heads. It is as if the malevolent spirits on the Îles du Salut are being released above us. By comparison, the storms we have had up until now were merely playing with the idea of a tropical storm.

Sheets of tepid water come at us forcefully from all sides. Waves threaten to swamp the little boat. The crew members rush around pulling down vast plastic sheets around the open deck as the boat plunges up and down on voluminous waves.

We are all totally soaked. Our baggage is literally pouring with water. Deep forks of lightning plunge down from a sky which is as dark and livid as a bruise. Cracks of thunder make conversation impossible. The boat ploughs on. When we arrive at the mainland, we cannot get off the boat for about twenty minutes because it is too dangerous to disembark. The little inflatable which will take us to shore bobs around helplessly beneath us. Odile, who doesn't look too worried about the turn of events, lines us all up. We are going to disembark in groups of four.

'*Alors*, is this your first visit to Guyane?' says a friendly Frenchman as we plunge up and down, as if on a giant rocking horse.

'Yes!' I shout above the thunder. 'Very, very interesting!'

'Are you in the space industry?' he yells.

'No!'

'Are you here tomorrow? '

'No! We are off to the swamps of Kaw!'

'*Zut alors!* You should stay here! There will be a *lancement*!'

'What is a *lancement*?'

'Take off!' shouts the Frenchman. 'A rocket is taking to the skies!' He gestures dramatically to the purple, pouring heavens. 'You know it won't be long before there is a *tricolore* on the moon!'

Guyane is where the European Space Agency has its headquarters. It's a good place for rocket launches, apparently.

It is near the equator, which gives it some sort of physical advantage. It is very unpopulated, which makes rocket launches safer. The headquarters are near the town of Kourou, just a few kilometres from us along the coast. The rockets fly up into space over the benighted Îles du Salut. Fancifully, I imagine the prisoners in their open air palisades looking up day after day on a square revealing only the empty sky over Guyane. They would hardly have believed that that only a hundred years later, powerful rockets blasting smoke and flame would soar right across that same vista on their way to space.

'*Allez-y,*' shouts Odile, lining us up beside the edge of the boat. We are almost the last group to leave.

'There are five of us!' I yell.

'Never mind!' she says. 'You must all go together.'

I grab Lucien and Honey and leap down into the tiny rubber dinghy, which is pitching back and forth with alarming force. We all hold on tight to our luggage, and start the perilous journey of about 30 metres to the pier. The dinghy is swamped by a huge wave, which narrowly misses carrying Lucien off my knee altogether. I hold him tight.

'Isn't this fun!' I shout into his curls. The children hold onto the rope handles of the dinghy tightly. They do not look as if they are having a great time, but they do look as if they are experiencing something unforgettable. When we finally reach the pier, they start smiling again.

We clamber up the stone steps, dripping wet, laughing, and toss our drenched bags into the car. Thank God we left the majority of our stuff behind at the Cric-Crac.

We drive back to Cayenne, relieved to leave the misery behind. We have two days now at the Cric-Crac to dry out before plunging back into the mysterious, savage countryside.

CHAPTER TEN

Allons Enfants de la Patrie

Honey's diary: *We were freezing and wet. My teeth were chatering. So wer everyones. We went straight into the shower. Now we wer worm and dry. We had rost potatos and water buffalo it was dlishose. And we wer in our pegarmes and hammoks and in about two minits we wer asleep.*

The pirogue, a long, shallow boat with an outboard motor, chugs on. And on. And on, through glassy water set about with miles of bright green plants, rushes, flowers and lilies. Enormous trees dip visible white roots far beneath the water's surface. The trees rise up hundreds of metres above the swamp in a green mountain that goes on for ever. Thin clouds of vapour circle their tops. Far away, we can hear the eerie laugh of a gibbon.

'*Alors,*' says Ondine from the stern of the boat, our glamorous (in a French rustic way, i.e. no make-up or bra) guide and pilot. '*Les vaches du marais!*' To our right, large water buffaloes wade up to their necks in the clear water, casually chomping on the greenery. They low intermittently, causing minute brown and rose-coloured birds to scatter up in disarray. Weaver birds fly in and out of their gourd-shaped nests hanging from tall plants. Egrets cling to the rushes, peering at us beadily down needle-sharp bills.

It must be about 90 degrees in the sunshine. There is no shade in the pirogue. I notice that all the French eco-tourists, unlike us, are properly equipped with hats. We are all slathered in suncream, but it is so hot that it seems to just be sliding off our arms and legs.

The men are all dressed in elegant green safari gear, and the women are all wearing white agnès b. linen. They are all doctors from Paris, it seems, having a bit of tourism on the back of a professional trip.

'I'm so HOT,' whimpers Gabriel, dipping his hand in the enticingly cool water.

'Please don't do that, darling,' I say sharply. 'Remember what Ondine said about crocodiles! Some of them are three metres long!'

'Caiman, actually,' he corrects me. 'Spectacled caiman. Maybe we'll see one tonight!'

We are in the Marais de Kaw, which is 140,000 square hectares and one of the largest French regional parks. I know this is a completely barmy way of looking at it, but here we are, 5 degrees north of the equator, cruising around a French regional park. It has a big brother, a French national park, just down the road. That's the Guiana Amazonian Park which comprises of 3.5 million square hectares of jungle and is, according to the French blurb, 'a jewel of biodiversity'.

My lovely sceptical husband has another way of looking at it. 'It allows the French to pump out as much pollution as they can at home, since by counting the Amazonian rainforest as a national park, they can just offset their carbon emissions,' mumbles Pip. He sits with hunched shoulders, filming the cows in the water as we chug by.

Well, it's a viewpoint.

Our guide Ondine, in the meantime, is channelling the spirit of Charles de Gaulle in a rather spectacular manner.

'This park,' says Ondine quietly, 'is part of the genius that is France.'

My children start giggling. The French tourists in the boat find nothing weird about this sentiment in the least. They nod their heads in agreement, swivelling binoculars expertly across the water.

'How can a park be a genius?' whispers Pip, shaking his head. 'Next thing you know, we'll be told that the Eiffel Tower has an intelligence quotient. Honestly. You would never get someone in the Lake District saying that this part of the countryside was part of the "genius of Britain". Even the most dotty of tour guides would agree that that would be insane.'

He's got a point.

'How can the Amazonian basin anyway be part of the genius that is France?' I whisper back. 'France only annexed Guyane as a proper department after the war.'

Ondine ignores our muttering and continues with her subject. She stretches out her hand to encompass the entire wet vista, of vapour and water, emerald plants, hummingbirds and a turquoise sky. It is an utterly magnificent view.

'Like Voltaire, Hugo and Zola,' she continues, 'this regional park is part of the illustrious body of national geniuses.' I casually ponder how Voltaire would enjoy being rated alongside a spectacled caiman. Let alone Zola, who lost his life as a direct result of writing *J'accuse*, the infamous newspaper article which indicted the French government for sending Dreyfus to life imprisonment in Guyane.

'These spiritual and national symbols guarantee the solidarity and pride of the French towards our country… they trace the contours of… eternal France.'

'They're always saying France is eternal, aren't they?' pipes up Gabriel. 'It's like General de Gaulle. He said France was eternal on that memorial in Saint Pierre et Miquelon. But I don't understand. What makes France eternal? Or more eternal than anyone else?'

'Oh, the French love being eternal, I think,' I say quietly.

I once gave my mother-in-law a cushion cover to embroider entitled 'The Eternal France'. I discovered it on an American craft website. It showed a map of France, with a giant Eiffel Tower in the middle and key icons such as cheese, champagne, chateaux and onions, all scattered about to indicate important places such as Bordeaux, Reims or the Loire Valley. I don't suspect any such cushion ever made its way into a French home, but the notion of their country as never-ending does seem a rather key concept to the French. Come to think of it, this is not unlike how the Americans see themselves, which perhaps explains the prominence of Eternal France, the cushion, on a site invented for an American market.

Soft furnishings aside, it seems that the French have a quite evangelical conviction about their eternalness.

'It's probably because they haven't got over Waterloo,' I whisper, only half seriously. Yet the more time I spend overseas in France the more I am convinced this is a country hanging onto its colonies partly because it mourns the loss of Napoleonic-style world dominance.

'Yeah, and perhaps because they nearly lost the war,' says Gabriel, who as a properly educated London child has been studying the Blitz. The French consciousness of their place in the European pecking order is of course another issue. They want to be eternal, and they want to be great. The United Kingdom, which actually has the appellation Great in one of its islands, isn't half so much bothered about being seen as great as France is. But as de Gaulle himself said, 'France cannot be France without greatness.'

'*La France éternelle* is actually part of the Gaullist far-right consensus. Now will you shut up,' says Pip. 'I'm listening to Ondine.'

'Here, you can find caiman of three metres long,' continues Ondine. '*Moi*, I find them *magnifique*.' The children look at her and gulp.

We have been chugging along a wide waterway for about three hours, when the pirogue suddenly diverts down a slim channel. As we approach, Ondine explains that we are about to arrive at Kaw, population sixty, one of the remotest villages in Guyane. She tells us that photographs of people who live in Kaw are *'interdit'* and bids us to be back in the pirogue in an hour. Is it safe? It looks it. We gratefully leave the blistering heat and head for a coppice of trees, and shade.

I love the village of Kaw. It is here that beneath a small enamelled sign reading 'Agence Postale' that I decide I have found the beating heart of France, in the form of a small yellow postbox. The box, as all proper French postboxes are, is marked POSTES and carries the insignia of *la République française*. Apparently a French postman turns up, by pirogue, once a week, on what must be the world's most extreme post round, to empty the yellow postbox and bring the people of Kaw their mail.

Beside the postbox are a series of directives from the Préfecture de la région Guyane. They are pinned onto a wooden board and marked with stamps reading things like *'Faction des Affaires Interministérielles'*, and evidently come from Cayenne. The letters are headed with the state picture of Marianne, and *'Liberté, Égalité, Fraternité'*. Even here, a perfect wilderness, Gallic red, white and blue, tape and legions of bureaucracy are alive and well. It's quite comforting.

We hang around by the postbox, taking photos of us beside it until the children start peeling away, leading us down the main street of Kaw. It is clear that although the French postal system is here, not much else is. An abandoned shack is marked *'Foyer Rural'*. A wild field has a long abandoned football goal. There is a church covered in peeling white paint. Inside, the modest pews are decorated with flowers and there is a strong smell of wee. Opposite the church, a cluster of Amerindian women are selling cakes and delicious almond bread. They clearly do this on a daily basis for the tourists.

We discover a primary school on the corner of the street.

'Well, kids, imagine going to school here,' says Pip, gesturing towards the École Élémentaire Mixte. A large noticeboard informs us that it is half funded by Europe, half by France, and that Hilaire Gober is the head. The wall outside is decorated with pictures of children holding each other's hands, and a song which starts *'Nous sommes les enfants de Kaw'*, written in that same looping handwriting. Presumably inside, the class has been ploughing through *'nos ancêtres les Gaulois'*. Before they get onto Sartre, Montaigne and Camus.

'That's assimilation for you,' says Pip.

'Well, in some senses it's a good policy,' I say. 'Giving these children a chance to read and write one of the world's greatest languages. Giving them access to the great French classics, to *Le Figaro*, to *Asterix*?'

'*Asterix* is legendary,' says Gabriel.

'Quite,' I say. 'It's a great world culture. Isn't it?'

'The people here should be learning stuff in their own language,' says my husband.

'Sure, but by learning French you can have access to French universities,' I counter. 'In France. I'm not saying it's the answer to everything, but surely it's an option worth considering. Children here have the chance to have tertiary education in the metropole. They even get one return flight to France a year, all paid for. You certainly wouldn't have had it if you were born up the road in old British Guiana, would you? All they have there, from their former colonial masters, is left-hand drive.'

'Yes, but they also have the power to determine their own future. And that makes a difference,' says Pip. I wonder what M Gober thinks about the opportunities offered to his pupils.

Our hour is up. We get back onto the pirogue and continue down the waterways of Kaw until we reach our hotel. It starts to rain, very, very hard. It's like we are moving through a massive, tepid power shower. Just as suddenly as they arrived, the sheets of rain switch off. We dry off in the sunshine and continue chugging down the river. Eventually, a vast boat, three storeys high with a giant arched roof, sitting impassively on the river, looms into view. This is our houseboat.

'*Alors,*' says Ondine, looping a rope from the pirogue onto a bollard. 'Lunch will be served in forty minutes.' She leaps off the boat and dives into the kitchen.

The children run upstairs, shouting with pleasure.

'Hammocks! Hammocks!'

Both upper decks are strung with brightly coloured, striped hammocks. There are about thirty of them.

I look at Pip. He looks at me. We have the same thought. The camera gear. It's too dangerous to leave it under a hammock.

'I'll go and discuss it with Ondine,' says Pip and beetles off. In the meantime, the children jump onto the beds, and swing. They are filthy, sweaty and barefoot, but they are alive with the sheer joyous prospect of spending the night in a hammock on a breezy 40-foot high houseboat.

Ondine and her colleague Gabriel serve us lunch, which is delicious and welcome. It's water buffalo stew, of course. The Parisian doctors crack open bottles of Bordeaux which they knock back with abandon. Baguettes, presumably made from French flour, materialise from nowhere; Napoleon butter is produced. Pâté appears. The whole is washed down with Perrier.

The doctors explain they are here on a fully subsidised trip, ostensibly to inspect the main hospital in Cayenne. Sending doctors over to Guyane is a good deal more sociable than sending convicts over. They are fascinated to learn about our project. At least, they are polite enough to appear fascinated.

'You know why we keep these DOM-TOMs?' says one.

'Is it because it makes you the world's second maritime power?' I venture.

'*Non, non*. It is so that the sun can never set on the *tricolore*, *vous comprenez*?'

I think I do. We gave up our motto of empire long, long ago. The French, it would seem, have not.

Suddenly, we hear a splash from the side of the boat. Oh God, I think, running to the edge. One of the children has fallen in. Well, not quite.

'Oh come ON, Mummy! It's lovely!' shouts Honey, bobbing up and down in the water.

But what about the 3-metre long caiman? I think, smiling gingerly down at her.

After lunch I am eventually persuaded that swimming in the Marais de Kaw is a good idea. Well, I'm never going to have the chance again. So I do it. The water is sweet and soft. It is deliciously refreshing, cool and clear. Yet after about 20 seconds of experiencing it, the notion of being pulled under the surface by something with teeth impels me to climb out.

That night, after a spectacular supper of chicken and couscous made by Ondine valiantly wearing a head torch (there is no power on the boat), and at least two bottles of rum, her assistant Gabriel takes us out for a midnight run in the pirogue.

The moon is giant and brilliant, the Milky Way a long, wide smudge of white against a sky of black felt. We chug through beds of reeds. After a while, we suddenly stop. Two red eyes are looking at us. There is a splash, a scuffle and suddenly Gabriel the guide is holding a small caiman which is about 1 metre long. He gives it to our Gabriel, who holds it up triumphantly. It is passed around the boat and then carefully slid back into the water. Presumably the 3-metre one has gone away for the weekend.

Thanks to his chat with Ondine, Pip has managed to secure a private room on the boat with some cupboards for the camera gear. We spend a night with bats flying in and out of the room, and serenaded by the roar of bullfrogs alongside inebriated doctors snoring. The children, swinging alongside each other in striped hammocks, sleep deeply and sweetly.

Next morning the sun rises through pinky pearl mist and light filters down through the myriad rivers and streams of the swamps. The doctors are up before us, with croissants, bowls of coffee, and presumably, colossal hangovers. They are singing. They are not just singing, they are singing their national anthem.

'*Allons enfants de la Patrie...*' they stand at the edge of the boat, bellowing to the jungle, ever present and misty in the gathering light.

They stand and sing, one hand over the heart, the other clutching a half-chewed croissant, these patriotic members of the Parisian bourgeoisie.

We are 10,000 kilometres away from the Place de la Concorde, where the antecedents of these guys cut the heads off their monarch and his queen, and yet here they are, in South America, lustily singing about the glorious Republic.

'Most odd,' says Pip, dipping his croissant into his coffee. The children are drinking hot chocolate. They have all taken their anti-malarial tablets without a peep. They roll their eyes at the sound coming from the aft deck.

'*Aux armes, citoyens...*' continue the French doctors.

I am going to get to the bottom of this.

'Ondine, can you tell us why these Frenchmen are singing all seven official verses of the Marseillaise?' I ask. 'I mean, is it a normal thing to do in the mornings here?'

Ondine looks at me as if I am completely mad.

'*Mais, non! Aujourd'hui, madame Millard, c'est le quatorze juillet!*'

Oh, *pardonnez-moi*. It's Bastille Day. Now I understand.

The French doctors, breathing heavily and beaming, repair to the dining area.

Slowly the egrets fly back to their perches.

An hour later, the pirogue arrives to collect the doctors and deliver an Englishman, James Prichard, who is staying on the boat with his Guyanese wife and their three young children. He clambers out and walks over to us. From his gait and his clothes I can tell he is not only English but also went to public school in England. It's the way his hair is cut, and the sort of unbranded, classic summer clothes he's wearing. The French doctors get into the pirogue with a lot of shouting and swaying. Then the onboard engine purrs and they depart, brandishing their binoculars at anything that moves.

'Hi,' says James to us.

'Hi there,' says Pip, shaking his hand. I can almost read his mind. He is thinking 'Thank God. No need for all that double-kissing crap.'

Pleasantries over, James sits down for coffee while his wife explores the spartan bathroom and their children do the hammock discovery thing upstairs.

'So, what are you doing here?'

We laugh.

'Investigating the DOM-TOMs,' says Pip casually. 'For a documentary series.'

James looks impressed.

'You don't say. I've been in the DOM-TOMs since I left Bristol.'

'I was at Bristol!' exclaims Pip.

'You don't say!'

'But what are you doing here?'

'I'm a French teacher,' says James.

Pip immediately looks a lot happier. He is clearly dying to have a simple conversation in English with someone who he could imagine playing cricket with. I leave them to chat and wander off to the side of the boat, whose open, wide wooden decks are about two inches off the surface of the water.

Lucien, in his *Death in Venice* sunsuit, is playing at the feet of our guide Gabriel. A black Guyanese, Gabriel is gentleness personified. Lucien loves Gabriel because he doesn't bark at him in French. He also loves Gabriel because he has tamed a white heron. It comes onto the deck of the boat when he knocks gently on the wooden deck.

This morning, he is teaching Lucien how to do it. Lucien is sitting on his haunches, bottom half an inch off the ground, in that way that only the very young can manage. Gabriel kneels beside him and taps on the deck. Lucien follows suit, using the back of his knuckles just as Gabriel does.

Tap tap tap. Tap tap. Tap.

Out of a cloudless sky, the heron descends. It folds its huge white wings into the shape of a teardrop on its back. It hops towards Gabriel, and then stands very still on thin, ebony legs. It folds its long white neck back like a hose. It has a sharp, yellow beak. A black, beady eye looks at Lucien. Gabriel moves away softly. Lucien is entranced. He looks back at the heron, and taps again. The heron comes a little closer.

Suddenly, Gabriel reappears, holding a fishing line. He baits the hook at the end of the line with a little meat, left over from breakfast. He drops it into the clear water, and waits. Lucien waits. The heron waits.

All at once, Gabriel pulls up the line. At the end of it is what looks like a tiny silver piranha, about two inches long. Not the stuff of bad dreams, but let's just say I'm glad one didn't flick past my leg when I was having my 20-second swim.

'Cousin of the piranha,' says Gabriel.

It is all mouth and eyes. He throws the flailing creature onto the deck. The heron follows it with its eye, and then stalks over to it. In one smooth movement, the heron picks up the fish and gulps it down its tubular white throat. It cocks its head at Gabriel. Gabriel grins at Lucien. Lucien smiles back, and regards the heron.

Back at the table, James is telling Pip what a great wheeze it is to teach French to Creole-speaking children in the DOM-TOMs.

'You get the teacher's salary, plus pension, holidays and so on, plus a 30 per cent uplift for working out here. France is a generous parent to all its departments. It has to be.'

He estimates the French government spends millions of euros sending teachers out to its far-flung territories.

'France wants everyone to speak proper French. Not their local language. It's a sort of steamroller approach.'

But what about the astonishing cost?

'But it's the old adage. If schooling costs too much, then why not try ignorance? Pretty soon you'll find out how much that ends up costing the state, in unemployment, teenage pregnancies, all the rest.'

He pauses. 'There's a moral contract going on here, too. France owes it to places like Guyane to stay here. The terrible history of its colonial past can, in a sense, be mitigated in a small way, now, by the vast economic opportunity of belonging to Europe. Perhaps its how France feels it can reconcile itself with the fact it exploited its territories for so long.'

Outside, vapour is rising from the rainforest as the heat of the day mounts.

'All the black Guyanese were brought here from the West Indies as slaves. But the sugar plantations here never really took off. And so they had to work alongside the prisoners, trying to tame the rainforest, building towns and roads. Terrible work. So now, when you have Guyanese women with eight or nine children, all on benefits, with a house provided by the state and university education freely available back in the metropole, it's sort of like just deserts. I just feel good when I see the mother of ten children raking in the benefits here,' says James. 'I imagine the slaves originally brought here will be looking down and thinking, well, at least my descendants are being looked after.'

It makes the French look a lot more noble than the rest of the European colonial powers.

'Plus, having all these places around the world makes France into…'

'Don't tell us,' Pip and I chime. 'The world's second maritime power?'

'Yes, well, I think it's extraordinary. Girdling the earth in this way gives the French an astonishing cultural footprint.'

'More than Hollywood?'

'Part of the reason they are doing it is so that they can offer an alternative to Hollywood.'

I understand. Rather than join in with the anglophone world, here is a system where one will not find re-runs of *Friends* on the television, or Angelina Jolie's latest movie at the cinema. It's a different offering, culturally and politically, with the French state still at the absolute centre.

'Beer?' says Pip.

'Don't mind if I do,' says James.

CHAPTER 11

Croissants in the Jungle

Honey's diary: *The Jungle Day. We drove to see turtles getting out of there shells which we call hatchlings. There were lots of moscitose. We saw lots of egg shells but we didn't see any hatchlings. Then we drove to Pauls house. We were amased what kind of House he had. It was made out of wood for sum resn he had four dogs. And he had 10 chicens I have no idea what there names were. AND he had Ducks. We went for a walk in the jungle. We walked on lots of logs. There were Ants biting Ants. We got bitn lots. Mummy got bitn on the bottom so we said 'you've got ants in your pants'. I got nineteen on my back they were like a needle ow ow, ow. Gabriel got bitn five times on the leg we were all crying except Paul. Paul is brave and he's been in the jungle lots of times all ready.*

Our stay in the riverboat was a delicious moment in, shall we say, the formal end of Guyanese tourism. The chap who promotes Floating Lodges in the Marais de Kaw, Jean-Louis, has a big agency, JAL Voyages, on the Avenue du Général de Gaulle in Cayenne. It's where you are directed if you are one of the few French tourists to visit. And it's more or less completely orchestrated for visitors, with caimans being hauled out of the water for your delectation, and encounters with cake-touting natives in distant villages.

So when we get back to Cayenne and the joyous surroundings of the Cric-Crac, we decide to push it a bit further. Turtles on the beach, we decide, should be next. We are off to witness baby turtles hatching out of their shells on the Plage des Hattes, about 200 kilometres east of Cayenne, at the point where the Atlantic meets the giant estuary of the Maroni river. Except this particular adventure is not quite so scripted as the houseboat on the Marais de Kaw. It's altogether far more chancy.

It's very dark. In fact, it's still night-time. We are creeping out of the Cric-Crac while the moon and stars are still bright in the sky. The armed guard pads around the compound of the motel. We putter away in our car, taking the remnants of last night's supper (a baguette and two mangoes) with us. No food is wasted. It's far too expensive here to indulge in throwing things out.

The Maroni is an Amazon tributary which forms the border of the country with Surinam. It's a long way to go, but as this is France, the main roads are good, straight, tarmacked and empty.

'Baby hatchlings!' I say with pleasure to the tousled occupants of the back seat who are wearing a combination of pyjamas and wet weather gear. It is, of course, raining.

Terrific gusts of water batter our small Peugeot.

'Better tell them it's unlikely that we'll see them,' says Pip grimly.

'But I thought Guyane was one of the world's big places for turtle hatching,' says Honey.

'Well, darling, it is, but life is not like a David Attenborough show,' I say, applying mascara in a hopeless attempt to look

178

soignée. 'The hatchlings may not get out of their shells at the precise time we want them to.'

Since the coiffed days of Saint Pierre et Miquelon, which I now regard as a terrifically sophisticated place, my presenter look has gone steadily downhill. Forget the smart skirts and jackets. I am now wearing giant linen trousers and Pip's T-shirt which reads 'Croissants in the Jungle' (our catchphrase), and appear for the most part like someone who has been living on a commune for the last five weeks.

Actually, staying in the Cric-Crac, what with its nightly visitations of cockroaches, lack of food and eternal humidity, has brought something of a communal spirit to our family. We have bonded together via the sheer experience of living in Guyane. This makes me worry slightly about the imminent arrival of Phoebe, who of course will have missed all of this entirely.

Two hours later we are knocking on the door of our nature guide, Sandra, who has a PhD in turtles. It is six in the morning. Sandra is in her mid-thirties, white, sporting a conspicuously 'biologist ' wardrobe of combats and an official-looking cagoule.

'Alors, on y va,' ('All right, let's go!') says Sandra, stubbing out a cigarette, the enjoyment of which, even for a French person, strikes me as somewhat early. We crunch over the sand in the dark, slapping away the mosquitoes.

'Mummeee,' cry the children in disarray.

'Pull your sleeves down. Pull your socks up. Keep walking.'

Two hours later, we are still on the giant Plage des Hattes, which is about 6 kilometres long, and 800 metres wide at low tide. Here, the Atlantic is muddy and calm. We have certainly seen traces of hatchlings. We have seen egg shells from whence hatchlings emanated. We have seen hillocks, where hatchlings are still incubating. We have seen flipper-prints from mother turtles about to lay eggs for hatchlings. But we have not seen a single hatchling.

It stands to reason, I tell the children. The probability of us standing beside a hillock when hatchlings actually start swarming out of it is about as likely as West Ham winnng this year's league, I say to Pip (an armchair Hammers fan). Still, we wait and we walk with hope in our hearts, and we talk to Sandra, while she smokes.

We all ponder on the existential quality of a hatchling, which only has one chance in a hundred of making it to adulthood. 'They can't even swim properly,' says Gabriel, who is fascinated by the entire saga, and who now wants to follow Sandra into Turtle Studies when he is older. 'They have to float on the top of the waves. For two years. Meaning that predators can easily eat them. Then there are the people who make them into turtle soup.'

'Oh, yuck,' shouts Honey.

'It's a local delicacy,' says Gabriel primly.

This beach is protected, Sandra assures us. It's certainly very empty. It's long and golden, yet the water which laps it is brown, shallow and really not very photogenic at all. Even so, Pip can't resist a few tiny shots. He is now so used to wielding his camera that he almost does it without thinking, hefting it to his shoulder and squinting down the eyepiece.

'Any thoughts?' comes the now traditional question from Monsieur le Directeur.

'Yes,' I say. 'I'm glad I wasn't born a hatchling. Here, on this typical Guyanese beach, is where thousands of turtles annually migrate to lay their eggs. For the visitor, however, the beach may be long but it is not exactly picture postcard...'

'Yet another nail in the tourism coffin of Guyane,' murmurs Pip from behind the camera.

'... yet as part of a French regional park it too will get protection from the state and EU funding, even though we are only 5 degrees from the equator.'

At dawn, the sun and consequently the temperature rises with astonishing power and speed. The children run around, writing their names in the sand.

'*Alors*, it ees too hot for the hatchlings now,' says Sandra, with finality. 'They will now not come out until the evening.'

She shrugs. We concede defeat, and underneath the hot water of (yet another) Guyanese downpour, leave the beach.

'Look, look, a rainbow!' cries Honey, and we all turn to see the rainbow shimmering across the sky. 'It's a double one!' she shouts, happily. 'I can see the whole rainbow!'

Very auspicious. Or perhaps not.

'Thank you Sandra, we have to go now,' I say. 'But really, so interesting. Even without the hatchlings. Actually, not seeing the hatchlings made it even more interesting.'

'How?' says Gabriel.

'Be quiet. I'm being polite,' I say, smiling furiously at Sandra.

Anyway, our eco-tourism experience is not yet over.

'We're off to the gîtes of Awala Yalimapo,' I say to Sandra. 'Do you know where they are?'

Staying in a gîte is going to be great, I've decided. The very name is to me so reminiscent of seventies family holidays in Brittany or Normandy: the diminutive dwellings clustered next to the large family holding, where Madame always, it seemed, had delicious *pâtisseries* and *bols* of hot chocolate steaming on the wooden farmhouse table. And you can stay in one here!

Sandra looks at me strangely. '*Les gîtes? Alors*, there is a *cabane* down the road.'

'Oh, well. That must be it! Thanks! Bye!'

We clamber, soaking, back into our car and bump off down the sandy track to the tiny village of Awala Yalimopo, which as its name indicates, is Amerindian in influence, rather than French.

There is a tiny shop perched on the half stony, half sandy beach front, underneath some wind-whipped palms and beside a rather large rubbish dump.

We walk into the shop.

'Do you know where the gîtes are?' I ask the Chinese man in French, who is manning the counter.

'Yes. They are my gîtes. In fact, they are *cabanes*,' says the man.

'Yes, yes, well, no matter, we are here. *La famille* Millard. You might find my booking. Here is my receipt.'

I produce my form for a six-bed *gîte*, and smile hopefully.

'Is this all your stuff?' he says, indicating our camera gear.

'Yes, why?'

There is a pause.

'Because you may need to leave it here in the shop with me.'

'Oh, really? Why is that?'

The man then does a most alarming gesture with his hand, as if he is holding a large knife.

'They could break in.'

'Who? What?' What is this man talking about?

'The local kids here. If they know you have stuff. *Alors*, they'll just slit the netting in the windows with a knife.' He gives me all this information in perfect French, and then smiles.

I look at Pip.

'What did he just say?'

'That our *gîte* is fundamentally insecure and that we, being obvious targets, are highly likely to be burgled tonight by locals with knives.'

'Ah.'

The Chinese storekeeper gestures for us to go right ahead and have a look, and gives us a giant (and presumably utterly unnecessary) key.

Our *'gîte'* is a hut behind another hut. It is constructed from bamboo struts and woven palm leaves. The windows have no glass, only ineffective, torn fly netting. There is a dirt floor. Our *gîte* is furnished with two bunks, each consisting of three skinny beds, one on top of the other. The mattresses are plastic. There is a single sink, a naked light bulb, and a broom. Is that it? No. There are also about four hundred mosquitoes in the room, all intermittently dive bombing the light bulb. There is an unidentifiable, fetid smell.

'This is fantastic,' shouts Lucien, instantly. 'Yay! Our very own hutch!'

With a radiant face wholly transfixed by joy, he grabs the large broom and starts sweeping the dirt floor.

'This is lovely, Mummee! Can we stay here forever? Can we? Can we? I like this hutch!'

I am almost choking with the heat and the odour. Stifled, I gesture to Pip. My gesture is not a 'knife through fly netting' mime, it is a 'knife across throat' mime.

There is no way we are staying here.

Even Lucien understands me.

'Oh Mummeee, please not! Please don't leave the hutch! No!'

We return to the shop.

'I'm so terribly sorry,' I say, handing him back the key. 'I've just remembered I'm on medication and I absolutely have to have a fridge in my bedroom. I'm so sorry. We won't be staying in your *gîte* tonight.'

'Mummy, please!' cries Lucien tragically.

We jump in the car, Lucien weeping copiously about a missed opportunity to stay in (to his mind) simply the nicest room in Guyane.

'God!' says Pip, hitting the accelerator and inadvertently piling through a giant puddle. 'That was good. Well done.'

I smile, and modestly accept the praise. 'Thank God we've got a car. And options.'

'Yeah, well what are the options?' he laughs.

I'm quite enjoying myself. One of the things which has happened on this trip, I've noticed, is that when we are really up against it, Pip and I operate rather harmoniously together. It's only when things are going well that we resort to bickering. Going off to the back of the French beyond has done wonders for our relationship.

I pull out a tourist guide from the depths of my bag.

'We are near a place called Saint Laurent du Maroni,' I announce.

'Looks quite big,' observes Pip, looking over briefly before cannoning into a pothole. It is now raining very heavily. 'Oh, bugger. Got to concentrate, now.'

'Yes, but you know what that is, don't you?'

'No.'

'That's where the bloody prison is. Le Bagne! The infamous Bagne! Very opportune. It's a crucial part of our film.'

'Not another prison, Mummy,' comes a squawk from the back seat.

'No, well, yes. This is the main one. Devil's Island was just an addition.'

'I feel sick.'

'Not long now, guys. Then we can stop for breakfast.'

It's still only about eight in the morning. The windscreen wipers cannot go any faster, but still the windscreen is deluged with water. We drop down to about 30 kilometres per hour, as the visibility outside is practically zero.

While Pip struggles with the driving, I indulge in a comic telephone conversation with a French representative of the Comité du Tourisme de la Guyane, in other words the tourist board (yes, it does exist, astonishingly), which goes as follows:

'Do you have any comfortable, luxury hotels in Saint Laurent?' (I'm not being a drama queen but I am not roughing it in another *gîte*, *cabane* or whatever they call it.)

'*Oui.*'

'Are they five star?'

'*Non.*'

'Are they ANY star?'

'*Non.*'

'But I thought you said you had some luxury hotels?'

'*Oui.*'

'Do they realise we are filming in Guyane for the Travel Channel? And that we might help promote it?' I say in despair to Pip.

Eventually, helped by the reluctant tourist board, we find a motel not dissimilar to the Cric-Crac. This is the Résidence du Relais Des 3 Lacs.

'Are there three lakes here?' asks Gabriel.

'No,' says Pip.

'I think there might be three swimming pools here, though,' I say reassuringly.

'Awesome!' says Gabriel, ever the cheery adventurer.

We leave all our bags in a locker in the locked rooms, and head into Saint Laurent, a town on the banks of the giant Maroni river. The rain has stopped. Steam is rising from puddles in the pitted roadside, thanks to the scorching heat. On the wide, brown river, which represents the border with Surinam, French policemen patrol on speedboats.

The architecture of Saint Laurent, which was constructed almost entirely by convicts at about the same time that Baron Haussmann was rebuilding Paris into the world's most modern city, is probably best described as 'butch empire'. In the centre of town, the French Establishment is represented in the grand style of Napoleon III. The now familiar buildings are all here; the *hôtel de ville*, *la poste*, the main school, the cathedral. They boast commanding pillars, pediments, wrought iron, and a sense of colossal, inescapable power. There is the obligatory statue of Marianne, emblem of the French state. There is a Boulevard du Général de Gaulle and there is a tiny airstrip, on which juddering twin-propeller aircraft occasionally land.

The largest and most impressive building in Saint Laurent is the prison, Le Bagne (so called after an Italian habit of putting their prisoners in a bathhouse). White, awesome, forbidding, Le Bagne is terrifying on a monumental scale. Beside the muddy Maroni river outside, a bronze statue of a despairing prisoner, head in his hands, summarises the feeling of horror and unease.

What used to happen was this. Having crossed the Atlantic, the French convicts would sail up the Maroni to Saint Laurent, and dock exactly where the bronze prisoner now sits. They would be shepherded off the boat, given white woven hats and incarcerated directly in this building. Those considered the most dangerous would be put on a separate boat and relocated to Devil's Island.

Life, for the *bagnards*, really was nasty, brutish and short. Malaria, typhoid, horrendous living conditions, barbarous working conditions; they had it all. In the first fifteen years of Le Bagne's existence, nearly half the deportees died almost immediately. But they kept on coming; right up until 1932. In the 150-year duration of Guyane's life as a penal colony, over 70,000 prisoners ended up here. At one point the prisoners represented a quarter of the country's entire population.

We stand, daunted, outside the prison. Directly opposite it is the grand mansion of the prison director. The prison, entirely constructed by its inmates, opened in 1851. We walk quietly beneath the giant arch and encounter the first courtyard. Giant doors, marked 'Quartier Disciplinaire' lead off into dark corridors which lead into vast holding spaces. In these spaces, men would lie on stone shelves. A long iron bar runs down the shelves, the length of the hall. Men would be shackled to this bar all night. Women were similarly cooped up in another hall. In the day, they would be given hard labour. The heat, the mosquitoes, the general despair shocks us all. We walk around in silence.

Further on, individual cells surround a grassy yard. This is the Quartier Special, where serious offenders were imprisoned. The cells are identical, stone, with a single barred window above each door. In one, the name 'Papillon' is scratched on the wall. The author of the best-selling autobiography, Henri Charrière, was incarcerated here (and subsequently moved to Devil's Island).

In another cell, a child-like image of a boat has been etched on the wall. Presumably it symbolised a longed-for release, never to be realised.

Beneath it, a single pathetic phrase; *'Adieu Maman'*.

La Belle France seems a long, long way away.

'Pitiful,' says Pip.

The children are silent and frightened.

There is a stone oval in the centre of the courtyard. This is where the guillotine stood. Anyone desperate enough to attempt escape would be guillotined here, publicly.

All the prisoners in the courtyard would be forced to open their cell doors and watch the execution. Afterwards, the severed head would be toured past every cell.

'That's what's on the pictures in the restaurant at the Cric-Crac, isn't it Mummy?' asks Honey.

'Yes, yes it is,' I say.

It's some distance from de Gaulle's fine words of the French overseas colonies representing 'summits of dignity and brotherhood'.

In the central square, a giant mango tree has grown. It is drooping with ripe, uneaten fruit. A single, rainbow-coloured hummingbird hovers in the heat beside the tree. Nobody takes a photograph of it.

The attention of the world was focused on this shameful institution after the pioneering work of a French journalist,

Albert Londres, who came to this place in 1923, after which he wrote a devastating book, *Au Bagne*. It was devastating largely because he told the world what was going on. He describes the prison as 'a factory churning out misery, without rhyme or reason'. His report caused an international scandal, but even so, the prison was only formally closed in 1945, at which point the last remaining *bagnards* were freed. A few photographs of the final prisoners still exist. The *bagnards* are a handful of old, confused, forgotten Frenchmen, stumbling out into the light of liberty, to the astonishment of the Western world.

We walk out of Le Bagne and back into Saint Laurent, which is just waking up to the day ahead. We have been up for five hours, but it is still only just gone nine.

'Breakfast, anyone?' I say.

After a somewhat greasy repast, which we eat quietly, we go and spend the rest of our money in the supermarket, where we have our now familiar engagement with our Gallic favourites; Yoplait, Napoleon, Perrier, Petits Filous. Using French brand names to wash away the grim past is somewhat surreal, but then Guyane is surreal, a country which France invented courtesy of a greedy dream, and which then turned into France's very own nightmare. Outside the supermarket, as I carry our goods away, we bump into someone from Hartleberry, Worcestershire. Of course you do. Well, we do.

'Hi there,' says Paul Griffin.

Paul Griffin is long-haired, tattooed and appears to be holding a can of lager.

'Keep walking,' I say to the children without moving my lips. 'This man is a weirdo. Plus, he's pissed. Plus, he's English.'

Unfortunately, I have bargained without Lucien's longing to hear the Queen's English. 'Mummeee! That man is English!' he says, rushing back to the gutter in which Paul is currently standing.

Before I know it, Pip has immersed himself in conversation with Paul, who has invited us to Sunday lunch in the jungle. Of course he has.

'Forget meetings with important French politicians, or Amerindians!' I shout, as we stumble to our car with our day's shopping, namely some pineapple, a six-pack of Danone stewed apple and a baguette. 'Let's all go and have Sunday lunch with a boozer from Worcester! Great!'

It turns out to be one of the most remarkable lunches I have ever had.

Paul Griffin does not live in a *carbet* (a sort of French summer house), or indeed a house in any formal sense of the word. He lives in a hand-built structure and sleeps in a hammock. In the middle of the jungle. I mean, really in the middle of an actual jungle. He came here about five years ago with his then girlfriend, who is French. Now he lives in the jungle alone. He has three dogs, some chickens and a 12-bore gun. This is to shoot the jaguar if it dares to come and eat his chickens.

'Would you manage to shoot a jaguar?' says Gabriel with awe.

'You bet,' says Paul, tossing his grey bunch back over his shoulder. 'I was a semi-pro clay pigeon shot back in the UK. I shot an ocelot here. Then I ate him,' he says, laughing. The children look at him, not quite knowing whether to believe him.

Paul, a former Hell's Angel, is also a practising cranial osteopath. He gives head massages and treatment to the stressed-out bourgeoisie of Saint Laurent, but he lives in 30 hectares of the neighbouring jungle. They are his to keep, these hectares, if he lives here for over a decade.

'After living here for ten years, it's mine to do what I want with,' he says, gesturing to the wild landscape around him of towering rainforest trees, lianas, palms and rushing water. 'The French government figures you'll be dead before the ten years is up.' He's already done about six years in the jungle. What will he do with a patch of rainforest? He wants to turn it into a sort of extreme ecological holiday camp, where people come and stay in hammocks, learn how to wash in the creek and cook food from locally sourced fruit and veg.

We park our car at the side of the road. After a walk of about ten minutes, led by Paul, we cross a plank over a fast-flowing river, and step down into a clearing.

Wide-eyed, the children inspect Paul's house, which consists, broadly speaking, of some planks, a Belling oven, a mattress and a rather torn mosquito net.

'We could give him our net, couldn't we, Mummee?'

We have of course come to Guyane with our own mosquito nets, which are huge, luxurious and tear-free.

'Of course we can,' I say abstractedly as I take in the style of Paul Griffin's living quarters. There is a tiny latrine, and a hand-built shower which takes buckets of fresh water from the nearby river.

'This is the soap, kids,' says Paul, showing them the leaves of a fragrant tree.

He dons a pair of oven gloves and darts down to the oven, proudly producing a tray of perfectly roasted potatoes. We eat the potatoes, a casserole of meat from an unspecified but delicious animal, which he has cooked on an open fire, and drink some fine French wine. We eat as if we haven't eaten properly for days.

'You've been living off bread and mangoes? And iguana?' he laughs. 'You poor English bunch!'

He pops Lucien down on a chair and proceeds to massage his neck and shoulders. By now Lucien has been exposed to so

much madness that he accepts this novel entertainment quite willingly. Then he treats the rest of us. The touch of expert human hands, massaging our backs and heads, is just what we need.

'The locals here think I'm a witch doctor,' says Paul, giggling. 'I mean, they know I'm not French. So they think I'm working with the spirits. Who cares.'

He then proposes a walk. We set off into the jungle; Paul with his gun and Lucien on his shoulder, the rest of us trotting behind. Pip insists on filming the whole journey. Paul explains how he got to know the jungle, which is intricate, unplanned, darkly beautiful and dangerous. Lianas hang down from massive trees. Birds and monkeys cry from perches which are probably 30 metres above us. Strange fruit and bright flowers brush against our clothes. Water drips. The air is fragrant and moist. Paul tells us he once got lost here, for three days.

'What did you live on?'

'Nuts. Fruit. And I had a tin of sardines on me.'

'How did you get them open?'

He looks at me oddly. 'With the key, you ninny!'

He is delightfully normal, and seems probably more so because his home environment is downright bizarre. He explains he lives on maize, pumpkin and pineapple, all of which he farms beside his hut. He fishes from the creek and occasionally eats one of his chickens. But he also has a page on Facebook which he accesses when he goes into Saint Laurent for his shopping.

'I'm thinking of running Healing Holidays here in the rainforest,' he says. 'Do you think British people will sign up for a couple of weeks here?'

We tell him they might. If they could cope with getting here, and don't mind insects.

The children talk to him about ants, snakes and spiders. He accepts all their questions and invites more, since he shares their innocent enthusiasm.

At one point, a rotten log blocks our route. Honey and Gabriel insist on standing on it before walking on.

'Don't do that,' says Paul.

'Why not?'

'Because it might be infested with black biting ants. And that is their home. They'll attack you if you threaten them by standing on it.'

'Come on, you lot! Off the log!' I shout. I go back to collect them, and in the process, manage to stand on the log myself.

Three minutes later, I feel a sharp stinging pain on my knee. No, this really hurts. It feels like a red-hot needle being plunged into my knee, a few times.

'Er, Paul?'

'Yup?'

'Does being stung by an ant feel like… ow… a red-hot needle? Ow! Ow!'

'Yup.'

Behind me, a scream from Honey, who comes rushing past, clutching her back.

'Ow, ow, Mummee, I'm being bitten!'

And there is Gabriel, yelling, shaking his legs demonaically.

'Help me! Help!'

Pip is shaking with laughter, filming us all.

I pull up my trouser leg. A giant black creature is running wildly around my knee. It seems to defy all attempts to brush it off.

'Die! Die!' I shout, squashing it with my hand. It continues to move, biting as it goes.

Honey and Gabriel are weeping spectacularly.

'I am certainly going to tell everyone about this at nursery,' comments Lucien from the refuge of Paul's shoulders.

We half walk, half run through the jungle. At last, the sunlight reveals the clearing and Paul's house, where everyone instantly takes most of their clothes off. I undress in what passes for Paul's bedroom, basically a tiny square with an elevated mattress around which hangs his moth-eaten mosquito net, dry the children's eyes and inspect their tender bodies. Honey has nineteen angry red bites on her back.

'Those ants really did not like you standing on their home, did they?' I say, hugging her.

'No, Mummy.'

Paul appears suddenly, biting on a croissant. I am so struck by the appearance of French patisserie in the Amazonian rainforest that I momentarily forget I'm only in my bra and knickers. Paul doesn't seem to worry about this, however. Presumably the fact he has five ex-wives and various assorted children across England might have something to do with his sangfroid. He doesn't seem to register any embarrassment at all. I put a T-shirt on, anyway.

'Do you want a swim? Shall I show you my own pool?'

'Yes! Yes!' yell the children, biting ants forgotten.

We venture to where the wooden plank crosses the river, and see that there is a gently flowing, natural pool down there.

'Just slide in. Underwear on, or not. No matter to me,' says Paul.

I choose the 'on' option, but the children take all their clothes off and jump in.

'Are you coming in?' I shout to Pip. He shakes his head, holding up a bottle of beer to explain his reluctance to get into the pond. But the water is heavenly. It immediately takes the pain away from our bites, and cools our sweating bodies. The children splash and shout and play in the crystal clear shallows.

'Are there any crocodiles here?' I shout.

'No. Don't think so, at least,' laughs Paul.

Washing in a jungle pool seems like the final act of submission to this strange world, equally appealing and repellent, a system of biting ants and Napoleon butter, glory and ignominy, of prisons and the transformative nature of culture. We now need to just cling on and let the French wave carry us where it will.

CHAPTER TWELVE

The Other Side of the World

Honey's diary: *The Day Of Phoebe. We were so anoid that
the flite witch had just landed wasn't Phoebes plane. It took
so long to wate that me and Lucien's legs were so tired. So
daddy was lifting both of us up at different times. We didn't
like it so we moand for ages. Finly daddy spoted Phoebe then
we all got out strayt away and all shouted 'Phoebe!' And all
huged her and she showed us her nice and new camra it was
eight.2 megapixels and it was red. I think Phoebes camra is
better than mummys. And we straghterway said 'Can we have
are presnts' so she let us have are presnts. Gabriel got a book
Lucien got a rubber duck and I got a wind-up thingy.*

It's our last night at the Cric-Crac and I am packing. You
absolutely have to pack the night before. And you have to
always pack the same way. Actually, packing bags successfully
is what enables you to travel. Honestly. If you can assign a
place for everything, zip it up and carry it, you will at least get
to the starting line. The other key thing is to always put the
washbag in first. Washbags refuse to be packed if they aren't
accorded this prime position.

Of course, if you've acquired stuff along the way, you simply have to jettison an equal amount. We've already thrown out our long-sleeved shirts and sweatshirts which were so vital in Saint Pierre et Miquelon. Well, I have to make space for the stuffed tarantula.

Bags are my domain. I'm damned if I will let anyone else touch them. 'No!' I shout, 'I'll find the scissors/duct tape/ pyjamas! Get away! Bags are My Area!'

There is a bag for each of the children. There is a bag for me. This contains the Hanover Primary School bag, which travels in a neatly folded state of emptiness, waiting for episodes of travel sickness, in which case it reverts to type and becomes a Dirty Clothes Bag again. There is a bag for Pip. There is the camera bag, which is very heavy, and can only be carried by adults. There is the tripod bag, which is generally cursed by all and will soon fall apart. There is the 'information' bag (this contains all our files, paperwork and our beloved copy of Aldrich and Connell). There is a 'games' bag (featuring the paper animals, and *Oui! On Fait du Coloriage*). There is a books bag, with a ration of five books per child and a book of poems by Michael Rosen. In this bag are the travel sickness pills, which have a special little poppered pouch all of their own.

Finally, we have Tror Lady Dor. Tror Lady Dor is a small bear in a Tyrolean costume which belongs to Lucien. It was given to him by my dear friend Jules who got it as a going-home present from a party at a friend of hers, namely Tracey Emin. When you press its belly, it yodels, making a sound which sounds a bit like Tror Lady Dor. Secure in Lucien's Trunki, Tror Lady Dor yodels to us from overhead lockers, on baggage carousels, in car boots. It seems as if he only yodels when the bags are all packed properly. When we hear Tror Lady Dor, that's when we know we are ready to leave.

I conclude that if I was as focused in other areas of my life as I am with packing, I'd probably be a far wealthier and more successful person.

After packing, I lay out the clothes for the children. T-shirt, underwear, trousers, socks, travelling shoes. I lay out the clothes for myself and Pip. They are soft and floppy with a residue of weeks of chemical travel soap. I go to the other bedroom and inspect the children. They are like the Three Bears, asleep in three adjoining beds, covered head to toe by sheets to avoid being bitten.

It's midnight, and pitch black outside. Faint tweetings and warblings come from the rainforest. I feel like a bit of French warbling myself, and put Carla Bruni on my iPod. Appropriately enough, she starts noodling on about going into a jungle where there has just been a downpour.

'Typical Carla,' I say.

'I wonder if she's ever even BEEN to the jungle,' comments Pip, who is reading a bit of Aldrich and Connell, in readiness for our next destination.

Carla warbles on about somebody belonging to her.

'She probably sings this to Sarko,' I suggest. I quite fancy the French president. I know this sounds peculiar, and that to some he is merely a control freak with built-up shoes, but to me this is not so. He's got a great haircut and I warrant beyond doubt that he has that peculiar French know-how with women.

I turn the air conditioning down from Violently Loud to Just About Bearable and settle down into our creaking bed. Somehow I've grown fond of the accoutrements at the Cric-Crac, which has effectively become our home in Guyane. The leaden, sweat-impregnated pillows, the giant air conditioning units, the cracked and mis-matched crockery, the naked light bulbs, the house cockroach.

'Will you miss the Cric-Crac?' I whisper to Pip in the darkness.

'No.'

'I will.'

'I'm just relieved we have all survived.'

'We've met the challenge. It's going to be easy from now on.'

'Yeah. Have you remembered we have a forty-seven-hour journey ahead of us?'

'I'm going to be quite sad to leave Guyane, though,' I persist.

'I'll certainly never forget it,' says Pip.

'Do you remember when Honey startled the burglar at the chief of police's house?' I whisper, and giggle. 'And that horror auberge which was really a prison?'

We both go to sleep, laughing. We will have to be up in four hours, get straight into our clothes, and leave for Cayenne airport. I'm not too worried. The children are now expert at this. On with the clothes, down with the malaria tablet, a bite of stale croissant, a gulp of UHT milk. If they have learnt anything on this trip, it is that in the hot, wet, black dark of a Guyanese morning it's best to put your shoes and socks on straight away, and take your malaria tablets. The croissant makes it bearable. That's the French Touch for you.

After breakfast, the rickety Peugeot which passes for a taxi arrives, and we all get in, silently. So silently, indeed, that we can hear Tror Lady Dor gently yodelling from the boot. As we pull off, I look out of the window and consider this strange, green, dangerously lush country which has been forcibly tamed by the French, at least along the coastline, into some sort of submission. We leave the suburbs of Cayenne and drive to the airport through the dawn-fresh jungle.

Suddenly the driver pulls to a halt. In the middle of the road, there is a spider about as big as a dinner plate. It is walking dauntlessly, delicately across the road. It tiptoes on its black, furry eight legs like an alien breed of prima ballerina. The children yell with pleasure. It is a fitting farewell to this giant, beautiful and alien country. Guyane, formerly a deathly prison, is now, more or less, a giant nature reserve.

We are flying 5,300 kilometres north to Los Angeles. Here, we will connect with Phoebe, our eleven-year-old daughter, at which point our family will be complete. It's been hard, communicating with our eldest child for six weeks on Facebook and the odd email. Yet she's been loved and cared for. Eve's mother Sarah has simply folded Phoebe into her family, with generosity and love. And for the last week Phoebe has been staying with my parents, who have adored spoiling her and having her to themselves.

'How on earth is she going to manage being one of four again?' I say to Pip.

During the ten-hour flight we decorate the walls and windows of our part of the plane with pictures of dragons and watch interminable Nickelodeon cartoons. Pip struggles with *Ulysses*. Finally, we arrive in Los Angeles. We are two hours ahead of Phoebe, who is arriving from London on a non-stop flight.

It's by far the longest journey she's ever made on her own.

We wait for what seems like hours for Phoebe in Arrivals, hanging off the railings with excitement, trying to spot anyone getting off a plane with LHR attached to their suitcases.

At last, just as I fear the children can't bear it any longer, she appears, walking into Arrivals escorted by a British Airways stewardess. She seems rather white-faced, and is walking rather stiffly.

'Hello!' we all scream, pushing the railings aside, and rushing up to her.

'Hi. I was sick into my blanket just before landing.'

'Oh, God, darling!' I say, embracing her proudly. 'Didn't they look after you properly?' I wipe my eyes and kiss her again.

'Mother,' says Phoebe. 'Please stop crying.'

The BA stewardess hands me a paper to sign, confirming I have received my child, who after all is still an unaccompanied minor, and melts away into the chaotic crowd of weeping, shouting and gesticulating travellers and their families.

I inspect Phoebe. She's grown; filled out, magically expanded. Formerly chaotic with her possessions, she is carrying a perfectly packed backpack and a small shoulder bag, neatly stacked with a diary and a gift from my parents; a new, red camera. Her younger siblings dance around her affectionately, patting her as if they can't quite believe she is here in person. Or that they can't believe that she is a person.

'I've got to tell you Mummy, I am starving,' announces Phoebe as we check into some grim hotel block at LAX airport for a night.

'Did you not have nice food on the plane?'

'Mummy. I don't DO airline food.'

Oh my poor daughter. That is going to change.

The next morning, we invade the buffet at the hotel. Everything is in dollars. It's not that much cheaper than overseas France, however. I spot that kids can have breakfast for $5 a piece. So, we'll all be kids for a morning.

'Right, everyone, choose your stuff and we will pick from your plates,' I announce.

Pip and I therefore have a tooth-rotting repast consisting of Coco Pops, chocolate milk and strawberry yoghurt. Still, we save about $50 this way.

Air Tahiti Nui TN01 is to take us 6,618 kilometres to Papeete, the capital of Tahiti, the main island in Polynesia. In the plane, there are flowers and garlands everywhere. On the walls are prints of famous paintings by Paul Gauguin.

'D'où venons nous? Qui sommes nous? Où allons nous?' is the inscription below one of them. Where did we come from? Who are we? Where are we going?

I might ask the same question.

Polynesia was formerly annexed to France in 1880, and the French lost no time in endowing it with almost paradisal qualities. At the 1889 World Fair in Paris, the gateway for which was the newly constructed Eiffel Tower, there was a special section for the French colonies. In the catalogue of the colonies of the Pacific Ocean by the French politician Louis Henrique, it is clear what quasi-mythological ideals Polynesia had begun to symbolise for the French.

'Born under a sky without a cloud on marvellously fertile soil, the Tahitian only has to raise his arm to pick a fruit of the tree, and the banana is a staple of his diet. He has never the need to work and fishing with which he varies his diet is a pleasure he is very fond of.'

Louis Henrique goes on; 'Tahitians, happy inhabitants of the unknown paradises of Oceania, only experience the sweet things of life. For them living means singing and loving.'

We know from correspondence that Gauguin went to the World Fair, and read the catalogue. Perhaps it was Louis Henrique's descriptions he had in mind when he wrote these grimly prophetic words to his wife Mette at the end of 1890:

'Let the day come (and maybe soon) when I can escape to the woods on an island in Oceania, and live in ecstasy, in calmness and from art. Free at last, without money worries I could love, sing and die.'

In another letter, of the same year, to his friend Jens Ferdinand Willumsen, he is more expansive.

'As for me, my mind is made up; in a little while I shall go to Tahiti, a small island in Oceania, where material life can be lived without money [...] Terrible times are in store for the next generation: gold will be king!! Everything is rotten, men and the arts alike. [...] Out there, beneath a winterless sky, on marvellously fertile soil, the Tahitian need only lift up his arms to pick his food; for that reason, he never works. In Europe, however, men and women can satisfy their needs only by toiling without respite...'

Of course it was not like that, even in 1890. After he got there, Gauguin, whose paintings indeed do depict Tahiti as a form of paradise, discovered to his cost what a great PR job had been done on him. In the end, he got so fed up with the place that he removed himself to Hiva Oa, an island in the farthest possible corner of Polynesia, where he fell out with both the colonial administration and the local missionaries. Plagued by a lack of money and continuing ill health, he died only two years after arriving on Hiva Oa. He was buried in a pauper's grave.

After what feels like forty hours in the sky, our giant plane lands in Papeete, Tahiti, and taxis gently down the runway, stopping at the airport.

'Oh, Mummee,' says Lucien tearfully. 'I think I can see ANOTHER French flag.'

His lip wobbles ominously. Rather than feel piercing pride that my youngest child can identify the *bleu, blanche, rouge*, which is indeed fluttering from the corrugated roof of Papeete's Tahiti Faa'a Airport, I feel sickening guilt. Here we are, in the South Pacific, and the poor child is so homesick.

'How many more countries until we go to London?' he asks.

'Oooh, about three,' I lie. Not for the first time, I marvel about how many foreign lands the French call theirs. How on earth do they remember them? The answer is that they don't, of course.

Take Polynesia. At first, Polynesia looked like a fantastic acquisition into the colonial deck of cards; a trump, one might almost say. At first. Having lost out on America, and watching the British move effortlessly into India, the French needed to plant the *tricolore* on some other tract of valuable land on the globe. The South Pacific looked like the perfect spot. It was what European nations seemed to do in the eighteenth century; go off on an enlightening exploration to discover new lands and push forward the frontiers of science. Then hard on the heels of the discoverers and scientists would come the flag-bearing generals and after them, the hard-nosed businessmen searching out sources of profit. The British were doing exactly the same as the French. So beating the British made the race even more heartfelt.

In the French corner was the explorer Louis de Bougainville, first Frenchman to circumnavigate the globe, and whose name is immortalised in the eponymous purple and pink tropical plant. In the English corner were the explorers Samuel Wallis, and more famously, Captain Cook. They didn't get plants named after them; they got actual islands instead.

It was Wallis who first spotted Tahiti in 1767. Bougainville appeared over the horizon a year later, Captain Cook soon after and Captain Bligh (on the *Bounty*) soon after that. The English, it seems, didn't think much of Polynesia. They nosed around, sent a ship or two back with some natives, paved the way for the London Missionary Society to come and do its thing, then powered off down to Australasia, again with the French in hot pursuit.

The French, led by the explorer Lapérouse, arrived in Botany Bay in 1788 only days after Captain Arthur Phillip claimed it for the British. Apparently a broken-down carriage stopped Lapérouse from getting there first. In 1840 the same thing happened in New Zealand, where the French apparently waited for some decent wine to arrive for their Naming and Claiming Party, and so missed their chance.

The moral of the story is make sure your transport is up to scratch, and don't be so choosy about your wine. French tardiness meant that the British ended up with not only New Zealand but also the spectacularly huge terrain of Australia. The French, in the meantime, continued to fight over Polynesia until its Queen eventually abdicated in favour of the French. So France got the consolation prize of Polynesia, which the British didn't really want anyway. It may be idyllic but it is wholly impractical, since it consists of hundreds of tiny volcanic atolls across a vast expanse of water, rather than a single, thumping great land mass. Such as Australia.

'Never mind,' said the French to one another, apparently, consoling themselves with the notion that once the Panama Canal was built, Polynesia would somehow come into its own as a South Pacific staging post. Did this happen? Er, *non*. The territory is only half linked up to broadband, even now.

The French inability to successfully colonise the South Pacific either led to, or is a result of, a particularly national characteristic, an unwillingness to shift away from the controlling nature of the metropole itself. While the British were energetically ruling the waves, the French, it seems, preferred to fold back on themselves.

We like to think of the French as extrovert, exuberant kissers and energetic lovers. However, culturally speaking, the national character is anything but. With its strict quotas for films in the vernacular, its apellations contrôlées for luxury goods and strict legislation stipulating how Gallic vocabulary must take precedence over an Anglo-Saxon equivalent ('*courrier électronique*', for example, should be used over the globally comprehended 'email') one can see this expressed again and again. Having carbon copies of France across the world, as represented by the DOM-TOMs, only reinforces the notion that Marianne is a woman who never refreshes her wardrobe. Of course, the irony is that having effectively lost the battle for global dominance (which even Napoleon could not revoke), the French have had to bear the experience of their language also slipping down the world stakes. It now prides itself on being 'the world's favourite second language', which is good, but not as good as being in pole position. Where English is.

Anyway, the French did eventually find a use for Polynesia, in the latter half of the twentieth century, as a nuclear testing ground, but that didn't go down too well with the rest of the planet. So now the French seem to regard French Polynesia indulgently, as one might a beautiful, indolent child who refuses to leave home.

It is rather stunning, though. If Guyane is France's Green Hell, then Polynesia must be its Turquoise Heaven. Plus, it has its own tourist board, which is very efficient.

'At last, we will be looked after,' says Pip as we arrive at the Radisson Plaza in Papeete, a wholly luxurious institution with lots of delicious food, proper beds with decent pillows, the total absence of insects and a spectacular view over a pristine beach which apparently was the first beach in Polynesia on which a Frenchman first walked. The whole package is not unlike something from the set of a James Bond film. We are garlanded with fragrant strands of creamy white orchids and hibiscus, and wander around in a daze sipping fruit juice to the tune of melodious ukeleles strummed by chunky, beaming

Polynesian men in straw hats who pop up in almost every corner of the hotel.

'This is... well... OK,' says Phoebe, who has arrived straight from London without any notion of what two weeks at the Cric-Crac really means.

'This is absolutely amazing! Sick! Legendary!' shouts Gabriel, who is by now quite aware of the wide quality threshold in the French hotel industry, and uses the best of his London vocabulary to express his acknowledgement of that fact.

We are even given a guide, who comes with a jeep. He is called Laurent, as all French guides seem to be. The very next day Laurent takes us up on a dizzying drive onto the top of the volcano that once formed Tahiti. Why does he do this? Because there is a famous French restaurant up there. We all hang onto the leather straps in the Range Rover and try to ignore the dizzying views of toy-sized airplanes taking off and leaving from Papeete's airport.

The French restaurant is called the Belvedere. It specialises in fondues and snails.

The menu starts off with French onion soup, then continues, via snails and moules, to steaks, fondues and coq au vin.

'Do you serve this sort of stuff because French people living here just miss it so much?' I ask Louis Giradou, ancient proprietor of Le Belvedere.

I am looking at a plate of snails. M Giradou shrugs, and touches the equally ancient menu with a bony hand.

'Per'aps.'

'How often do you have a, er, snail delivery, then?

'Ze ship comes in every week. Full with ze snails. Burgundy snails, of course.'

I'll say it again. The French are really quite barmy.

Understandably, since it is the biggest island of the lot, they have seized Tahiti as a serious contender for the 'Paradise on Earth' beauty parade. Everything is floral, fragranced, and branded as such. No public toilet is without its bowl of white orchids, no phone box goes untouched by a poster of a spiky orange flower, no municipal railing is left unloved by a swathe of bougainvillea. Art has similarly been commandeered into the Polynesian story, in particular anything touched by Gauguin, who first came to Tahiti in 1891. Gauguin has been turned into a street name, a conference hall, and countless hotel rooms and cafes. I even found myself utilising a 'Paul Gauguin' lavatory at one point. Essentially, Gauguin, who came here to escape, has been turned into a rather glamorous signpost.

His grandson Marcel Lai, who still lives here, has taken a pretty dim view of this.

We are due to interview Monsieur Lai the next morning. But suddenly the lean, mean filming machine which is the Millard family seems to have broken down somewhat. We discover this on arising at our normal *réveil* of around 7 a.m. Early morning starts have become essential to our filming programme. They mean a) we can do most of the work before it gets too hot, and b) we can have an extraordinarily long feast at the breakfast buffet.

Our eldest daughter, however, is ignorant of this policy.

'Will you please GET UP!' yells Pip, pulling away the duvet at the appropriate hour.

'Leave me alone!' shouts Phoebe back, no less energetically. 'I don't HAVE to get up! You don't OWN me!'

'Darling,' I remonstrate. 'We have to go filming with Laurent.'

'I don't care about filming!' says Phoebe. 'I didn't ask to be here! I didn't ask to fly over!'

'Come on, Phoebe,' I plead.

'I didn't ask to be born!'

'You have to care about the filming,' says Gabriel, in a bored tone. 'That's why we're here. THEY insist on it.'

Who are THEY? THEY are the parents who forced you over to the other side of the world.

'Come on,' I wheedle. 'There'll be lots of lovely *pain au chocolat* downstairs at the buffet.'

The promise of the breakfast buffet does the trick. After which we are taken by Laurent to the vast indoor market in Papeete where we drink some spine-tingling raw cane sugar, shot with lime. This comprehensively wakes us all up, probably thanks to industrial amounts of sucrose.

After the market, we are off to interview Marcel Lai. Laurent takes us to Lai's low, white house which is surrounded by a garden full of pink and red flowers. The studio next door to his bungalow is packed with copies, reproductions of Gauguin's paintings that he has commissioned. This is the nearest you will get to seeing an actual Paul Gauguin painting in Polynesia, as all the originals are in America or Europe.

'I never let journalists see these works normally,' says Lai crossly. 'People are always asking me to host groups of tourists. I never do.'

'Oh,' I say, unsure how to greet this advertised hostility. 'Why have you, er, allowed us in?'

'Because of the Travel Channel,' he says. 'I want to show people how we have nothing here. Not one of my grandfather's works is in Tahiti, or in Hiva Oa. Not one. They are all in Vienna, Paris, London.'

'Well, maybe it's the humidity,' I suggest.

He looks at me candidly as if to say 'humidity my arse'. Lai stands proudly beside the copy of one of his grandfather's self-portraits. He has exactly the same aquiline nose and hooded eyes.

After about fifteen minutes, Laurent arrives in the studio, panting heavily.

'*Madame, je suis désolé*, but your children, they are locked in the car!'

I rush out. All four are howling with laughter, jumping up and down so violently in Laurent's Transit that it is rocking gently.

I knock furiously on the window.

'Will you behave!' I shout. 'I am trying to do an interview! What are you doing?'

'We were filming. I was interviewing Gabriel,' giggles Phoebe.

'Yeah, we were talking about your sex life with Daddy,' says Gabriel.

'Yay!' shouts Honey.

'Yay,' chimes in Lucien, somewhat unconvincingly.

The dog of Gauguin's grandson starts barking and running around the passion flowers like a mad thing.

After a few minutes' more filming, we take our leave of Marcel Lai in his studio full of reproductions and head off to another giant hotel where we are going to get lunch out of the ground.

This, apparently, is the way Polynesians ate before the arrival of Burgundian snails, *pain au chocolat* and McDonald's. Polynesian wizards would bury an entire lamb in the ground, alongside some oven-heated rocks, and let it cook for three days in the soil.

Then, with great ceremony, they would disinter it. This is what we are about to witness. We arrive at the Sofitel, a luxury French hotel where this event is to happen, and encounter a traditional Polynesian 'priest' who is white-haired, covered with dark blue tattoos and smells very strongly of tobacco. He waves a priestly hand at us.

'I will now walk over hot fire, and bless the meat from the ground,' announces the priest.

'How do you not burn your feet?' asks Lucien.

The priest, who is sporting a feathery headdress, blue tie-dyed robe and plenty of flower garlands, gives him a withering look.

'I have Holy Powers,' he announces. 'I have the power of the Polynesian gods. They will protect me. The coals are six hundred degrees hot.'

He then walks over the coals, which fizz in a very satisfying way.

'Awesome!' shouts Gabriel.

Everyone applauds. Beautiful Polynesian women, in bikini tops and skirts made of palm leaves, shimmy around the priest, shaking their bottoms with seemingly impossible speed. A roast lamb and several whole piglets are excavated from a leaf-lined oven in the ground. Men pat animal-skin drums. They have palm leaves strung around the calves of their legs, and their biceps. They are wearing minute G-strings. Their bodies are simply flawless. A youth wriggles up a palm tree and throws his arms out, laughing, when he gets to the top. The whole display is of youth and extreme physical beauty.

Yet everyone we see over the age of, say, thirty-five, is rather large and lumpy. Laurent sees us looking at the crowd. 'You see how fat we all are?' he says, grinning.

'Oh, no, no. Actually, yes,' I say tactfully.

'Do you want to know why that is?' asks Laurent. 'That is the presence of France. Before the French arrived, we ate all our own food. We grew it and we ate it. And we had our own ceremonies. We had our singing, our tattoos and our dancing. Then the French arrived, and we had to stop all the singing and the dancing. Tattoos were forbidden.' That's all changed now; singing, dancing and tattoos are very much part of the tourist package. However, the Polynesians started to become a European satellite in other ways. They grew to enjoy being paid for by France. 'We began to eat McDonald's and drink Coke. That's the legacy of being a French territory.' He laughs. 'And we perform in French hotels to the entertainment of French millionaires.'

We eat the lamb, which is delicious, roasted and tender and, along with about a hundred others, watch a 'native' show which involves a lot of drumming and a lot of bottom-shimmying.

Some of the guests are plucked from the dining area and forced to dance with the beautiful women. Everyone has smiles on their faces, and flowers in their hair. Everyone, essentially, is participating in the giant branding exercise which is French Polynesia. Are the locals smiling because the joke is on us; or is it on them? I can't decide.

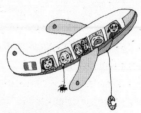

CHAPTER THIRTEEN

Ne Me Quitte Pas

Phoebe's diary: *We are going to Hiva Oa (another miniscule island) to see Gauguin's GRAVE. I hate Mummy and I hate Daddy. As usual there was a massive fuss about me not eating my food on the plane and Mummy said she wouldn't let me OFF the plane until I finished my food. See? Always about me because I am the eldest. This stinks. Mummy said if I didn't eat then I would have to go hungry as she wasn't going to buy ANY MORE FOOD FOR US. I'm not going to tell her I'm hungry, even if I am, so she will get a little surprise! Apparently I am ruining this trip so I might as well go home. I wish this damn plane would arrive. Jesus.*

After three hours rocking around in the sky, and the usual tussle with Phoebe about eating her food (perfectly nice cheese sandwiches and a carton of pineapple juice), our tiny biplane comes racing down through the clouds over Hiva Oa, chief isle in the Marquesas group of islands, 5 degrees south of the equator and as far from Tahiti as Britain is from Moscow.

It lands with an almighty thud on the thin, red airstrip. We are on the ground, but the airstrip appears to be on the top of

Hiva-oa los-angeles

australia

tiki

cemetery

a mountain. I estimate we are still around 3,000 metres above sea level. We all clamber out of the plane. It is hot, and windy. Around us tower high craggy peaks, covered with bright green foliage. Within the peaks are deep, dark crevasses and silvery ribbons of water.

The airport building is a single corrugated iron shed. Inside the building a group of Scouts, in green scarves and yellow shorts, are very loudly performing a Polynesian 'haka', yelling and dancing. Drumming thuds from the building. Someone steps forward and garlands us with flowers.

I glance at the airport sign, which reads 'Aeroport Hiva Oa – Jacques BREL'. We are further from any major land mass than we could be anywhere else on the planet, wearing hibiscus necklaces and surrounded by chanting, drumming Scouts. Yet the French have named the airport after a Parisian-based Belgian cabaret singer of the fifties. Is this charming? Or a signal of the French refusal to engage?

Brel died in 1978 in Paris, wife on one side of the bed, mistress on the other, but his body was brought back here. It seems that the Marquesas in general and Hiva Oa in particular was his spiritual home. 'In these islands of pure solitude, I have found a sort of peace,' he wrote here, lying naked beside the ocean.

I marshal the children into some sort of order, pick up our bags from a long table, and look across at the marvellous emerald forests covering the mountains. In his book *La Tour du Monde*, published in 1902, the writer Pierre de Myrica describes the palpable misery of living in the crepuscular lands of Northern Europe, as if it were a specifically French affliction, and the subsequent joy of going to the tropics:

We have become attached to darkened homes, to a lazy life under an annoying climate [...] it must be noted that this feeling weighs most heavily upon the French and that the Anglo-Saxons usually put up with it. Smitten with the exotic ideal the mental state of our race is so unresistant no sooner as it is transplanted to a foreign land.

'Do you think the French are smitten with the exotic ideal?' I gasp to Pip as I shoulder one of our colossal bags. We've chucked out so many clothes, but these babies don't get any lighter.

'Well, they have so many rules and regulations at home, perhaps they just need to have the idea of an available wilderness, in case they get fed up with it all,' says Pip, fighting with the tripod.

I ponder this. Perhaps the DOM-TOMs are like a glossy Club Med brochure for the French. Whenever they get fed up with tax demands, and receipts in triplicate, and stamps which are only available from a *tabac*, and all the other glorious red-tapery of *la République*, they can always know there is the possibility of running free, and naked, in an ordered wilderness. Well, it seemed to work for Jacques Brel.

When we have arrived at our hotel, a wonderful eco-lodge high up above the ocean, I quiz the manager about why he thinks the airport was named after Brel and not Gauguin.

Gerard Bourgignon, whose name is about as Gallic as you can get without actually being called Charles de Gaulle, considers the issue over a mint julep in the sun. We are sitting beside the pool, which is perched on a giddying shelf high in the mist-topped mountains above the turquoise ocean. The children are playing in the water. It's a perfect moment for Gerard and I to have a proper chat. I know this tranquil scene will last about four minutes.

'They still disapprove of Gauguin here,' says Bourgignon sadly. 'They don't look at his artistic legacy. The church is still very strong here.' Gerard has adopted the granddaughter of Marcel Lai, whom we interviewed in Tahiti, and hence is parent to the great, great granddaughter of Gauguin. He tells me he is intending to return to France with her, in order to give her a decent education. Perhaps his aim is also to remove her from the local view of Gauguin, too, which appears to be a troubled one.

'Gauguin is not popular. He had so many problems not with religion, but the church. It was difficult for people here to follow him, to accept him. He was living with a fourteen-year-old girl and had children with her. Yet the image of Paradise that they use is the image of Polynesia as depicted by Paul Gauguin.' Quite. In life, Gauguin was rejected; in death, he's become the entire brand.

'Whereas with Brel, it was quite different; oh, they love him in the Marquesas. But not as a singer.' Apparently Brel's anthems were just too sad for the Polynesians. They did not love Brel because he was a sex god with big deep chocolate eyes who sang 'Ne Me Quitte Pas'. In Polynesia everyone under, say, thirty, looks pretty much like a sex god anyway. So forget the French fanciability stuff.

'They loved Brel because he was mad on flying,' says Gerard. Apparently Brel would sometimes collect the mail from Tahiti for the Marquesas in his little bi-plane, *Jo-Jo*. After his death, *Jo-Jo* was rescued from a dilapidated state and restored by the islanders. She now sits in a hangar in the village of Atuona on the island.

This is the reason why the airport is named after Jacques Brel.

There is a sound of aggrieved screaming from the pool. Honey is doing 'starfish' jumps. Every time she goes to the edge of the pool, Gabriel taunts her by popping his head out of the water, and laughing at her. She daren't jump in, for fear of landing on him, and so the moment is gone. She screams with frustration and fury, which of course makes him laugh all the more.

Since Phoebe has arrived, there is a Herculean power struggle going on in the middle of the family to be her particular playmate, and Honey is not giving up easily. Pip trots over, tempting Gabriel away with a pair of goggles.

'There are only five Frenchmen who have been honoured similiarly with a named airport, you know,' smiles Gerard.

'Who, who, who, who are the others?' says Gabriel, who loves a quiz, and a list.

He has got tired of teasing Honey and is standing, dripping, beside me.

'Guess,' says Gerard.

'Charles de Gaulle?' says Gabriel.

'*Oui. Très bien.*'

'Er, oh, I know another one. Aimé Césaire airport in Fort de France, Martinique.'

'*Oui! Formidable,*' says Gerard, with evident surprise.

There is a long silence.

'There are three more,' says Gerard, hopefully.

'I don't know any other famous French people.'

'*Alors*, we have Lyon Saint-Exupéry Airport, named after the famous aviator and writer. Then in Saint Denis, La Réunion, there is the Roland Garros Airport, named for the World War One ace, and then here, in Hiva Oa, we have the Jacques Brel Airport. Voila!'

'Awesome.'

We arrange with Gerard to film Brel's plane *Jo-Jo* tomorrow. I scoop up Lucien in a towel and we repair to our rooms in which there seems to be an entire family of geckos in full cry.

'Gecko! Gecko!' shouts Lucien.

The next morning, Gerard takes us to see Brel's tiny plane. We go down to Atuona in a jeep, and park up beside the aircraft hangar. Gerard slides open the vast doors and there, brilliant in immaculate white and red paint, is *Jo-Jo*, whose restoration was paid for by friends and admirers here in Hiva Oa. Around it on the sides of the hangar are hundreds of posters, drawings and images of Brel; Brel at the Olympia, Paris; Brel singing in some gloomy, smoke-filled bar; Brel, 'L'inaccessible Étoile'. And as we walk around the plane, Brel's voice is booming out of the speakers, that dark, deep hoarse voice, with its Belgian twang, begging us not to leave him. His most famous number, 'Ne Me Quitte Pas', was written for one of his mistresses even though he had already dumped her, apparently.

Listening to Brel's peerless voice in the world's most seductive language, I'm overwhelmed by multiple sensations. I look at Pip delightedly, hoping he will feel it too. He rolls his eyes.

'Too French for me,' he says.

Although I want to be consumed by the romance of it all, I'm quite proud that Pip refuses to lie down and be conquered by the bewitching allure of, not so much France herself, as the whole carefully marketed *idea* of France, which singers such as Brel have plundered wholesale. Or maybe they didn't do it so knowingly. Perhaps it is just innate for French adults to behave like this, to be hopelessly romantic, yet chronically unfaithful; maybe it is just part of the French national spirit, as acceptable beneath the *tricolore* as *liberté, égalité, fraternité*.

'Are you cross with me that I'm not so smitten?' asks Pip, ever the courteous Englishman.

'No,' I say fondly. 'Never. *Ne me quitte pas.*'

He laughs. This trip has bound us together like nothing else. 'Not likely.'

'Oh Mummeee, this is boring! Why do you always have to go on about Jacques Brel?!' shouts Honey. 'Why can't we go back to the pool?'

Gerard is standing in the door of the hangar.

'Let's go to the Maison du Jouir,' he says, referring to the house which has been built on the exact place where Gauguin lived, and which represents how he lived here in Hiva Oa.

Oh, fabulous. Two French icons in a morning! I ignore the children, who are playing tag around the palm trees, and shouting, and trot over to the Maison du Jouir with Gerard.

'Maison du Jouir, what's that?' says Pip.

'House of Pleasure, House of Fun,' I say. 'Actually, it's more accurate to call it the House of Orgasm.' I'm still in a Brel state of mind.

'Yes, well I don't think the Travel Channel needs to have quite such an accurate translation, to be quite honest,' says Pip.

Gauguin turned up here from Tahiti in 1901. The French missionaries, who had arrived here some time earlier, disapproved of him hugely. The things which sustained Gauguin, namely wine, girls and art, were not the things which sustained the missionaries. However, in order to purchase land on Hiva Oa, one had to attend church. For a year.

'So he did,' said Gerard. 'Every Sunday. Then when a year was up, he bought this house, or a house very similar to this, right here, called it the House of Pleasure, La Maison du Jouir, and never went to church again, aha ha!'

The land was right next to a missionary school. Having bought his land, Gauguin built his house, and decorated it with a pair of big-breasted nudes outside, specifically to irritate the nuns who ran the school. That was the art. He dug a well outside, just so he could keep bottles of wine well chilled. When he wanted one, he would cool it by dangling it out of his window on a fishing rod into the well. That was the wine. Having left his family in Tahiti (let alone the wife in France), he then seduced a young girl, Vaeoho, who bore him a child when she was just thirteen. That was the girl. Several of Gauguin's grandchildren from this line (as opposed to the line of Marcel Lai in Tahiti), still live on the island. Gauguin only had two years in the House of Pleasure, before he died of a heart attack brought on by syphilis in 1903. He had been desperate to go home.

On 12 June 1892, he wrote back to the man whom he had originally importuned.

'Dear Director of Fine Arts,
   You were kind enough, at my request, to grant me a mission to Tahiti [...] however frugal one is, life is very expensive in Tahiti and the journeys are very costly.
   I have the honour of requesting that you repatriate me to France. I count on your good will to assist with my return home.
   With all my deep respect, Monsieur le Director, I remain your devoted servant,

Paul Gauguin'

When he finally died here of a stroke, alone in Hiva Oa, on 8 May 1903, Gauguin had pathetically few possessions; a chair, a table and some bottles of wine. He had run out of money, health and supporters, his body ignominiously tossed into a pauper's pit. (It was exhumed and buried in the cemetery some years later.) It took three months for the news of his death to reach Paris. As the cemetery is directly above the village, we decide to drive up there.

The cemetery clings to the side of a giant wooded mountain. It takes a while to locate Gauguin's grave, because it is so understated. Actually, it takes so long that we put the children back in the jeep where they can be fanned by the air conditioning and escape the mosquitoes.

Eventually, slapping insects off my legs as I walk down the cemetery's steep slopes, I come across it. It is decorated only with a copy of the sculpture Gauguin intended to be here, a naked, long-haired woman half-kneeling, half-crouching.

There is a large stone, decorated with white beads, on which someone has daubed in white paint 'Paul Gauguin 1903'. The paint is faded and the stones on the grave are covered with lichen. The whole thing does not have any of the pomp or gravitas one would imagine appropriate for the last resting place for one of the fathers of modern painting. I begin to see why Gerard Bourgignon said what he did about Gauguin's reputation on Hiva Oa.

Close by Gauguin is the grave of Jacques Brel.

Now, this is much more like one would expect the grave of a famous French person to look. There is a little poem about Brel, engraved on a marble slab, a proper name check, with birth and death dates which are respectfully surmounted on a brass plaque, even a small bas-relief portrait. There are also quite a lot more flowers and beads around his grave, which is in a proper space and dignified by the presence of some tall, large-leafed plants.

Palm trees are gently waving in the azure skies. Far below, rollers crash onto the sand. Slowly, I am aware of the cemetery's peace and tranquillity being disturbed. There is a wholly fiendish noise coming from a car parked below the cemetery. I look down and recognise our jeep. Why are my children such horrendous travelling companions?

'I'm with Gauguin on the cost of living here, frankly,' comments Pip as we walk, rather sadly, down to the jeep. 'Remember that £85 chicken and chips lunch we had the other day in Papeete. I just don't know how on earth people survive here.'

When we get back to the hotel, I look out over the balcony at the giant valley, the valley Gauguin must have looked at many times. It stretches out far below us. It is full of moist, verdant foliage, bright green trees, purple-leaved flowers, red blossom, huge palms, creamy magnolia, moist bananas and pink bougainvillea. Above, mist encroaches down the mountain tops, and above the mist, the sky is turquoise. When compared to the silver grey skies over Paris, and the tidy French countryside, Polynesia must have seemed, to Gauguin, a paradise of almost overwhelmingly brilliant luxury and power.

He never got to see the other side of the island, however. The next morning, we are due to take a trip to see the 'tiki'; statues of ancient Polynesian gods which the French missionaries (of course) had taken against and which Gauguin (of course) found rather inspirational. The tiki are situated in a verdant forest on the other side of the mountainous island. Our guide is a local. He is covered with inky black tattoos, and for once is not called Laurent, but Tematai.

'Is that like Timotei shampoo?' asks Phoebe.

'Will you shush,' I say to her.

'Will you give Mummy a tattoo, Timotei?' asks Gabriel. 'I think you know she really wants one.'

'Do you, Mummy, do you, do you? Go on, have one, have one,' says Honey.

'That is so gross,' says Phoebe. 'And sad. You are far too old for a tattoo.'

'I don't know, darling,' I remonstrate mildly. But I'm tempted. 'I think it might be fun. At least, it would be unforgettable.'

'And unerasable,' says Pip.

'Shall I?' I'm quite serious about it.

'Are you mad?'

'I thought it would give me one of those "I am alive" moments. You know, like when we decided to come here in the first place and bought the tickets.'

'I think we have had far too many of those "I am alive" moments recently,' says Pip.

We continue bumping along a terrifyingly vertiginous road for about two hours. Eventually, we reach the sacred spot of the tiki.

'This is where human sacrifice would take place,' says Tematai, as if he is talking about the weather.

'Would people really be killed here?' asks Gabriel urgently.

'*Ah, oui,*' says Tematai, a bit more sombrely now that he is talking to a child. 'They would be killed and their bodies eaten. Their heads would be put there (gesturing to the statue) and given to the tiki as an... how you say... offering. The bodies would be shared amongst the people.' It seems that this sort of practice, as well as formal orgies, dancing and tattooing, went on for centuries in the Marquesas, at least from the fifteenth century until the missionaries turned up in the 1840s and put an end to all the fun.

'Eeeeeewww,' says Phoebe.

Gauguin longed to come here. But he never saw these monumental sculptures. His legs, by then covered with syphilitic sores, were too far gone to support the journey, which in those days would have to be on foot, and would have taken about five days.

After arriving, we walk reverently around the grassy plain on which the six or seven giant stone tiki are situated.

There are about five gods, a goddess and something crouching on the ground which looks like a small animal or a frog.

'Maybe this was a tiki pet,' says Phoebe, patting the lozenge-shaped stone sculpture.

The tikis have all been decapitated, and castrated. Apparently the chaps were extremely well-endowed. Sexual prowess was a key element of religious ritual.

'And they were also in what you might term Go Mode,' comments Pip, switching the camera on.

'Any thoughts, darling?'

'Timotei, sorry, Tematai, do tell us, ahem, about the male sculptures,' I say.

'They all had erections,' says Tematai. 'This is what gave them their power.'

The French missionaries took a bit of a dim view of such overt masculinity, it seems, and thus promptly chopped off their genitalia as well as their heads. Apparently there are body parts in many museums around the world.

'Poor tiki,' says Honey, stroking a giant lichen-mottled and grey stone thigh with her small hand.

After several tours of the tiki, and inspections of their mutilated bodies, it's time for lunch. We follow Tematai to a house, or *carbet*, where a friendly woman in an apron comes out and bids us *'Bonjour'*. She has lunch ready for us. The *carbet* is huge and light, and festooned with flowers and plants which come bursting through the windows on either side. We will be eating fried banana, fried breadfruit and goat curry.

'Goat curry, how delicious, Tematai.' I pile the children's plates with food.

'It tastes like old socks.' Told you.

'When will our children become adventurous with food?' I say in despair to Pip.

'Never,' says Gabriel. 'I hate French food. Can I have a Coke?'

'Only if you ask the waitress. In French.'

He groans and trots over to the counter, where I hear him deliver the desired phrase. To my satisfaction I note that his accent is rather good.

'He'll make the Lycée yet,' I say to Phoebe.

'What, with just *"je voudrais avoir un Coca, s'il vous plait"* under his belt?' she snorts. 'I don't think so.'

I ponder on the seemingly invincible barrier against the learning of foreign languages that English children, or at least, my children, seem to possess. And their dislike of foreign food, which is incredibly annoying. They are all toying with their goat curry and making faces of loathing. To avoid the shame of four full plates being returned to the shy yet friendly woman who has been bustling around in what looks like a tiny kitchen, I eat half their food too, even though I'm really not at all hungry.

'I'm going to get home really fat, absolutely enormous actually, and it will all be your fault,' I tell them.

They laugh and drink more Coke.

We end the day beside the sea, in a perfect tiny cove lined with white, silky sand. The mountains come right down to the water, covered with tropical plants and trees of dark green. Long aerial roots hang down from the branches of the trees. Palms and bananas wave their fronds in the wind, which is kicking up perfect rolling waves of azure blue.

A man gallops past us, on a pony. The pony has no saddle and he has no shirt; they are both, quite literally, bare-backed. As he clatters away, the children jump out of the jeep, pleased to be away from the rigours of filming sequences, big thoughts, pieces to camera and all the other accoutrements which go along with making a documentary.

They struggle into their swimsuits and run across the beach, leggy Phoebe, Gabriel hard on her heels, Honey yelling with a desire to be accepted by the older two, and the warm bundle which is Lucien, hardly knowing whether to rush after them or stay with me. I follow them towards the surf; Pip hangs back, filming us. Eventually, he packs the camera away and we all end up in the water, diving over the waves which crash and foam around our legs. All the exasperating, frustrating, expensive, incomprehensible elements of our trip are washed away in the Pacific surf as we all experience a bit of French wildness, the ecstasy Gauguin craved and the peace Brel loved.

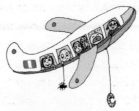

CHAPTER FOURTEEN

Mad World

Phoebe's diary: *Things Mummy and Daddy have promised me. Mummy: to have a dial phone in my bedroom. Daddy: to take me on a clothes shopping trip when we get back to London. Mummy: to sit next to me in a plane.*
This has never happened.

'Excusez-moi mais avez-vous le pomme compote?' ('Excuse me, but have you got the apple sauce?')

Although my grasp of French grammar is still, frankly, rubbish, we have now been away in the French universe for about eight weeks. At this point in our journey, the original aim of escaping normal life has in itself become the norm. We have stopped questioning why we are on this trip – at least, Pip and I have. The children continue to wonder.

'Why are we here really, Mummy?' Honey will pipe up, as I am in the middle of some tortuous moment in a tiny grocery, trying to find out whether they sell stewed apple.

Or Lucien will settle down into his seat on a plane, yawn, look at me and ask 'When are we going to be back in London?' before putting his head on my knee and going to sleep. As far

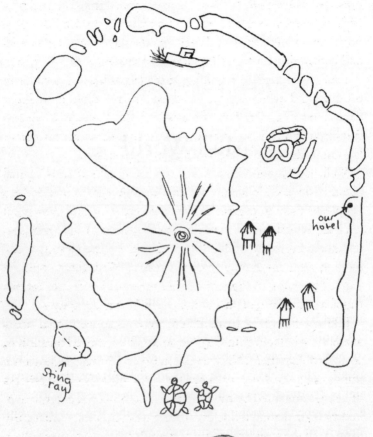

sting
ray

our
hotel

Bora Bora

as Pip and I are concerned, all we can think about is that we are working our way through the journey, and that the journey must be completed. We have gone beyond the confines of a holiday, even a long one. It's how I imagine the Galileo space probe might feel (if it had feelings), leaving the solar system and continuing on trundling into deep space.

'I feel as if we are trundling into deep space,' I confide in my husband when we are installed on our three-hour flight from Hiva Oa, a tall, mountainous palm-fronded island, to Rangiroa, which is a flat, round one with pink sand and a giant lagoon in the middle. He looks at me quizzically.

'Well, don't for goodness' sake leave me and the Travel Channel behind,' he says. With no communication with home and no people to meet and greet us, we must exist in our own small nucleus, which means new invented structures and routines. It's taken a journey of 30,000 kilometres for me to start really looking after my family myself, I realise. Well, there could be worse places for an Induction into Parenting, I suppose. Yet this trip is a *'grand projet'* in stamina, as well as geography.

Take the notion of treats. There were no conventional treats available whatsoever in Guyane, apart from stuffed tarantulas, so no problem there. Now we are in French Polynesia, however, things are quite different. Since the entire place is in the process of being reinvented by the French as a commercial enterprise in luxury (rather than a nuclear testing station), treats practically drop from the trees. If you are prepared to pay, of course, which we are not. Since we have arrived in Polynesia I have been driven half demented by repeated demands from the children for hats, plastic turtles, furry dolphins, T-shirts, key rings with crazy frogs on them, and so on.

At one point I go into a fit of rage, and actually hurl the entire contents of one child's suitcase into a nearby hedge.

Then, feeling rather like Jack Stanton in *Primary Colors* when he throws his mobile out of the car window, and then has to spend the next 30 minutes finding it, I have to shamefacedly climb into the hedge to retrieve all the stuff.

The constant demands of a 90-day shoot combined with the 'trip of a lifetime' around the world mean that slowly but surely, I have metamorphosed into a sunburnt, insect-ravaged woman who spends her life packing and unpacking, occasionally brushing her hair and donning a radio microphone for a piece to camera. There has been the frequent use of foul language. There have been threats. There has been the denial of fizzy drinks, at least if Good Behaviour is not instantly forthcoming. I'm certainly a different kind of mother from the London version, but I'm not really sure it's an improvement.

'Never mind,' I say to Pip. 'We haven't had a disaster. Yet. '

'I know,' he says lovingly.

The tiny biplane thuds down onto the runway at Rangiroa.

'Where are we going NOW, Mummy?' says Phoebe. I worry that she's not got into the peripatetic vibe just yet.

'We are staying in the Pension Henri, sweetie.'

This turns out to be probably the most hideous bed and breakfast in the entire Polynesian archipelago. It's on a level with the Hotel Robert, the only major difference being that it is hot.

The Pension Henri is a set of rooms on shingle next to a family house. It is run by a timid, terrified-looking Frenchman called Monsieur Gilbert. M Gilbert is from Bordeaux and looks as though he wishes like hell he was back there. He is married to a large Polynesian woman who clearly brooks no nonsense.

The deal at the Pension Henri is simple. We have one room, with two bunk beds and a double bed. The bedroom has no other furniture. There is an ensuite bathroom, with a floor packed with loose, razor-sharp pieces of coral. If you have no shoes on, this means you must leap from the bedroom floor (cement) onto one of two miniscule mats, one beside the basin, the other by the loo, in order not to seriously lacerate your feet. There is no glass in the window of the bathroom, so life in the room represents a sort of insect free-for-all.

There is a pitiful kitchen with no furniture other than one counter. The kitchen table and chairs are outside on a railing-free ledge, with a 10-foot drop onto the ground beneath. There might have been a view of the ocean, which would have made things a little better, but M Gilbert has for some reason grown a huge hedge of leylandii in front of it.

The children start playing on some plastic chairs. Madame Gilbert rushes out of her house and shouts at them to get off.

'This has got to be the world's worst bed and breakfast!' says Gabriel happily. 'Wow! Do you know,' he says, 'I'm quite nostalgic for the Cric-Crac!'

There is no air conditioning.

'*L'année prochaine,*' says Monsieur Gilbert.

'What does that mean?' asks Honey.

'It means he's going to have air conditioning next year.'

The hopelessness of this statement silences her.

'Hey, guess what?' says Pip, wandering into the dark room.

'He's got those pillows here! The same that we had in Guyane!'

After a supper of Weetabix (them) and red wine (us), we try to go to sleep, but nobody can. As the hours of darkness tick by, everyone is crying and sweating on the sweat-soaked pillows and under the nylon, slippery sheets. Mosquitoes bombard us all night. Honey and Gabriel, who rushed to claim the top bunks, are regretting their enthusiasm, since they are now roasting in the heat. Eventually we move them down and they end up in our bed. Pip goes to the top bunk, and I find myself curled up under a nylon sheet with Lucien in his bunk. Actually, this is a treat, since it means I get to inhale his sweet baby fragrance throughout the night.

In the morning, breakfast is no better.

'We now hate French things,' announces Phoebe. Oh, great.

'Not another croissant!' yell the others. They commence to wail for an industrial load of products from Nestlé, preferably Cheerios, to arrive.

'Why can't we have Cheerios?'

'Shreddies?'

'Rice Krispies?'

'Because we've got croissants,' I say, through gritted teeth.

Eventually, after the croissants are grudgingly eaten, we are carted off by a man in a jeep who arrives to take us on an ocean experience, which involves walking for what seems like 3 kilometres over a blistering coral beach to the sea. This trip has been prearranged by the tourist board, I think. It is one trip too many, I grumble inwardly. I don't want to sound spoilt but I'm starting to envisage sitting down for a long time rather like a man dying of thirst envisages an oasis in the desert. I am carrying Lucien, who refuses to walk over the sharp corals. Pip is carrying the camera, and cursing. Pouring with sweat, we eventually reach the shore, where we are allowed to put some of our things down.

'*Alors,*' says our guide. 'We must swim round 'ere.' What?

He gestures to some rocky outcrop around which some shallow water is swirling.

'Why?'

'To see the ocean flood the lagoon. You can still carry your camera, you know.'

All right, then.

We set off around the rock, wading through the clear water. Gabriel and Phoebe, both good swimmers, run off, giggling and splashing. After them goes Pip, carrying Honey. For some reason, I am carrying both the camera and Lucien. There is an extremely strong current pulling at my legs. This is the tide coming in with a rush, I later learn. Suddenly, a huge wave smashes against the rocks. A vast amount of water comes immediately pouring through a gap in the rock and swirls around us both. I am suddenly in water up to my waist. Lucien cannot swim. We only have one camera.

'Help! Help!' I shout. Nothing happens.

Then, after a few seconds, *'Au secours!'*

Our guide reappears.

'I can't do this! What do you think you are doing?!' I yell frantically at the guide. I'm actually crying as I shout at him. 'We could have been swept out to sea! Why are we going around here? It's too deep!' I shout, my French collapsing into English.

I'm tired, and hot, and terrified about losing Lucien, or the camera, or possibly both. Tears are pouring down my face.

The guide smiles genially, and grabs both Lucien and the camera, almost at the same time as another wave pitches over the rocks and sweeps me off my feet into the water.

I struggle round the rock, weeping silently, and meet the rest of the group on the other side. We continue wading through some endless sandy corridor, only to come out onto the beach at precisely the spot where we left it. Indeed, there are all our other bags, carefully piled up on the sand.

'Well, what was the point of that?' I sob to Pip as the children start throwing sea cucumbers at one another.

He shrugs his shoulders.

'A French moment,' he says, by way of explanation.

That night I brave the costs and call my father.

'It's tough!' I wail. 'Today I was asked by our guide to wade with him around a small inlet and I burst into tears. All right, he looked like an Adonis, but what a berk! The inlet was being pounded by some giant ocean waves, and I was carrying a) Lucien, who cannot swim and b) a camera. God! The French will have it their way.'

My kind father sympathises. He can't swim either, you see.

Yes, French moments. There are quite a few here. It's almost as if Rangiroa is so remote from the metropole that its expat French community has gone slightly crazed.

Probably the most extreme example of this is Vin de Tahiti.

The atoll of Rangiroa, which surrounds a lagoon so vast that Jacques Cousteau called it 'the world's greatest aquarium', is completely covered with dead, or fossilised, coral. Unsurprisingly this is 'a soil difficult for wine-growers'. Yet here we are, in Polynesia's very own vineyard.

'Well, if it's so challenging, why are they doing it then?' grumbles Gabriel as he slumps into the boat which is taking us to the vineyard. We've had another night in Pension Henri, we are all tired and covered with mosquito bites.

'Because the owner is determined to have French wine bottled in French Polynesia,' I tell him. Apparently the owner, Dominique Auroy, is a French wine fanatic. He trialled around a hundred different grape types before finding ones which would grow in such a challenging environment. He's also got a vineyard in Rwanda for much the same reason.

'What's the reason?'

'Love of proper French wine.'

'Stupid.'

Gabriel is very cross. He wanted to go on a shark-feeding experience, not spend his morning filming in a vineyard on coral soil.

The boat cruises alongside a tiny pier, where the wine master, Sébastien Thépenier, is due to meet us. M Thépenier is dapper and relaxed in a Ralph Lauren shirt and chinos. By contrast, I am sporting an old T-shirt from a 1998 exhibition at the ICA, and a skirt which used to be white.

'*Enchanté*,' he says. He's pretty gorgeous.

'*Enchantée*,' I say.

'Stupid man,' says Gabriel under his breath.

We all walk along a thin path to the vineyard. It spreads out before us, looking just like something you might find in Bordeaux, only with a fringe of palm trees and a lagoon behind it.

'This looks totally surreal,' says Pip. 'How can I get a wide shot of the whole vineyard?'

'*Alors*, you can go on top of this tank, here,' says the wine master.

Pip climbs up a small ladder on top of a vast vat. Gabriel follows him, singing loudly.

'Gabriel, could you be quiet for a few minutes,' says Pip testily. 'I need to do a GV.' (General view, in other words a nice long shot showing off the landscape and surroundings.)

'Alice the Camel Had Five Humps,' shouts Gabriel in response.

'So sorry about this,' I say to Sébastien.

'*Alors*, the wine, she is grown on the coral soil. This is very difficult and we have had to enrich it with plant compost grown on the atoll,' says my guide.

'Alice the Camel Had Four Humps!' shouts my son from the top of the vat.

We do our best to ignore my son.

'We have had to have many visits from specialists from the metropole to test whether the wine, she is all right for drinking.

And I brought all the wine roots from France, of course. People love this wine. They think it is crazy and very special. The minerality of the coral soil is our best friend.'

What is the point of this? No point. It is merely valid because it is a legitimate extension of classic French culture, like the series of French films at the cultural centre on Saint Pierre, or the foie gras production on Miquelon. Its only role seems to be that it is a continuing promotion of the glory that is the French Republic.

'Alice the Camel Had Three Humps!' yells Gabriel.

'Gabriel, will you shut up!' shouts Pip murderously.

'And Rosie, stop walking down the lines of the grapes. Stay still with Sébastien, I can't focus on you otherwise.'

We stand stock still beside a vine. Sébastien knowledgably pulls down a bunch of grapes and discusses the particularly rare, mineral-tasting bouquet gained from grapes grown in coral. Suddenly, I have a pain of imaginable sharpness on my bare foot. I know that pain, I think. I inspect my foot. Yes, as I suspected. Hordes of black ants have charged out of the undergrowth by the vine, and are biting my heel.

'Aaagh!' I yell, leaping away and brushing my foot. 'I have to walk, I have to move! Can't you SEE that!' I shout to Herr Director.

'Alice the Camel Had No Humps! Because Alice Was A Horse!' shouts Gabriel.

'Shut up! Shut up!' yells Pip.

Sébastien looks around him at this supposedly respectable British filming team, who seemed to be so professional, and seemed to have such an overt interest in oenology, at least that's what he thought when he recieved our original fax from England.

We eventually achieve something approximating a report from the vineyard. We taste the wine back at Sébastien's HQ.

He's right. It is very... minerally. By which I mean it tastes of rocky chemicals, in the same way that Badoit water does. Only it's wine.

A very thin woman in pale linen comes into the shop. She is clearly a regular.

'I need some Sauternes... I'm having some people round tonight, and we're eating foie gras,' she explains to Sébastien, who assists her in a purchase.

'Sixteen thousand kilometres from Paris, and they operate the same way,' mutters Pip.

The day after the vineyard experience, we make the decision to stop filming.

We put down the camera and embrace the sun and the wind and the air and our four children. We have recorded hours of fluttering French flags, people playing pétanque, cycling, eating croissants, and singing 'La Marseillaise'. We have even recorded dolphins leaping through the waves of the ocean coming into the lagoon.

We are all getting on each other's nerves. Gabriel's demonstration on top of the wine vat reveals that we have now got to pay some attention to our children. Perhaps we must offer them something other than my fascination with French culture, which I used to think was virally contagious but which I realise, now, has not been inherited by my offspring.

The next day, we leave the Pension Henri, wave adieu to the anxious M Gilbert and go to Bora Bora.

How can I describe Bora Bora? A series of tiny *'motu'* (sandy islands), Bora Bora rings a magnificent lagoon, out of which an extinct volcano rears its summit. There is golden sand. Turquoise skies. Clear, shallow water in which turtles and stingrays swim. Our children have flowers in their hair and shell necklaces and think that their parents have at last understood how to arrange a proper trip.

The island was turned into a holiday resort after the war, largely for exhausted American GIs, and is a totally different proposition from the dark, luscious wilderness of Hiva Oa or the resourceful vineyards of Rangiroa.

We arrive at our hotel by boat. The hotel is full of French and Japanese honeymooners. The newly-weds spend their time cuddling up on sun loungers, and whispering tête-à-tête over candlelit suppers. When we sidle into the restaurant, our four spirited children marching behind us, the couples glare and hide behind the flower arrangements, as if afraid to come too near to a living representation of what they might eventually become. They wear different outfits all the time, sometimes two or three in the same day.

By contrast, we are wearing the same old stained rubbish that we brought from London. Not that I'm too bothered. Gone is the groomed, cosmetically enhanced reporter I hoped to represent in my dispatches from Saint Pierre et Miquelon. In her place is a frazzled human being in thrift store clothes and whose make-up consists of, basically, bright blue eyeliner, borrowed from Honey.

I even manage to leave my sandals behind in the catamaran on which we take a sunset cruise.

'That shows you are relaxing,' says the pilot of the boat, who is of course called Laurent.

'You have to keep the pace slow – to feel the love.'

Laurent says he never wants to leave the island. The cruise shows us how heavenly it is. The children sit on the catamaran, their faces upturned to the sky as it turns pink.

'Of course, it was better here before,' says Laurent. Before what?

'Before satellite TV.' He shrugs. 'Before, we were content. Now everyone watches cable and satellite TV and spends all their money buying things they see on TV, so we are all in debt.'

Yes, but you can always be bailed out by Paris. Laurent shrugs.

'I don't want to think about Paris.'

Eric Moll does. Eric is the French-born manager of our hotel, and he misses Paris so much that he's had the Eiffel Tower tattooed on his arm, Polynesian style.

'Can we see, please, please?' clamours Honey.

He obligingly rolls up his sleeve and produces an inky bicep.

'Would you ever find a British hotel manager with the Tower of London on his arm?' I giggle to Pip.

'Of course it is wonderful here,' says Eric. 'When you have the colour of the lagoon here, it's like you are looking at a dream. Or Photoshop, but you are in the postcard. There are, however, some things about Paris that I miss.'

Like what? I think about Paris. Which of its many delights would I miss the most? The grey light filtering through a bedroom window in the morning? The rigidly perfect Haussmannesque streets? The smell of rat poison in the Metro? I suggest these to Eric.

Eric laughs. '*Non.* Christmas. I am missing Christmas in Paris. And the cold weather, the window displays in Galeries Lafayette, the Champs Élysées...' We sigh nostalgically together.

'Will you please pull yourself together,' whispers Pip. 'You only went to Paris first when you were FOURTEEN.'

At this point, Phoebe runs up.

'Gabriel has fallen off a bridge,' she gasps. 'He's in his room.'

Did I mention the hotel was designed for honeymooners? These are people who spend so much time gazing at one another that they don't care what is going on around them. Nine-year-old boys care very much about what is going on around them. And so when Gabriel was walking across a low bridge over a pool, he leaned over the weedy white rope handrail (again, built with uncurious honeymooners in mind), to see what was beneath the bridge. At which point he spotted a turtle in the pool below him, and so leaned over to inspect it. And a bit more. The turtle moved away. So did Gabriel, leaning over further still; the rope gave way and he fell off the bridge and onto the coral reef of the pool. We find him in his room, slightly shocked. His knee is bruised and his arm has been deeply grazed by the coral, from wrist to elbow.

'Are you all right?' I ask, rather unnecessarily. He smiles feebly. On balance, he seems all right, although Eric immediately summons a paramedic who rushes up with a giant bag from which he extracts tincture of iodine and vast strands of bandage.

Eric announces that by way of compensation, Gabriel can officially adopt a turtle (not sure what this means, but it sounds good, a bit like France being the second maritime power).

I chat to the paramedic as he dabs Gabriel's arm. This is probably the most action he's had all year, I think. 'What else are you called to do?' I ask.

'There is no hospital on the island. So sometimes I assist women in giving birth, if there is no time to get to Tahiti,' says the paramedic casually. I look at him with increased respect.

'He'll be fine,' says the paramedic. 'But no swimming.'

'What?' shouts Gabriel after the paramedic leaves. 'What about our shark trip?'

'Ignore him,' I say. Because we are going on a shark trip tomorrow.

What is the best thing to say about the shark trip? For the children, the best thing was the sharks (obviously). For Pip, it might have been the lunch, which we ate on a trestle table in the water. We sat at the table, our legs dangling in the lagoon, eating freshly harpooned langoustines off plates made from leaves.

'Your hands are your forks, your teeth are your knives,' says Marcello, our chef and guide, as we embark on this spectacular feast.

Whereas for me, without wishing to be overtly cheesy, the best thing about the shark trip is Marcello. Long blonde tresses, blue sarong beneath which is a nut-coloured body covered with tattoos, neck adorned with a string of pearls and a manta ray's jawbone, Marcello is a walking advertisement for masculine perfection. He picks us up in a flower-festooned boat and takes us to a deserted, Robinson-Crusoe-style beach where the trestle table is already in place in the water.

After cooking us lunch, he takes us in a motorboat across the lagoon. Driving with his feet, because he is playing a ukelele. Serenaded by the warbling strings of the uklelele, we eventually arrive at a specific spot outside the lagoon in the ocean, whereupon the boat is anchored. The sarong is casually removed to reveal a perfect body enhanced only by a rose-coloured thong. Then, Marcello dives in. While we English weeds are still messing around, attaching our snorkels and not knowing how to enter the water, Marcello is diving down, without so much as a mask, to a depth of about 12 metres. Anyway.

Pip is the first of the family to jump in. After about 2 seconds he reappears.

'F***! There are about twenty sharks down there!'

Marcello, by this time, has resurfaced. I swear his hibiscus is still behind his ear.

'*Mais, oui!*'

'Is this normal? Are they safe?'

'*Mais, oui!*'

And yes, circling the boat with long, whipping tails, are about fifteen to twenty black-tipped sharks. About six foot long. They seem extremely menacing.

Never mind. We all jump into the ocean, apart from Lucien, who stays on board, looking nervously over the side.

Marcello produces a dead fish, slashes it with his diving knife (kept in the thong), and chucks the fish in. Chaos in the water ensues, as the sharks dive for their food. Down on the seabed, however, there is a greater commotion. An enormous lemon shark, the length of the boat, casually cruises up and grabs the fish from its smaller sharky brethren. As it swims away, Marcello dives down to it and strokes it on the nose.

'Are these sharks dangerous?' asks Pip.

'The lemon shark, oh *non, non.*'

Fifteen minutes later, after swimming around with hundreds of other tropical fish, we are back in the boat, laughing and shouting. Marcello, who is clearly used to all this attention (he obviously does this routine with French honeymooners most days), laughs and gets out the ukelele again.

'You drive,' he says. To Lucien. Is the man mad?

But no, here is Lucien, aged four, suddenly in charge of a rather large, fast motor-powered vessel. We power back into the lagoon. Lucien is beside himself with joy. Eventually, much to Lucien's anger, Marcello insists he stop the boat in a specific, shallow spot. Around us is a family of giant stingrays, cruising around the boat.

'*Allons-y*,' says Marcello, leaping out, giving us once more a perfect view of his thong-enhanced behind. The idea is that we all get out into the water and kiss the stingrays. Well, Marcello does the kissing. We just pat the vast square fish, which swim around us rather eerily.

On the way back, each child takes a turn at steering the boat. I can hardly thank Marcello enough. I'm almost crying with the sensation of it all, the shocking proximity to the sharks, the delicious lunch, the spectacular location, but above all the knowledge that we are here, and we can never not be here; my children will never forget this day, a day which is already ebbing away, the sun setting behind the peak of the volcano, the lagoon suddenly turning black.

On the shore by the hotel, Marcello's wife is waiting for him to take her home, cook her supper and serenade her with his ukelele. Is she a beautiful Polynesian? She is not. She is an extremely middle-class-looking French woman who works at the hotel spa. Well, lucky old her.

We clatter into our room and collapse on the bed. Pip lazily turns on the television. Great! A programme about sharks! How fitting.

A giant shark fills the screen. It looks very nasty.

'*Le requin citron,*' intones the presenter. No! A lemon shark! '*Un des requins les plus dangereux de l'Océan Pacifique.*'

The children squeal about this all night.

CHAPTER FIFTEEN

A Little Piece of France in Australia

Phoebe's diary: I've decided I'm not going to whine in my diary about Mummy being horrid and annoying. Although I cannot even begin to explain how much she aggravates me sometimes. Air New Zealand is wicked. The multimedia system is COOL and I FINALLY watched 'Angus, Thongs and Perfect Snogging,' and love, love, love it. Yay!

Long-haul travel has vastly improved since Jacques Brel chugged across the Pacific. Let alone poor old Gauguin. Now there are super-fast jets, with films, and games, and nursery rhymes and little packs full of cards and crayons to while away the hours. Families have never had so much with which to occupy themselves. However, while travel conditions may have changed, human nature has not. I have discovered that if you are a parent and travelling with your other half, and that other half absconds entirely from looking after the family group, a veil of incandescent fury will descend over the half who is doing all the work.

'Yes, but Lucien and Honey only ever want to sit next to you,' says Pip, quite reasonably, as we settle down into our seats and I realise that once again, I am going to be expected to salute the world of Peppa Pig for the next twelve hours.

'And the others are quite happy watching films and playing Tetris. I think that silly Thongs and Snogging film is on, which Phoebe has been asking to see for weeks. It'll cheer her up. She's in a right fluster about not being in London for her birthday as it is,' says Pip.

Yes, Phoebe will be twelve in a matter of days. I don't care, though. It's just not fair. To have something approaching 500 minutes of undiluted Peppa Pig and then to catch a glimpse of my dear husband vaguely watching a good (well, an OK) film (*How To Lose Friends & Alienate People*), while fingering a copy of the *International Herald Tribune* (albeit the international edition and one a few days out of date), prior to nestling down for, as he puts it, a spot of zeds, is enough to send me into a total rage.

At one juncture in the journey, in order to alleviate the barrage of death stares going towards my spouse from my seat, he actually sends me a mini bottle of champagne down the aisle. Of course, I send it back.

Plus, I have left book nine of *A Dance to the Music of Time* in Papeete airport when Lucien was having a (now customary) pre-boarding tantrum. Twelve hours on a plane to New Caledonia and all I have to amuse myself is origami. My Crowned Crane is amazing. That doesn't help my mood. I have been prevented from watching *How to Lose Friends & Alienate People*. I have had to sing 'The Grand Old Duke Of York'. I have read *Daddy Pig's Old Chair* so often I can practically recite the bar code numbers on the back page.

Pip, on the other hand, has been laughing his head off at *How to Lose Friends* etc. I feel like telling him he's achieved the promise of the film's title, but of course we haven't lost each other. We can't.

Something else is disturbing me. When we were leaving Papeete, amid the tantrum from Lucien, Pip actually told me my interviewing technique had started to go downhill. Indeed, as he put it, 'your interviews are becoming rather beta minus'.

I take a moment to muse on this as we pass over Wallis and Futuna, two minuscule specks in the South Pacific which belong (of course) to France and are accessible only by oil tankers, or something. Maybe he's right. Maybe I am the wrong person for such an epic. Maybe I'm so concerned with packing, and washing clothes, and keeping the children safe, that I have no energy for Scott-of-the-Antarctic-style leadership and poetry in my interviews.

On the positive side, the demands of our journey are at last bearing fruit on the imagination of our offspring. Halfway in the journey I give Gabriel an English text book, as part of a vague ambition to keep a notional amount of education in his head. His school was not overly worried about him keeping up, which is good, but I am, and have brought some books with us. Gabriel's task is to fill in the blanks in a small questionnaire entitled 'Description of a Real Place'. It's clear his time in foreign climes has certainly sharpened his mind somewhat. Words in italics are his.

'It was *very busy in the swampy market.* There were *people rushing around with mangoes and papayas.* Here and there *were disguised policemen arresting thieves.* Close by *I spotted a person stealing some fruit. Gun in hand and armed with a deadly spider, I made eye contact with him and shouted "Thief!"'*

I flip through the (Kiwi) in-flight magazine. 'Why does everyone hate the French?' begins one article. What an extraordinary title. So prejudiced, and so... Anglo-Saxon. Well, I don't. But do I understand them any better, now I have lived in their midst for a few months? Have I managed to get beyond their stereotypical facade? The problem about the French, I realise, is that the stereotypical facade really does exist. So is it a facade, or is it really them? I mean, who else in the world would have their cuisine officially protected as a World Heritage Site, or pass by-laws about the amount of obligatory bakeries per square metre in city centres. Some of them even wear those striped Breton jumpers in an unironic manner. And they all love cycling. Yes, it's easy for us to snigger when the reality matches up with the film version. Plus, in the DOM-TOMs they are more French, and therefore more amusing, than anywhere else.

Yet am I verging on the racist by such thoughts? Yes, the French can be snobbish and blinkered and hemmed in by rules and regulations in a way that other (English-speaking) countries are not. Yet they are also charming, cultured, enthusiastic bon viveurs who generally disdain modern-day horrors such as ready-made cuisine, speak one of the world's greatest languages, have the world's most beautiful capital city, and prefer watching intellectual movies over low-quality television (French TV shows rate far lower than their British counterparts). I find that rather appealing.

It's the rules and regulations bit of the French character which comes to the fore, however, when we finally arrive at Nouméa's La Tontouta International Airport, Nouvelle Calédonie.

'Stand back! Your child has a fever!' a man in uniform and a de Gaulle-style hat announces.

What? You must be out of your mind, Monsieur.

'*Mais non*! Our camera has shone in her eye, and *absolument,* she has a fever.'

He pulls out a small piece of paper from the photosensitive device.

'*Alors*, it is 37.2 degrees. She must go to the camp outside the hospital.'

Nouvelle Calédonie was claimed by France in 1853. Peopled by Melanesians, known as Kanaks, for two thousand years, it was officially named by Captain Cook, who was reminded of Scotland when he saw its mountains and lakes. Geographically, it is a long, thin island rather like a cigar, about two o'clock off the coast of Brisbane, and its acquisition must have settled some amount of French pride, since it is one of the South Pacific's largest islands.

At first, the French used it much the same way that Britain was using Australia, i.e. as a conveniently distant place to which convicts might be shipped. Around 22,000 criminals and political prisoners were sent there, including 4,500 key members of the Paris Commune who routed Napoleon III, barricaded Paris and burned down the Tuileries Palace in 1871. After this, the French geologists realised how very rich it was in mineral deposits, particularly nickel. So they gradually closed down the prisons and sent over loads of pioneers, labourers and settlers instead. Now, the French like to call Nouvelle Calédonie the Côte d'Azur of Oceania; or 'a little bit of France in Australia', and paint it in glowing colours. They certainly don't want to start importing little English girls with potentially nasty infections into it.

'Ha ha! Honey's got swine flu!' Her brothers and sister make instant mileage out of our predicament.

'Stop! I haven't! I haven't! Shut up!'

Honey writhes and screams at the top of her voice, before a queue of about four hundred horrified-looking people.

'Take these children AWAY!' I shout at Pip.

'She must go to the hospital and be examined,' says the official.

The rest of the family shuffle away towards the taxi rank, leaving me and Honey, who has been forced to wear a face mask, to wait for instructions in order to go to the hospital. Insisting on wearing a pair of sunglasses over her mask, Honey looks rather like Liz Taylor coming out of a Beverly Hills hospital after some health scare. Big, silvery tears cascade down her cheeks at the humiliation of it all.

'Come on, Hearty,' I say, using her baby nickname. 'We'll go to the hospital, and it will be FUN.'

Of course, it is anything but. We eventually find the hospital. It looks like it was built by the convicts who were sent here in the nineteenth century. It's large and forbidding. Outside the main compound is a giant white marquee, with about three hundred people in it. They are all queuing up to be seen by a solitary nurse. They are all wearing face masks. It is about 200 degrees inside the tent, and there are no chairs.

I find an official. We have the following conversation.

'*Excusez-moi.*' ('Excuse me.')

'*Oui?*' ('Yes?')

'*Ici, c'est la queue pour l'examen medical de la grippe?*' ('Is this the queue for swine flu testing?')

'*Oui.*' ('Yes.')

'*Mais combien de temps doit-on rester dans cette queue?*' ('How long is the queue going to take?')

'*Trois heures.*' ('Three hours.')

We check out of the queue.

It's the one thing you need when you are going around the world with children: the confidence to bail out when the going is not good. There is no way I am standing in a queue for three hours in the blinding heat with Honey, aged six, in a face mask.

'All right, Hearty. We will go and find a doctor. Maybe we'll find a funny one like the man who sorted out my ear in Martinique.'

I demand the address of a doctor from the official. We leave the hospital and after about ten minutes' walk, eventually arrive at the reassuring green cross of a *pharmacie*, above which is the surgery for Dr Richard. Dr Richard is a very charming and sophisticated Frenchman, with posters for London contemporary art galleries in his waiting room. He charges me £60 to tell me Honey has a throat infection.

'Pas de grippe, Madame.' ('No swine flu, Madame.')

Then he charges me another £60 for an assortment of what my father, a chest physician, would call 'hokum'. We collect up all the hokum (syrups, linctus, nasal sprays, etc.) and carry it back to our apartment, walking back down the steep inclines of the Avenue Charles de Gaulle to the Baie de l'Orphelinat.

The Baie de l'Orphelinat is so called because this is where hundreds of young orphaned girls arrived by boat from Paris. They had been sent here by Empress Eugénie, wife of Napoleon III, in order to mate with the new settlers of Nouvelle Calédonie. One can almost imagine them walking bewildered down the gangplanks, in their white smocks and Parisian haircuts, ready for a new life.

Nouméa is now full of their descendants. It has an elegance which belies its earlier status as a country for pioneers on the make. It is full of white villas, and characterised by hills leading down to bays ringed with palm trees and full of glittering yachts.

High above the city are five giant softly pointed metal spires. This is Renzo Piano's Tjibaou Cultural Centre, a gift from President Mitterand to the indigenous Kanaks in order to placate them after a messy and bloody insurrection in the eighties, which reached its apex in 1989 when their political leader, Jean-Marie Tjibaou, was assassinated.

We walk past a variety of classic French cafes. I note that a *menu fixe* is £70. I start to panic about how much money we have left. Paul Gauguin, I note, felt the same. He came here on one of his frequent escapades away from Tahiti back home to France.

Writing to his friend George-Daniel de Monfried, on 30 August 1893, he has the following observations;

'I arrived today, Wednesday, at midday – with four francs in my pocket! [...] I was forced to stay in Nouméa for 25 days where the hotel and shipping were very expensive.'

Plus ça change, plus c'est la même chose.

Honey and I arrive at the apartment, which is on the ninth floor overlooking the lagoon. We spread out the new medicines in the bathroom, and tell everyone that Honey has not got swine flu. Cries of disappointment from the rest of the children. To my pleasure, Pip and the children have already unpacked and arranged everything in its set place. This is an essential part of our regime, since it gives everyone a sense of order and continuation.

'And, there's an aquarium just next door!' says Gabriel with joy. He's right. About a hundred yards away is the National Aquarium of New Caledonia. What a relief to sit down in front of a giant tank of water. I know it sounds bizarre, but after days of travel, of zips, picnics and boarding passes, the notion of sitting on a bench watching fish hanging in the dappled water before me is pure heaven. The aquarium is dark, and big, with room after room displaying giant tanks full of fish, turtles, molluscs and sharks.

In one area there is a long pressurised oval tube containing two nautiluses, creatures which normally live on the bottom of the ocean. Extraordinary things, tangerine striped with alien faces and exquisite curved shells, they mesmerise Lucien, who stands before them for about twenty minutes. Classical music is playing. There is no sense of commercialisation. There is no sense (or not much) of scientific research. It's simply all about sitting on long leather benches and watching fish doing their thing.

The next day, we have a date with Max Shekleton. Max Shekleton is the British consul to New Caledonia. His ex-wife Hilary was one of the people who first pricked my interest in the DOM-TOMs, and she insisted we visit him.

Shekleton lives in an exquisite house with a terraced garden overlooking the Baie de l'Orphelinat. There is a large Union Jack on a flagpole in the garden. 'Hooray!' shouts Gabriel as we approach the house. 'Something English!' Honestly, the more my children stay away from Blighty, the more doggedly patriotic they become.

There is much to delight them in Max's house. There is an official portrait of the Queen in the front hall, copies of *Country Life* in the loo and Josiah Spode's 'Italian Blue' crockery on the dining table.

Max, however, has not been airlifted straight from Mayfair. Born and bred in Australia, he has pretty much unrivalled knowledge of the French in Oceania, and a fascinating archive. Downstairs in his cellar there are boxes and boxes of black and white postcards of New Caledonia back when it was a destination for convicts. The *bagnards* stand before the camera with their white straw hats, the postcards showing how they built the city, dug the roads and, in some unfortunate cases, lined up to face the guillotine.

These were the bad times, of course. In 1864, nickel and a host of other metals were discovered under the mineral-rich soil of New Caledonia, after which the penal colony was phased out and quite quickly closed down. The difference between New Caledonia and Guyane, you see, is that New Caledonia is no soggy mosquito-ridden jungle, but a geological marvel, a slice of the Earth's crust which appeared out of the mix several million years ago almost intact. And the French were jolly chuffed they had planted the *tricolore* on it.

We sit out on the terrace watching the windsurfers on the turquoise lagoon, eating perfect French bread and cheese, with freshly squeezed orange juice. Max talks to us about the whole post-war, post-colonial, post-empire phenomenon of the DOM-TOMs.

'It's about a concept, rather than a need, I suppose. Without these overseas territories, France would feel she had lost a limb. The French are very proud to have this network. They are the only European country to have a leg on every continent. Living in New Caledonia you could almost be in Aix en Provence,' he continues.

We tell him about Honey and the attitude of the officials in the airport. He laughs and nods his head.

'Look at the French civil servants in their uniforms, the customs men in their tight shorts, and the gendarmes on their flashy motorbikes. It's French civilisation. The French attitude to everything is here. And the mission to civilise is still in the back of everyone's minds. If you want to excel here, you have to speak French. If you want to go into politics or trade, you have to be a perfect French speaker.'

All right, I will. The day after this, we have an exciting appointment. Twenty minutes with the charismatic prime minister of New Caledonia, Philippe Gomès. I am determined my interview will not be beta minus. As I get dressed in my only smart outfit, I decide it's going to be in perfect French. I'm pretty confident about my French by now, and M Gomès is by no means the first politician I have interviewed.

We arrive at his residence, and walk up to his office. Our babysitting arrangements have collapsed and so we have left Phoebe in charge back at the apartment. We are therefore rather tense, and late. No worries, however, as we discover M Gomès to be extremely laid-back, for a president. There is almost zero security here. After a few minutes, we are issued into the presidential HQ. M Gomès has a giant office almost entirely decorated with framed posters of classic nouvelle vague films, plus the obligatory vast portrait of President Sarkozy in a sharp suit.

'M Gomès,' I kick off, with a knockout question (in my mind) about the power of French culture.

M Gomès looks rather like Kevin Kline. He is attractively dishevelled, tieless and unshaven. Of course, he has a perfectly cut suit too.

'*Encore? Je ne vous comprends pas,*' says the president.

Pip giggles behind the camera. 'C minus,' he murmurs.

Oh, blast and damnation.

'Er, M Gomès,' I continue in my mother tongue. 'I would like to know how you think French culture can exist down here on the other side of the world, in New Caledonia.'

'New Caledonia has a particular personality,' he responds, also in English. I feel like a worm. We continue.

'There is the Kanak culture, the Pacific identity. And then we have the French legacy. Our legacy of human rights,' he says, glossing over not only the horrors endured by the convicts first sent to Nouméa, but also the Kanak struggle for authority. 'Then there is our culture; everyone understands it. French culture has traversed the centuries. It is a message. A cultural message, of artists, *auteurs,* musicians, of everything we have done, everything we have made... the French splendour which has gone around the world. And then the luxury.' He leans forward. 'French luxury,' he whispers. 'And then, our women. French women. Women are very important!'

Honestly. It's not even akin to good old British sexism. It's not about politics. It's not about feminism. It's just about sex. French men just cannot help themselves.

Is he proud to be here? *Dans le monde, on dit que la France a cinq océans,* he says, diving happily back into his language. *'Et on dit que dans la France, le soleil ne se couche jamais.'* No! Not the sun never setting on the *tricolore*! Again! *'C'est une belle image, n'est-ce pas?'* grins M Gomès.

We wrap up the encounter.

We get back to the apartment quickly, hoping there have been no disasters. Phoebe's only support system was a large piece of paper reading *'Au secours. Nous sommes dans la chambre 182'.* Just in case she needed to call someone in a panic.

To our relief we find them all safe and watching a film about Clipperton. Yes, Clipperton! The empty atoll of my dreams, hundreds of miles off the coast of Mexico, and acquired by France in 1858.

'Ooh, Clipperton!' I squeal. 'I'm so sorry we never got there!'

'Mummy you are slightly deranged,' says Phoebe drily. 'Who wants to go there? It is completely uninhabited. There is no hotel. There is no airport.'

'Well, did you enjoy the film?'

'It was OK, actually.'

'You see?' I say to Pip. 'Phoebe has been given extra responsibilities, and they are all learning something about another culture. They are picking things up. And Phoebe, you have been great, looking after everyone like this. Well, you are nearly twelve.' I grip Pip by the arm. 'In two days' time! It's her birthday. We mustn't forget.'

Phoebe is extremely unimpressed about having her birthday in New Caledonia.

'What will we be doing on my birthday, then?'

I look at our itinerary.

'Look, darling, we will be with Melanesian tribespeople.'

There is a tremendous silence.

'How could you DO this to me, Mummy?'

'Well, I can't help it,' I said.

'Can't we go back to England?'

'What, for your birthday?'

'Yeah.'

'That is obviously impossible, my sweet. Be reasonable.'

There is a silence.

'But don't you think it's cool? Having your birthday in such an extraordinary place?'

'No.'

The next morning, I'm in the back of the car again. Gabriel, pleading travel sickness (with some accuracy), is in the front. Everyone else is on the back seat.

'I hate being here!' I shout from the boot.

Forget all about a Dream Trip. This journey has become Torture in Transit.

'When we get back to London, I'm never travelling ANYWHERE OTHER than in the front!'

Nobody listens to me.

'When we get back to London, things are going to change!'

Zero response.

I glare out of the window. We are driving past the central square, Place des Cocotiers, which has flame-coloured trees, formal French flower beds, fountains and a small patisserie selling croissants. This is where Jacques Chirac once stood when he was an opposition candidate for the French presidency, after violent insurrection from Kanak *indépendantistes*, and bellowed 'You are strong and determined. You are France.' Today, there are also a lot of people marching around the Place des Cocotiers.

They are all bearing placards and chanting about *'une représentation juste'* (fair representation). What they are agitating about concerns the forthcoming independence referendum. They want Philippe Gomès to slap a five-year restriction on who can and who can't vote. They are afraid that just before the vote Paris will ship over thousands of loyalists and thus rig the mandate. Does New Caledonia want to be independent? Theoretically, independence has a lot of support. In reality, the thought of having to fund its own judiciary, security and military services, rather than getting a bumper handout from Paris every year, puts most people right off the idea. It's not so much about being called 'strong and determined' as a fear of going it alone in the South Pacific which I suspect stays the wish for New Caledonia to stray from Paris.

We leave Nouméa behind and drive through a sequence of tiny villages called things like Bourg Paris. At one point we drive through a village which boasts a pétanque square right next to a traditional Kanak totem pole. I'm speaking to the head of tourism, Patrick Moreau, on the phone as we sweep past the *hôtel de ville*, with its fluttering *tricolore* and obligatory statue of Marianne.

'It's a pretty patriotic place here,' I say to Patrick Moreau.

'Aha!' says Moreau delightedly. 'The sun never sets on the *tricolore*!'

Yes, we KNOW.

After two hours, the road becomes thinner and the soil around us redder. Eventually, we trundle up a steep rocky road which is almost bright orange in hue. At the crest of the hill, Pip stops the car. Everybody gasps.

Before us is a scene which could have come straight out of a science fiction cinematic masterpiece. The road goes straight down into an industrial quarry of spectacular dimensions. Vast steel towers churn out white smoke. They are linked to one another with rolling escalators, tubes and metal walkways. They stride across an enormous compound dominated with giant silver buildings. Enormous black trucks, dwarfed by the cathedral-like size of the silver sheds, reverse into the mouths of gateways to be loaded up with some material, after which they pull away again. Red lorries crawl along the layers of rocks.

Teams of workers, all dressed in bright blue jumpsuits, march through the dusty terrain. Behind the plant, the open earth is carved into colossal slabs where even from a distance of about a kilometre and a half, one can see the different layers of mineral deposit. This is the Goro nickel mine, one of the world's largest opencast mines.

Two hours later we are all clad in bright blue jumpsuits, even Lucien. We are to have lunch with Christian Tessarolo, head of geology at the Goro mine.

'*Bonjour!*' says Christian, hoving down on us in a titanic corridor.

He leads us companionably into the canteen where a collection of his colleagues are all eating lunch. This being France, the meal consists of a starter, proper French bread, coq au vin followed by crème caramel.

'Are three course lunches on the French bill of rights?' asks Phoebe cheekily. Luckily Christian finds this hilarious. He has clearly been told all about the British working habit of chewing sandwiches at the desk.

'*Alors*, do you know our cuisine is now a World Heritage Site?' he chuckles. We indicate that we have heard about this advance.

'This is our patrimony,' he says, energetically mopping his plate with crusty bread. Alas, no wine is allowed here,' he sighs. 'Come with me and I will show you the drinks array.'

We follow Christian to a soft-drink dispenser, delivering green, blue and red fizzy drinks respectively.

'*Alors,*' says Christian, pressing each button in turn. 'It is like this. We have garnierite, nickel and chromium, *n'est-ce pas*?!'

I ask you. Associating a fizzy drink dispenser with his beloved mineral deposits. This man is a complete rock anorak. 'I have mining in my blood,' acknowledges Christian happily. 'My grandfather was a miner in Alsace.'

After lunch, we go outside where there is already a small demonstration prepared for us. Ten or so brightly coloured rocks are arranged on a trolley.

'We start with the garnierite,' he says, holding up a sample of it. 'This is what the nickel is inside. Named after Jules Garnier who discovered it here in 1864.'

'Is that the same as Laboratoires Garnier?' asks Phoebe. 'You know, the shampoo people?'

Christian looks at her with mild incomprehension, and continues.

'Then we go onto the cobalt. Then the laterite. Then the chromium. Then the saprolite. And the further you go down, the more you find.'

After about fifteen minutes of rock demonstration I begin to worry that viewers of the Travel Channel might not find this element of our trip altogether gripping. I start rolling my eyes at Pip. Then I remember one of the very contentious issues about the Goro mine.

'Christian, can you tell me about the spillage of acid waste products from the Goro mine into the lagoon which surrounds New Caledonia?'

At this point the PR woman, who has been following us throughout, steps in.

'This interview is OVER! *Fini!*'

'He was lovely, though,' I say to Pip after we have left Christian, with double kisses on each cheek.

We drive through miles and miles of endless blue-green forests and over mountain pass after mountain pass. Eventually, we arrive in the palm tree-covered, silvery haven of Nouméa.

That night we blow red dust out of our shoes, our hair, our jeans. Our mouths taste of metal. However, we are full of excitement because on our way back, we stopped off at the market in Nouméa and bought a chicken. And some potatoes. While Pip and I rush around the flat, trying to find a baking dish, the children build a den of cushions and blankets.

'Roast chicken tonight, children!' I say with enthusiasm, stooping underneath the den.

Ninety minutes later we are all sitting around the dining table eating a roast dinner. Is there any other better food to give a notion of home, stability and comfort? Our menus have ricocheted from stale bread to foie gras and back again. Now we need simple, plain home cooking. The children are quiet as they apply themselves, with knife and fork, to meat, potatoes and gravy.

For some reason, I notice as I'm eating that my jaw is stiff and hurting.

'Maybe it's lockjaw,' I say to Pip.

'Look it up online,' he says. We have bought some Internet time in our apartment. Five minutes later, I wish I hadn't.

'Maybe I've got tetanus of the head,' I quaver. 'A rare form of the disease, apparently. Turns up in the facial area. Well, for 10 per cent of the population. What should I do?'

'Ignore it,' says Pip.

I start doing mouth excercises, moving my jaw this way and that, and opening it excessively wide. This seems to help, although I obviously look half crazed when I am doing it.

'I think it's because I'm so tense,' I announce, during the washing-up. 'Too much packing and unpacking, and nobody ever helping. Do you hear that, guys?' I shout over to the children. No response. They are all ensconced in the den, watching a French shopping channel.

After everyone has been installed in their various beds, I look through our itinerary. We are on Day 65 of our shoot. I flip through the next few pages which, in precis, read as follows:

'Depart for the Tjibaou Cultural Centre... interview the director... view an animation of Melanesian myths...

visit the endemic vegetation of the Blue River Park, with special arrival of the flightless kagu bird... visit to the Bourail Rodeo and interview a stockman... go underneath the lagoon of Poe...'

So much to fit in. So much to organise. It's the fifth of our documentaries. I feel as if this project will never end.

I lie back on the bed, groaning while doing mouth excercises.

'Who thought this trip was the best idea they had ever had in their life?'

'You did, darling.'

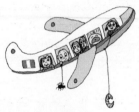

CHAPTER SIXTEEN

Tribal Life

Phoebe's diary: *We met this chief of a tribe and by coincidence he brought out this mahoosive cake and then Mummy just HAD to tell him it was my birthday! He has this great laugh and when told this, he laughed A LOT! We sang 'Joyeux Anniversaire' which is always so embarrassing. Before that though Mummy made us go to SCHOOL. Aaagh. Three reasons why we didn't want to. 1. It's our holidays. 2. We can't speak French. 3. We don't know anyone.*

'We are on our way to live with tribespeople, children,' I announce as we board a modestly sized plane to the island of Maré, largest of the three Loyalty Islands which are just off the coast of New Caledonia. There are about eight other people on board. I swear, these biplanes are shrinking as we continue getting further away from civilisation. I do a couple of mouth excercises. My jaw is feeling a lot better. I'm now quite ashamed that I actually thought I had a fatal strain of tetanus.That's what travelling for weeks and weeks does to you. Makes you get everything out of perspective. Quite the opposite of what it is supposed to do, in fact.

The Isle of Mare

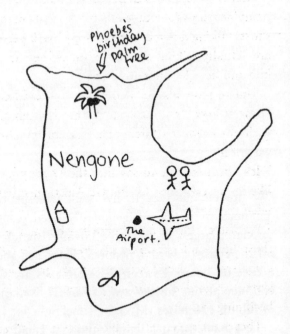

Phoebe's birthday palm tree

Nengone

The Airport.

NEW CALEDONIA

French assimilation hasn't been spread quite all over the DOM-TOMs. There are some places where the French clearly don't think it's worth building a *hôtel de ville*, or erecting some yellow postboxes, and the Loyalty Islands is one of them.

In order not to offend anyone on the Loyalty Islands, where Melanesians live in an 'authentic' tribal way, visitors have to get to grips with some local traditions. These are explained in a special pamphlet. Once we are ensconced in our seats, I begin to read it to everyone.

'Ethical charter. We are about to witness nature in its primeval state, and search for authentic human values.' The pamphlet shows a couple of white tourists in immaculate beige shorts talking down to a very happy black person. I mean, they are actually talking down to him, as they are kneeling above him and he is looking up to them.

'Unlike some places,' I continue, 'our landscapes are neither "deserts" nor "untouched". We are the centre of this system with our *chefferies* [areas ruled by chiefs], our tribes and our way of life.'

It's not quite fair to say that the Loyalty Islands are rather like the reservations for Native Americans, but this is exactly what they seem like.

I consult Aldrich and Connell, who summarise the islands thus: 'little understood by the French'. Why? Because 'neither colonists nor social scientists took great interest in social systems regarded as difficult, primitive and in the process of becoming extinct'.

They were never settled by Europeans, largely because they weren't worth it, as there is no easily accessible fresh water. Nowadays they are populated by indigenous Kanaks in a supposedly subsistence-type wage-free economy.

'Exchanges are not measured in currency,' continues the pamphlet. 'Money is not the centre of human relationships.' The truth is that tourism apart, most of the tribes are funded via remittances; money sent from their relations who have migrated to the *'grande terre'* (New Caledonia) and work there in places like the Goro mine.

Two hours later, we arrive. 'Remember,' I say to the children as we disembark in blinding sunshine at Maré Airport. 'When we enter a district we must make ourselves known to the chief. It is a mark of courtesy to bow when we meet the chief. We then have to give the chief a piece of fabric. It's a way of thanking the invisible guide. And, then we must remain silent while the chief thanks us. All right?'

Max Shekleton had told us about the fabric deal, in an email before we left the UK. We have brought with us some London Underground T-shirts, which I'm told will go down very well. There are some other things I have not explained to the children. One of the standards in the tribal system here is that women are treated as second-class citizens. 'Let's not talk about that,' as Honey might have put it.

Maré has several tourist options; well, two. You can either stay with a tribesperson in one of their gîtes, or you can stay in a luxurious eco-lodge. After our experience of the 'gîte' in Guyane I'm a bit nervous about the former option. Thanks to a key contact of Max Shekleton's, we have been booked in at the eco-lodge. It is full of middle-class French people sitting sipping coffee with their immaculately behaved children. They are instantly recognisable types who wouldn't go for living in a hut with a tribesperson either but who would also shun the marble grandeur of an InterContinental. Is this like us? Maybe, bar the immaculately behaved children.

The eco-lodge is full of hardwood furniture and palm leaves and surrounded by small chalets on stilts. Ours opens out with a little terrace facing the shore of the lagoon. The children run out onto the beach and gather white shells, which they then painstakingly put into long lines on the wooden terrace. The more chaotic and diverse our trip gets, the more they seek to impose order on it, I think.

After a few hours of this, we meet our guide, Joce Sioremu. I recognise his name, and quietly consult the pamphlet. As I suspected, he wrote it. A large, calm man, he takes my hand and pumps it up and down.

'*Bienvenue!*'

We all smile back at him.

Joce then assesses the group.

'*Alors*, the three elder children, you have got school today, *non*? It is a school day, you know!'

Without any more to say, he hurls open the doors of his Transit van and pats a welcoming hand on the seats within. The children dutifully clamber inside. Pip joins them. I am accorded the front seat! I like this place more and more. We set off down an impossibly bumpy road.

'Where are we going, Joce?'

'We are going to school!' announces Joce.

'Really? Have you arranged this? It's not on our itinerary.'

'I have set it all up for you,' says Joce, laughing his head off.

Cue chorus of moaning and groaning from the back.

'Mummy we are NOT going to school. It's my birthday tomorrow, remember?' says Phoebe in a low tone.

'Well, what does that have to do with anything?' I reply sunnily. 'I think school is a marvellous idea.'

Five minutes later, we turn into a dry, open field marked with a red gate, and pull up underneath a wide, low mango tree. The field is ringed with one-storey concrete buildings. A few of the buildings have been adorned with sprayed graffitti. There is a football goal in the field. That's it. From somewhere within the buildings, we hear a bell clanging and suddenly children pour out of the doors, running across the field in the directionless yet focused manner all children seem to have.

As we pile out of the Transit, a young white woman comes sauntering over to us. This is Jordane, the head of English. She's from Paris, and she's got missionary zeal. Truly, she has missionary zeal, since she's been sent here from her church.

'*Bonjour, bonjour,*' she says, smiling. 'Are you here to help my children speak English?' The children laugh nervously.

'They already have a few words of English here, because of the first missionaries who came. They were English,' she says.

(Indeed, this is true. What's more, all the English words seem to be about drinking tea: teaspoon, saucer, fairy cake, etc. Well, maybe not fairy cake.)

'How much of the French curriculum do you teach here?' I ask Jordane.

She looks at me in surprise. Here is where I realise that while there may not be a *hôtel de ville* on Maré, French assimilation is alive and well, albeit in a slightly less pronounced way.

'We teach the same here as in France, the exact same.'

'Is that relevant here?' I ask. Is knowing about Monet and reading Sartre really necessary under a South Pacific sky, in a place whose closest neighbours are Australia and Japan? But then again, why should the reach of these cultural giants be limited to France? The mission to civilise sounds very old-fashioned today, but perhaps its ambition wasn't altogether a dreadful thing.

'The French education system is great,' says Jordane coolly. 'We teach the moments of great French culture, sure. But we also teach lots of Oceanic culture. And yes, they speak French here in the playground as they do in the classes. Otherwise they don't learn it. You must be able to speak French here. You know, there are over thirty Kanak languages spoken in New Caledonia.'

'Do you live in a tribal way?' I ask her.

'You mean do I accept the low status of women here?' she says, crisply. 'I don't want to talk about that. We have just got married,' she says, pointing out an intense-looking bearded young man who is walking up behind her. He is head of history. 'And no, we haven't shared our wedding presents. And we don't pool our salary. But that's what people do here. And now, *les enfants, allez-y*. Classes have begun.'

Our three elder children simply melt away into the hordes of Melanesian kids.

This leaves Pip, me and Lucien alone with Joce.

'*Alors*, we now go and see Le Grand Trou!' announces Joce.

'Wot's that?' says Lucien.

'The Big Hole,' replies Joce.

'Oh, bonkers!' says Lucien, delighted.

Ten minutes later we get out of the car beside what looks like a large jungle, and follow Joce into it. After a short walk, we arrive at a cordoned-off area. Peering over, we can see the ground beneath our feet suddenly dropping away. This is Le Grand Trou. It is certainly very, very big. And it is certainly a hole, a vast dark hole in the middle of the lush, woody and crowded jungle, about 60 metres wide and 37 metres deep with bright blue, fresh water at the bottom. It's a geographical phenomenon, caused by a river at the bottom, but this was, for many years, the only available source of water on the island of Maré.

'My grandparents would come and get water here,' says Joce. 'They would boil banana leaves to make them supple, and make buckets out of them, put a stone in the bottom of the bucket and throw them over, attached to the lianas which grow out of the rocks. Then they would drag them up, full of water.'

'I'm good at throwing. When did you do this?' asks Lucien.

'Every day. This was before we had taps,' replies Joce.

'Oh,' says Lucien, silenced.

'It was very, very dangerous. You had to stand on the ledge just before the drop, and throw the bucket out and down. You had to be careful not to fall.'

The hole is protected now by a fence. About ten years ago a young man decided to go and taste the water for himself, with a cup. Having climbed down, he was physically unable to climb up again. Mercifully, his cries were heard by a passer-by, and a helicopter was scrambled from Nouméa to come and save him.

Lucien absolutely loves Le Grand Trou. We stay there for quite a long time, doing some filming. Our latest craze is to do a series of little televisual introductions to the whole series. This essentially involves saying *'Bienvenue en France'* in a sequence of impossible locations. Hence I find myself beside Le Grand Trou, leaping out from behind a large fern, shouting *'Bienvenue en France'*, while Joce holds Lucien by the hand and looks on politely. It almost goes without saying that these 'stings' (as they are known in televisual parlance) are never used when we get home.

After doing about twenty *'Bienvenue'* moments, it's lunchtime. Joce takes us to a local *carbet* which is selling food. At least, there is food for us to buy. It's probably someone's house which has been turned into a restaurant for our benefit.

'Have they got any Cheerios?' asks Lucien optimistically.

'You might get an egg sandwich,' I say.

When we get to the table Joce is talking quietly to the woman whose house we have invaded.

'What language is that?' says Lucien.

'It's our local dialect,' says Joce. 'But you will recognise some words.'

'Will I?'

'Yes.'

'What words?'

'Sipoon, for spoon. Blanket, for blanket. Horse for horse. Donkey for donkey. Sugar, bread, potato. All English words, just like the ones you use. All from the missionaries.'

After lunch, we wander along an immaculate beach. Far out the waves break on the coral reef which encircles the islands.

'Do you wish you were independent from France?' I ask Joce. He shakes his head.

'Oh, *non*. They give us an infrastructure. They pay for our schools. They built the mines, and bring jobs.'

According to Aldrich and Connell, it's precisely remote, economically fragile places like Maré which are the most ardent supporters of France. In Maré, the *indépendantiste* movement does very badly. In French Polynesia, it's the far-flung Marquesas, not Tahiti, which love being French the most, and as we know, Saint Pierre et Miquelon is ardently loyal.

We collect the children. School wasn't as dire as they had feared. 'Even though we were all split up straight away, Mummy,' said Phoebe.

Apparently, the thing which had sealed the children's popularity was their revelation that we pick up the droppings of our family dog, Disney. The way we look after dogs in Britain is simply hilarious to the children in Maré, where dogs are not pets, do not have their poo picked up by humans, live outside and must fend for themselves. 'They couldn't believe we buy special dog food for Disney,' says Gabriel.

'Or toys! Or shampoo! Or poo bags!' says Honey.

'Don't you wish Disney was with us here, Daddy?' asks Phoebe.

'No,' says Pip with feeling.

Actually, our pet is having a wonderful time back in London with Nicola Baird and her family. We met Nicola in the Islington Music shop two weeks before we left. I was moaning to the proprietress of the shop about the fact that we had no one to look after our lovely Border terrier, and that we didn't know what to do about it. Nicola, a complete stranger who happened to be standing behind us, piped up and suggested that she, her husband and their two young daughters could look after him. 'I like having dogs on a temporary basis,' she said. 'Hooray!' said her daughters. Her husband Pete just smiled and shrugged. So that's where Disney is at the moment. Nicola Baird; what a star.

The next day is Phoebe's birthday. I've managed to smuggle a box of several sets of tiny stud earrings from London in my luggage, and we make a bit of a ceremony, giving them to her over breakfast. They seem to please her greatly.

I look over to the foyer and see that Joce has arrived.

'We're going off to the tribal chief now,' I announce. The children don't respond in any specific way, since they have never met a tribal chief before and thus don't know whether to laugh or groan.

We arrive at the tribal hut of Monsieur Kenneth (or Keciehni) Wagada about twenty minutes later. M Wagada, who has no teeth and a very dirty laugh, appears delighted to see us. We give him our London Underground T-shirt. He bows and thanks us formally. We remain silent, as instructed. He then gives us a bolt of blue printed cotton. We thank him formally. He remains silent. Then he summons his wife, who seems about thirty years younger than he is. She brings us all coconuts out of which we are meant to sip the foul-tasting water within.

The children roll their eyes desperately at me but there is nothing I can do about it; it would be thoroughly rude to refuse.

'How lovely,' I say. 'Coconut water! Our favourite!'

'*Très bien*,' says Mme Wagada. 'I will get you another whole coconut.'

Before I can say anything she charges off and brings us another coconut which she chops at expertly with a machete. Oh, God. We now have industrial quantities of coconut water to drink.

There is, however, a cake, which is delicious and creamy and full of berries. We sing '*Joyeux anniversaire*' to Phoebe and eat it in handfuls while M Wagada talks to us about tribal life. Mme Wagada sits on a tiny stool several metres away from us all. It is clear she is not expected to join in the conversation whatsoever.

'But we share everything here,' says her husband. '*La joie et la tristesse. Voilà*.'

After twenty minutes of chat about the future of life as a tribesperson, which ranges from how little money and material objects are needed here to the importance of the mine at Goro for employment ('Surely the two are inextricably linked?' murmurs Pip at this point), M Wagada beckons us all to walk with him in his jungly back garden. He pops into his house, which has two rooms and no windows, and comes back with a spade and a coconut from which there is a large verdant shoot, about 30 centimetres long.

'We are going to plant this tree for you, Phoebe, on the day of your birthday,' he announces.

Phoebe looks suitably delighted. Actually, I think she is genuinely surprised and pleased that a fuss is being made of her.

'Well, it's a LOT more original than going to see a film at the local shopping centre, with dinner after at Nandos,' I whisper.

'Yeah, I suppose so,' says Phoebe.

We walk over to the jungle. I quietly pour our coconut water over a shrub as we go.

M Wagada starts digging the soft, sticky soil, and hands Phoebe the coconut with its leggy green growth.

We all watch as Phoebe places the coconut gently into the hole, and pats it down. The green shoot stands happily amongst the trees, banana plants and lianas of M Wagada's back garden.

'We'll come back in ten years and see how big your tree is,' I say. Ten years. By which time my lovely big daughter will be twenty-two. To my amazement, I discover I'm crying.

The next day it's time to leave Maré and fly back to Nouméa. As we are unloading the trusty thirteen bags from the taxi and preparing to go through to Departures, who should arrive but M Wagada. He rolls up in a battered jeep, and leaps out. In his arms are six handwoven headdresses, made from long fronds of palm leaf. We each put one on. They look utterly hilarious and charming. The children run around, screaming with delight at their marvellous new hats. Mme Wagada, who I warrant made the hats herself, is absent. M Wagada smiles a big toothless smile and giggles, before kissing us all and driving off.

We take off from Maré, flying over the turquoise lagoon to Nouméa. Lucien is asleep on my knee. I think about Phoebe's palm tree in the jungle of the island of Maré, growing tall as she will over the years to come.

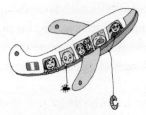

CHAPTER SEVENTEEN

My Academic Heroes

Phoebe's diary: *We got a taxi to Sydney Uni to interview the two guys that wrote mummys 'Bible' so she was really excited about that. We played charades with Alex, the girlfriend of the cameraman. She's really funny and nice. Then we had to get up early to catch a 12-HOUR flight. It's the longest flight I have EVER BEEN ON. I will just watch MOOVIES!*

And so we go to Sydney, to catch our next flight on around the French-speaking globe. 'Has everyone got their books?' I cry when we are all settled aboard NZ735. Even when the going's good – and on Air New Zealand, with its four-course meals in Economy, the going is very good – I have taken such a limited amount of child-centric amusement that each book has totemic status.

Lucien has about three hundred books to choose from at home; here he has five. We are off Peppa Pig now and back onto the gripping adventures of *Little Red Train*, by Benedict Blathwayt. Oh, Benedict, I know your entire canon in intricate detail; every single page. Honey gets Pippi Longstocking, the bumper edition, all good stuff, and the older two are wading, with me, through *David Copperfield*, six pages per outing.

That's all they can stomach. It is mesmerising, though. God, but Dickens is good for long-haul. I can see why people wept when they greeted him in America. In the days before email and mobiles, let alone electricity, he must have saved them all from going bonkers. Thirteen weeks in the company of Micawber, Steerforth et al., and time just flies past.

It's easy when you are in the presence of an epic. We are now in the closing stages of our own epic, and during our Sydney stopover we are actually going to meet Aldrich and Connell. I've interviewed some famous people in my life. I've even met David Bowie. Meeting Aldrich and Connell in the flesh, however, is a most engaging thrill.

Aldrich and Connell, Connell and Aldrich. Two academics at the University of Sydney who have taken it upon themselves to write the only English-language book on the French overseas domains. My Bible.

Robert Aldrich is from Boston. Associate professor of economic history, he is a French history expert. John Connell is from Leeds. Associate professor of geography, he is an anthropologist and expert on the South Pacific.

When I realised our schedule meant a 15-hour stay in Sydney, I emailed them and begged for an audience. As our August arrival would be halfway through their winter semester, they were only too happy to oblige.

As soon as we touch down at Sydney we dump our stuff and shoot off to the University of Sydney. The University of Sydney is red-brick and enormous, with legions of hearty-looking students striding about, their arms full of books, their heads full of 'potential'. I feel as if we have just landed here from the

Blue Lagoon which, come to think of it, is quite an accurate description of the balmy, turquoise waters surrounding New Caledonia. New Caledonia is only three hours' flight away but feels very far off. The point is that fitting in with the trenchantly independent beat of anglophone capitalism feels extremely different from how life is under the watchful maternalism of Marianne.

After walking up several flights of stairs and along about a mile of dusty corridor, we hail Aldrich and Connell, who are waiting to greet us, rather donnishly, in neighbouring offices.

'I feel a bit like Stanley meeting Livingstone in Africa,' I whisper happily to Pip, who is struggling along the stairs behind me with tripod and camera. 'You know, the intrepid journalist tracking down the grizzled experts out in the bush.'

'Oh, calm down,' he snorts with laughter. 'They are just a pair of academics. And downtown Sydney is hardly the bush.' Well, I'm still excited.

We repair to a tiny library full of ancient hardbacks and a poster of some South Pacific island peeling off the wall. The professors are both wearing tweedy jackets. Aldrich has leather patches on the arms of his, and an intelligent, East Coast manner. Connell, who I would say is slightly older, has a beard and an equally smart, Yorkshire manner. They are both probably in their early fifties. They are exactly as I imagined them. I have not been let down in the least. This makes our meeting all the more thrilling.

After chats about shared experiences on Hiva Oa, we venture into the university kitchen to source some coffee.

After about eight minutes, the instant coffee is found. After three months of perfect French coffee made from freshly ground beans, this powder makes a potion which tastes wildly exotic. We go into the allocated meeting room.

Pip tinkers around with the camera. A cameraman tinkers around with the lights.

Imagine! Another cameraman. Really, no expense has been spared for this interview. Very sweetly, the girlfriend of the cameraman has agreed to come along and play charades with the children, so we won't be disturbed by inopportune cries of 'I'm bored!'.

'And... action!' says Pip.

What joy; talking about our subject with two acknowledged experts who aren't French. Quite apart from the ease brought by conversing in English, it also means the interview will not be derailed with explanations about France being the world's second maritime power, or the likelihood of *tricolores* on the moon. I'm not jealous of the French pride in their own national status. It's just it keeps getting in the way during interviews. Plus, A&C can give a bit of perspective on the whole phenomenon.

'Why does France need, or want, an empire?' I ask Robert.

'People don't like giving up on grandeur, do they?' he responds. 'In some ways it's like an aristocrat having a collection of old family jewels. It's not a question of needing, or wanting, these countries as much as it being difficult to get rid of them.'

It hadn't really occurred to me that France might want to get rid of the DOM-TOMs, since every single person we had met spent most of their time furiously arguing in their favour.

'Yes, well, some have a strategic value, but it's limited. They are very costly. There is an extreme dependence on Paris, and it's very difficult to reconcile the level of subsidy they receive with the actual resources of the places themselves.'

'So, have you been to absolutely every one of the DOM-TOMs?'

'I don't think so, no,' says Aldrich.

'You mean you have travelled mostly in the South Pacific?' I suggest modestly.

'Yup,' says John Connell. 'I have never been to Saint Pierre et Miquelon.'

'And I don't think John or I have been to Guyane, have we John?' says Robert.

'Nope,' says John.

'Have either of you been... to Clipperton?' I ask.

At this, they merely laugh. The truth is plain, however. It looks like we have been to more of these crazy French territories than Aldrich and Connell have! Ha! I begin to view my long-term lodestars with a bit more equanimity.

'Well, that's very interesting,' I say, 'as in my belief, both Guyane and Saint Pierre et Miquelon really are MOST important in the overall...'

Pip starts coughing behind the camera, and kicks me.

'Sorry, sorry. Where were we? Ah yes, how is the French view of colonialisation different from that of the British? Robert?'

'Well, historically France has this mission.'

'The mission to civilise?'

'The very same.'

I think of the *tricolore* fluttering on the reed rooftops of beach-side houses in Bora Bora, the *À Bout de Souffle* poster in the office of the president of New Caledonia, the Paul patisserie in Fort de France, Martinique, the lessons on French culture in the school in Maré. Even Guyane, with its many outlets of Mr Bricolage. Is Mr Bricolage a civilising force? Maybe. It could just be good old commercial outreach, of course. Isn't the mission to civilise a bit outdated these days?

'In a global world where English has taken over, it's not surprising that France is keen to hang onto French culture,' says John Connell. 'It makes sense as a symbol of the presence of France against the global power of English. Look at it from their point of view.'

'Do you have sympathy with that?' I ask Robert Aldrich.

'Look, I'm a Francophile,' he says, as if admitting to something rather dodgy. 'And the French had the idea that their culture was universal. Paradoxically it goes, in their viewpoint, with the notion of equality, and indeed, democracy. Anyone can have access to French culture. The trouble is that we don't share that world picture any more. We think more of a migration of cultures; the French learn English now, don't they? It doesn't mean that French will necessarily disappear. The DOM-TOMs have been isolated, in their Frenchness, for years. They need to integrate, now, and mix with the culture of the area. You can see it's already happening with Creole, which is mixed together like a curry.'

We go through each of the six destinations, in order of our trip.

Saint Pierre et Miquelon?

'A consolation prize. And if they belonged to Canada, those islands would be utterly deserted.'

Martinique?

'A French boutique, the ancestral home of Josephine, close to America and with the *savoir vivre* of being French, yet unemployment causes great social tensions.'

Guyane?

'Well, it was known as Green Hell. But now, putting a European space station there means that Guyane is an integral part of Europe, so Brussels can be asked to provide subsidies from the rest of the EU.'

Polynesia?

'France was looking for a good South Pacific base. Testing atomic bombs there did nothing for French reputation around the world; twenty years on, France has improved its image somewhat.'

New Caledonia?

'Becoming an independent state is a bit of a dream, a very difficult exercise and the Kanaks fear a future without France and no money.'

La Réunion (our next stop)?

'A honeymoon destination, but you know, most French don't think about it. Tahiti is the main and first destination for newly-weds.'

'It's hard to imagine President Sarkozy will carry on subsidising them,' says Aldrich, 'but by the same token, it will be impossible for him to stop doing so. Imagine pulling out. It would cause social devastation. Perhaps the French should arrange a new status for its overseas departments. Although, if that happened there would be a significant migration from people in the DOM-TOMs back to France.'

We finish the interview, and thank Aldrich and Connell. I'm sad to say goodbye to them.

Our next and final flight to a new *département d'outre-mer*, La Réunion, is fourteen hours long. I'm looking forward to it as I hope it will give me time to reflect on what this collection of people who live in the DOM-TOMs represent. Some are blissfully happy, some discontented, others envious of the life enjoyed in the metropole. Yet apart from a few rebels in Martinique, they all agree independence from France is not the answer. When it comes to a choice of going it alone, or living under the shadow of the Eiffel Tower, everyone seems certain that life within the republic is preferable to life without. Should a DOM or a TOM walk to the brink and look over, everyone starts saying 'remember Haiti', the former French colony which chose freedom and is now one of the poorest places on the planet, isolated in its Creolephone status.

Every five or so years, following a strike or other indication of public discontent, one or other of the DOM-TOMs will carry out a referendum. Every time, the plebiscite comes to the same conclusion. Give us a bit of autonomy, but keep on paying our bills, *merci*.

Meanwhile, as far as the Élysée Palace is concerned, the Republic is going to keep on paying. No French president is going to have his legacy stained by being remembered as The One Who Lost The DOM-TOMs. 'As long as I am president, the question of Martinique's... separation from France, will not be broached,' announced President Sarkozy in 2010.

So the whole costly business just keeps going on, for no reason other than to ensure these tiny places around the world can *be* French. Recieving the French euro, you see, means you have to get on the French bus, and sit down as if you mean it. This is not the same with other tiny communities funded by a larger Western power.

If France is in charge, then Gallic principles of life (proper grammar, foie gras, identical handwriting, decent coffee) must continue to be upheld; French culture will continue and in return, France will remain the world's second maritime power, whatever that means. *Vive La France!*

I think the notion, to the French, of France's eternal culture is bolstered by having this mini empire. Britain used to boast about ruling the waves, and in Napoleon's day, she did. However, come the twenty-first century, it is our old enemy who has more square metres of salty water circling the globe. As our interviewees constantly remind us, 'the sun never sets on the *tricolore*'. Is this a sarky reference to the very similar phrase once used about the British Empire? It's certainly a coincidence. I think the presence of so many parenthesised initials (Fr) around the globe is a rather nice taunt for the old assailant at Waterloo. Is France still piqued about losing at Waterloo? A suggestion by Britain to commemorate the 150th anniversary of the battle was firmly squashed by the French, who don't necessarily find it amusing that so many places in London – a station, a bridge, any number of pubs – are named after their most humiliating defeat. Let's not forget that Waterloo Bridge leads to Trafalgar Square, incidentally, a memento of another crushing Napoleonic loss.

And so an imperial presence, even such a tiny one, is clearly important to the French self-regard. In formulating the DOM-TOMs after the war, de Gaulle was perhaps acknowledging this. While Britannia has been divesting itself of its far-flung children, and considers places such as the Falklands as an overseas territory, so not officially part of the United Kingdom, Marianne has hugged her overseas children even closer, turning them into full departments and turning a blind eye to the enormous cost this entails.

As post-colonial answers go, it is a remarkably different one to that of Britain, who devised the Commonwealth as an umbrella organisation for its former overseas territories. Yet the Commonwealth is not a political union paid for by Britain, but a club whose members are there from free association. When you see pictures of the Queen in an Indian office, she is there in a purely ceremonial guise. Not so with the many, many portraits I saw of President Sarkozy across the DOM-TOMs. Le Président is a strict yet generous parent.

When Commonwealth countries get restive, a conference is called. When the DOM-TOMs get restive, the Élysée Palace sends in the gendarmes. Followed by money. After violent protests against the cost of living broke out in Martinique and

Guadeloupe, President Sarkozy sent over 300 military police, and gave an extra €850 million to the troublesome islands.

There's no question, they are costly. Working out how much the whole string of shallots costs France is a bit like guessing the amount of bonbons in a jar, and then gluing on about seven zeros. Paris picks up the bill for almost everything, including the *grands projets* (bridges, hospitals, cultural centres) and a carillon of benefits.

Yet in their time, the colonies were rather useful to France, and not just as dumping grounds for political prisoners or criminals. Their produce of fur, fish and sugar, let alone manpower, historically boosted the French economy. Why abandon these tiny territories now they are no longer useful? There is an undeniable moral position here, as well as a post-Napoleonic desire for a continued global presence. In Barbados, a former British colony, impoverished people beg on the beaches, desperately selling tat to wealthy tourists. In the French Caribbean, social security ensures such a vista would never happen. When we visited Aqualand in Martinique, a water-themed park, I was struck by how many local families were there. Taking the day off to go to Aqualand with the kids was perfectly acceptable in an island where tourist culture is practically non-existent.

Everyone is asleep as we fly above Antarctica. I scrabble around in my bag and produce a child's textbook, *Le tourisme en France*, which I have borrowed from the library of the French Cultural Institute in London.

Amid the descriptions of Normandy, Provence and the Massif Central, the confetti of empire is described in nothing less than beatific terms. Temperatures never dip below 24 degrees and there are 'numerous beaches of fine sand'. Never mind Green Hell; Guyane has *'une extraordinaire richesse floristique'*. La

Réunion and Polynesia get much the same treatment; according to *Le Tourisme en France*, these places all have delicious, unthreatening tropical climes, wall-to-wall Gauguin, and coral reefs teeming with brightly coloured marine life.

It's only when you turn to its companion volume, *La géographie de la France*, that the picture gets distinctly darker. *La géographie de la France* reveals a wholly different profile of the DOM-TOMs. Volcanic, unstable, unproductive, financially helpless, these vulnerable, violent rocky outcrops are less pockets of paradise, more places of banishment. Forget about Gauguin and swaying Polynesian babes; Tahiti is brusquely summed up in *La géographie de la France* as '*23 hr 20 d'avion de Paris*'.

Which view is the right one? Heaven or hell? Probably neither. Perhaps the DOM-TOMs should be seen in an entirely political spirit, as a construct devised by Charles de Gaulle as a sort of salute to Napoleon.

To her neighbours in Europe, the DOM-TOMs might appear laughable, the dregs of a once mighty empire. To the French, these tiny holdings are positive proof that the *tricolore* represents the continuing presence of a globally important force. It's rather like the way the French continue to insist that their language is the official language of the Olympics, or protect their cuisine as a World Heritage Site. The extrovert, anglophone world may snigger, but introvert France has a trenchant belief in its culture that economically speaking, at least, is not necessarily a bad thing. They drive French cars, watch French films, go on holiday in France and consume the produce of their own country. Whereas the English middle classes are defined by their ease in importing culture, from holidays in India to Tuscan olive oil, the French middle classes place great importance in defending the home product.

Middle-class, mainstream France is not involved in a crisis about being French; there may be a crisis of this nature in France, but this is more to do with the inflexibility of France to achieve true racial integration, which is the unsavoury flip side of being the world's second maritime power.

When *Time* magazine put a sad-looking Pierrot on its front cover, under the headline 'The Death of French Culture' (published 21 November 2007), and wrote that 'France is a wilting power in the global cultural marketplace', the French responded with an astonishing salvo of condescending derision.

The loose-shirted Parisian intellectual Bernard-Henri Lévy suggested in a long piece published by *The Guardian* that the article said more about American cultural nervousness than anything else, and that its anti-French posturing was 'a displaced form of panic which dare not speak its name'.

Although there is a sector who rail against the metropole out in the DOM-TOMs, the *tricolore* is still being vigorously waved around the globe. This could be due to homesickness, for some, but I think it runs deeper than that. Having suffered a chaotic, bloody history, a revolution and several invasions, and courtesy of a directly accountable head of state, the French have hammered out a sensibility of who they are.

This is not quite the same as patriotism. It is more a clear understanding of what it is to be French, wherever you may be, and an unwillingness to get outside *l'Hexagone* and see things as others may see them. To the French, there is nothing extraordinary about the presence of a *République française* postbox in the middle of the rainforest, or a strict national curriculum in schools from the Indian Ocean to (say) Avignon. Napoleon codified France and its empire, and the remains of that empire is still operating under it, 200 years later.

BONNES VACANCES!

As Flight QF63 prepares to land in Johannesburg, everyone on the plane starts performing that imperceptible yet significant shift of putting on shoes, finding books, yawning. The children sit up, tousle-headed and curious. We are on our way to our final stop, La Réunion, the spectacular jewel in the Indian Ocean.

Honey's diary: *We played boxes. Then we waited a little. Then we read some books. I am getting very bored here. We went over Antartica but didn't see it.*

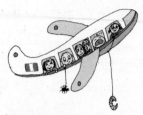

CHAPTER EIGHTEEN

The Home Stretch

Phoebe's diary: *In La Réunion we went to the Aquarium and it was really cute. NOSE FISH are officially my favourite fish! LOL. There was this mahoosive shark looking at me with these beady eyes. Then we went to the garden of palms. It was called Folio's Palmiste cozz it was owned by Mr Folio (not rocket science), but I didn't see very many palm trees. Outside the garden though I saw about 9,00000,000000,0000000,002 of them. :S*

La Réunion is the most gorgeous of all the French confetti. It is an island with perfect beaches, vast rolling ocean waves, two huge volcanoes, mist-shrouded mountains, lush ravines, tropical birds and silver rivers. It burst out of the ocean about three million years ago in a vast volcanic explosion. Like its neighbour Mauritius, it too had a dodo (with longer legs). That's the only similarity. Mauritius, which brings in jumbos from international airports on an hourly basis, is simply a large rock full of fanatically luxurious hotels perfect for newly-weds. Whereas La Réunion, which only gets internal French flights from Paris-Orly Airport, has yet to be discovered by the honeymooners. It is wild, mysterious and spectacular.

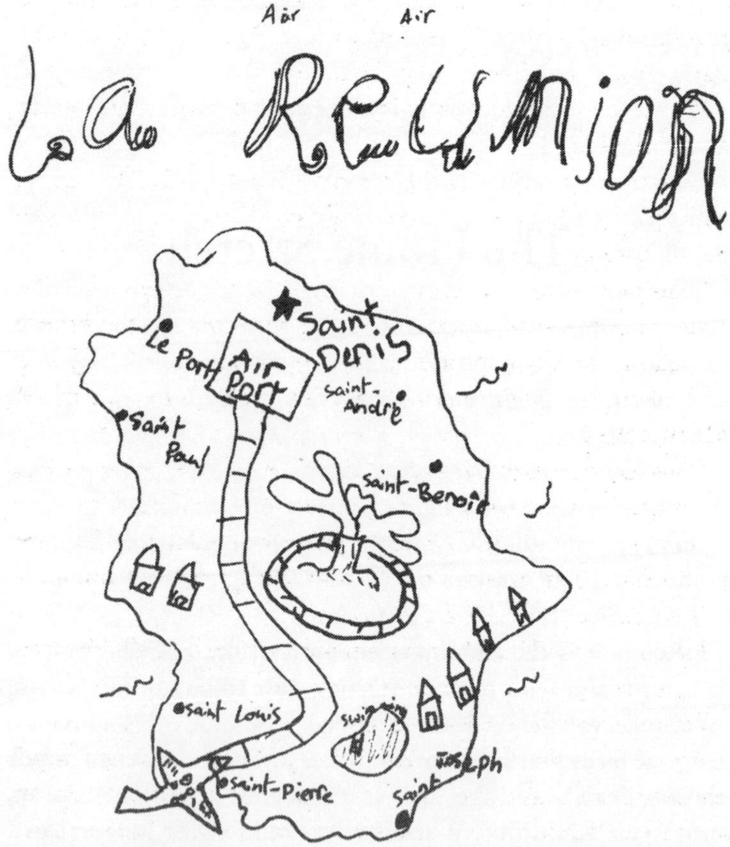
Air Air
La Reunion
Saint Denis
Le Port
Air Port
saint-André
Saint Paul
Saint-Benoî
saint Louis
saint-pierre
saint joseph
indian ocean

You would have thought that by now our senses would have been saturated, but nothing really prepared us for the knockout splendour of La Réunion. It was colonised by the French in the seventeenth century and named to commemorate the union of revolutionaries from Marseilles with the National Guard from Paris. Yes, a rather obscure political detail.

Rather less obscure, but no less political, is the new motorway across the island.

We are collected from the airport by our guide. Who is, of course, called Laurent. Laurent only wants to talk to us about the motorway.

'This motorway, she has just opened!' says Laurent excitedly as we shoot past sugar refineries (La Réunion has the French EU quota for sugar production), large branches of Hyper U and, of course, giant buildings bearing the logo for our friend Mr Bricolage.

'This journey used to take us about four hours. Now we can cross the island in forty minutes.' He sighs with pleasure.

We come to a minuscule traffic jam and slow down. Laurent points out a sign above a bridge and reads proudly from it.

'La Grande Route de La Réunion'

He doesn't read out the next bit, but we take it in all the same.

'Construit grace à l'Union Européenne 2008.'

Pip snorts in the back of the car.

Above us in the sky there are hang-gliders swooping around the mountains, and we can clearly see the clouds of vapour above La Réunion's one active volcano. Piton de la Fournaise has erupted more than 170 times since the mid seventeenth century, because it is directly connected to one of the earth's 'hot spots' leading down to the molten core of the planet. The heat-blasted, lava-strewn terrain around it resembles a moonscape. It even erupts underwater, causing the geographical wonder of 'pillow' lava on the seabed.

BONNES VACANCES!

'Your hotel, there is a running track beside it,' announces Laurent as we swing past a small village (offering a Paul patisserie, a Jean Louis David hairdresser, a *pharmacie*, a pétanque square and a yellow postbox). La Réunion is not about lounging on your beach towel, painting your nails and reading a trashy novel, it seems. You can do that in Mauritius. As the hang-gliders attest, this island is about action. Surf contests on the beaches, jogging around the hotels, canyoning, running or climbing on the volcanoes. You can even slide down the waterfalls which cascade from the mountain tops; one, which splashes onto a road, is rather delightfully known as Pisse en l'Air.

La Réunion markets itself as a sort of exotic Action Island.

That is just as well, frankly.

Thanks to our thrifty living policy we have been focusing rather too much on a menu comprising only croissants and chips, let alone the gallons of red wine consumed by me and my husband after the children have gone to bed. We now represent a flock of fat French chickens rather than a lean, trim travelling machine.

'God, I'm almost glad there's a running track here. I am so fat,' I say to Pip as I flop fatly down on the bed after unpacking, which now only takes about 3 minutes since most of our clothes have died and been thrown away, thanks to immersion in industrial quantities of New Caledonian dust.

'I simply MUST go for a run.'

The children are contentedly pulling down every single towel from the bathroom and getting into their swimsuits. Pip will take them to a deserted pool which we have spotted in the hotel grounds. I'm going to work off some of those croissants.

I put on my trainers and my running outfit, which consists of a sports bra, a (mercifully quite long) London Underground T-shirt and a pair of bikini bottoms.

To my relief, I discover the track is no more than a largely deserted path amongst the trees which crowd the water's edge.

I set off. In the tops of the trees, hundreds of weaver birds flutter furiously above me, darting in and out of little woven nests which hang like dozens of tiny oval baskets. On my right, Indian Ocean rollers crash onto the beach. A couple of middle-aged Frenchmen pad past me, going the other way.

'*Bonjour,*' they gasp.

'*Salut,*' I reply, in the split second of sweaty togetherness which is maintained by runners across the world.

I try to keep an even pace, stay in the shade and clear my mind. We still have one more documentary to shoot, one more location to understand, one more community to summarise. Whom shall we interview, what sequences must be shot? Our first shoot in Saint Pierre et Miquelon seems like it happened a very, very long time ago. However, it is still fresh in my mind, and I am now rather fond of it. Perhaps because the weather was so British, I think, as I sweat and gasp in the tropical heat.

When I stagger back into the hotel, I see Phoebe sitting outside our room in the sun.

'Hello there,' she says, as if witnessing the arrival of a scarlet-faced parent sporting an old T-shirt, bikini bottoms and trainers is quite normal.

'Water,' I croak. Afterwards we sit down together and talk. What do we talk about? Going home, of course. Normally, two weeks in somewhere like La Réunion would be a wonderful span for forgetting about home and enjoying a break. But after nearly four months away, the Arrivals terminus at Heathrow is all we can really think about.

Phoebe and I talk about her next term at school, about what her plans are, what sports she would like to do, what clubs she would like to join. Our chat is detailed and precise, not vague and world-encompassing. We both know that soon we will have to start reacclimatising from 14-hour flights over Antarctica to short journeys on the No. 91. I stroke her downy cheek and tell her she has been plucky. She's had to join us midway and has done so with great humour and verve.

We will probably never live like this again, all roped together like climbers on a mountain. But the shared experience has been so profound, so demanding that I sense its invisible ropes will remain, linking us together even when we recommence our different paths at home.

Our children have been changed by this trip. They've become naughtier, certainly. But they are all well, and safe. At least we've managed that. Furthermore, I sense they have also become more united, and ready for a certain sort of independence.

'Would you like to do the interviews today?' Pip says to the children the next morning.

'Yes, yes, yes,' they clamour.

We are due to visit the distinguished Creole poet Axel Gauvin in his eyrie of a house far above the beautiful beach of Saint Leu. Gauvin welcomes us in most courteously, and allows the children to raid his fridge. He shows us his poetry books, which are published in English, French and Creole. The insistence that the French language must rule supreme is blighting people's lives, in his view. 'France thinks the only solution is to give us money, but cash won't resolve the problem. It costs a lot of money to fight illiteracy. A hundred thousand people here cannot read.'

Really? We look at the surf crashing onto the beach far below while Gabriel and Phoebe fiddle around with the lights.

'What France must do is recognise our cultural differences, and give us lessons in Creole. *Nos ancêtres les Gaulois* is still hovering in the background,' says Gauvin ominously.

'Monsieur Gauvin,' begins Gabriel. 'Why do you write in French as well as Creole?'

'That is the whole point, *mon petit*,' smiles Gauvin kindly.

'Why?' asks Gabriel.

'Because I need to show the French readers that there is another language here, a language that Réunionnais children speak. And that they should know it too.'

'And the English?'

'We all should speak English as well. Alongside French.'

'Here speaks an enlightened Frenchman,' Pip murmurs to me.

The next day, we have to go into the capital of La Réunion, Saint Denis, for an interview with Gauvin's counterpart Jean-Marc Boyou, the head of cultural affairs. M Boyou's office is in central Saint Denis. The capital is extremely elegant, with a gold and white *hôtel de ville*, a beaux arts war memorial and delicatessens whose windows advertise that they sell wine from across France alongside *conserves*, *fromages* and the rest of the protected luxury hamper that is French cuisine.

The office of cultural affairs is in a beautiful pale blue empire-style building, with long shuttered windows and an open-air terrace in a white colonnade. If there were an epitome of a colonial building in the tropics, this would be it.

M Boyou has an even nicer suit than the president of New Caledonia. Plus, he is wearing a silk tie. I can envisage him strolling down the Boulevard Saint Michel in Paris.

He is rather dangerously attractive.

'He's not going to make the film,' says Pip.

'He's certainly going to make the book,' I respond.

'Tell me about La Réunion, Monsieur Boyou,' I ask.

'*Alors*, this image of La Réunion, it is much more modern than the African cities which are its neighbours. There is an effort from France and indeed Europe, to bring Réunion alongside them. This is why we have the new road, the bridges across the ravines and the many *grands projets*.'

Don't make the place look Third World, in other words.

What about the Creole heritage you have here, however? What about Axel Gauvin's points? Réunionnais Creole is different from Caribbean Creole, but no less important. Is it taken seriously by the head of cultural affairs? Monsieur Boyou may be good looking, but he is far too educated to start spouting on about *nos ancêtres les Gaulois* and the importance for local children to speak perfect French in the playground.

'Even if they call it a patois, there is a real love for us here for the Creole language. It is like wild honey, more perfumed and sweet than anything else. And it is complicated, because people here want to eliminate it. It's important that the French know that Creole is important. We can't abandon one or the other.'

Boyou leans forward in his perfect suit, beneath the roof of the pillared sun-terrace. Outside, brightly coloured birds hop about on a luxurious lawn fringed by palm trees and bougainvillea.

'People shouldn't all eat McDonald's and speak American English around the world,' he says smoothly. 'Diversity of life is important. And with France, well you know, the sun never sets on the *tricolore*,' he smirks. God! Stop it! Napoleon, you can rest happy on your golden catafalque in Les Invalides, since you have at long last beaten *les rosbifs* with your confetti of Empire, your string of shallots around the world. Don't forget greatness, however, warns M Boyou. It all comes down to the enduring glory of France. Just as de Gaulle said, France is nothing if she is not great.

'France is a great nation with principles. With a certain vision of the world. And the background of our vision of the world is that we are more liberal than America. It is part of the liberty which we give the people here. *Liberté, égalité, fraternité*. It is a dream. A rainbow.'

Again, I remember the Parisian doctors singing 'La Marseillaise' to the swamps in Guyane, and in Saint Pierre et Miquelon, the memorial to Charles de Gaulle with its stirring salvo: '*Vive La France!*'. Like it or not, the French know they have a vision, and out here, thousands of kilometres from Paris, even here, they know what that vision is. It's a country with its own tropical wilderness which in harsh economic terms is utterly useless, but which in a spiritual sense is vital to the French pride and sense of itself as a key world power.

We climb back into the van.

'I am holding Gabriel's turtle HOSTAGE!' shouts Phoebe.

'Mayday, Mayday!' says Gabriel.

'*Ferme ta gueule!*' ('Shut your trap!') responds Honey, who has picked up this piece of French argot from Laurent, who occasionally bellows it in an aggrieved fashion at other drivers.

'We are going to find out how coffee is made here, you guys. Just calm down now.' The screaming from the back seat continues. Everyone is in a high state of excitement, counting down before our return.

Coffee. It's a very long process, on La Réunion. Particularly Bourbon coffee.

'Hello, dear children,' says a lovely man, Alexander Dijoux, who runs a heritage arts centre and gives courses in how to make traditional 'Bourbon' coffee, from the roasting of the beans to the eventual arrival of the beverage.

Lined up on chairs, the children quiz him about the making of the coffee. He helps them hold a round straw mat on which the roasted beans are put and blown so their husks fly all around them in the warm spring air.

'Blow, blow!' enthuses Alexander. 'And fight with the fire, fight with the roasting of the beans. If you burn them you lose your coffee.'

The children look at him patiently. In terms of crazy French traditions, this one is probably one of the most relaxed they have come across of late.

'At the vertical,' encourages Alexander, holding the percolator up.

'Yes, yes. You blow it.'

About one hour after we first roast the beans, the coffee is bubbling in the percolator.

'Now will you taste it, dear children?' asks Alexander.

'No,' they all chorus.

The next day we meet Clovis, a gentle, unassuming Creole named after a Gothic French king and given to long walks high in the Réunionnaise mountains. First, we are off to the original volcano which formed La Réunion, the extinct Piton des Neiges. It is in the centre of the island and dominated by its three giant caldera, or cirques. They are now a World Heritage Site, vast natural amphitheatres high above the ocean, streaked by water and abundantly fertile, with luxuriant vegetation as far as the eye can see. For extreme sports aficionados, there is a nigh-impossible race, the Grand Raid of La Réunion which takes place every October; a crazy 24-hour, 125-kilometre experience where 200 fitness freaks don headlamps and trainers and charge across the volcanoes and the cirques from one coast to the other.

'Runners have to take a sleeping bag and a whistle,' explains Clovis.

'Why?' asks Honey.

'In case you fall down a crevasse. But it is very, very popular. Lots of runners come from *la Métropole* to take part.'

'Who wins?' asks Gabriel.

'*Alors*, always someone from the island. A Creole. Never a Parisian,' says Clovis with unconcealed pride.

The colossal Cirque de Mafate has no roads, and is accessible only by foot or helicopter. There are small villages within the cirque, with electricity provided by solar panels or diesel generators. Unsurprisingly, the cirque is a hiker's heaven; there is no traffic, but there are gîtes, a few shops and some fairly rudimentary restaurants.

We drive beneath the Pisse en l'Air, which satisfyingly splashes on the roof of our car, causing much laughter from within, and continue up to the edge of the cirque, where the roads peter out. Our guide Clovis points to the rim of teetering peaks around the bowl-like cirque. With a bit of imagination, they look rather like a man's sleeping face.

'That is the face of Mafate,' says Clovis. In the mid eighteenth century, Mafate was a famous runaway slave who escaped from the sugar plantations and took refuge with his family in the teetering ramparts of the cirque. He was eventually hunted down and killed, but his immortality is assured by his profile, eternally sleeping in the mountains.

We are in the village of Hell-Bourg, which proclaims from a roadside sign that it won the accolade 'Most Beautiful Village in France in 2000'. The village clings to the side of the volcano, its brightly coloured Creole houses looking almost like ski chalets with their gingerbread designs on their roofs and shutters.

One of the most famous, the Maison Folio, is a perfectly preserved nineteenth-century green and cream Creole house whose garden is packed with flowers, medicinal herbs and ferns. Only the perfect French fountain, and a certain regimental formality about the beds, give away the nationality of the owners. Madame and Monsieur Folio, both in their eighties, come tottering out of the house as we approach.

'*Voilà!*' says Madame Solange Folio. '*Notre salle de bain.*' We are standing outside the house, in a sort of garage, and looking at an ancient metal construction connected via a series of tubes to a very vintage boiler. I suspect Madame Folio has something far more *moderne* indoors, yet once upon a time this would have been the very latest in bathroom luxury, the boiler packed with hot coals to deliver hot water to the guests.

Inside, the house is an elegant wonder of lace curtains, parquet flooring and beautifully engraved glass.

In the nineteenth century, it was the done thing to have a holiday home up here; the French bourgeoisie would have their businesses along the coast, whether in coffee, vanilla or sugar, and escape to the mountains at weekends, in a sort of eighteenth-century version of a spa break.

We spend quite a long time with the Folios, interviewing them and doing (in my mind) endless walking shots where I have to peep out behind a fern or some other garden adornment, spouting some piece of information about the French.

'The children seem very quiet,' I say to Clovis. 'Do you, er, know where they are?'

He smiles softly and beckons me around the back of the house, where a couple of garden buildings have been decorated for children and furnished with doll's houses and a pram. On the back wall there is a large blackboard.

'How many vowels in these words?' Phoebe is saying before her sibling audience.

She has chalked up a selection; No Smoking, Hiva Oa, Shell Necklace, Tummy, School.

'Three!' shouts Honey.

'Twenty-eight!' shouts Lucien.

'Two!' shouts Gabriel.

'Lucien doesn't know what a vowel is,' taunts Honey.

The younger children are all sitting on chairs at tiny desks. It's as if, having been denied a school structure for so long, they are determined to find one and replicate it themselves.

'Hello, Mummy,' says Gabriel patiently. 'Have you finished yet?'

'Nearly. Two minutes.'

'You ALWAYS say that.'

'Yes, but this time I mean it.'

'I've got some important information for you about Réunion,' he says, waving a yellowing brochure he has picked up, presumably from the floor of the Folios' house.

'Oh yes?'

'One day in 1952, La Réunion received 1,869.9 millimetres of rainfall, the greatest 24-hour precipitation total ever recorded. And it holds the record for the greatest rainfall in 72 hours.'

On cue, the rain arrives. We hear it pattering on the giant ferns and palms of the Folios' garden long before we feel it, so lush and crowded are the plants.

We take our leave of the Folios and rush back into the van, the children moving as a team trained into expertly leaving one situation and immediately regrouping somewhere else.

'Oh, wow, Rue Charles de Gaulle!' I cry from the back of the car.

The children groan.

'Clovis, would you mind stopping the car,' I say. 'I simply must take a photo of this sign.' Throughout the journey I have built up a not insignificant collection of snaps of Rues, Avenues, Boulevards and Places du Charles de Gaulle. It is, I admit, rather a peculiar specialisation.

'Come ON, Mummy,' someone yells from the car while I dance around the sign outside.

'*Alors*, President de Gaulle, he visited La Réunion,' says Clovis, when I get back in.

'Really?'

'Of course. But he was so tall, he had to have a bed made especially for him.'

Across the French world, away from the hub of France herself, there seems still to be an almost palpable love for the General. Equally, French grandees seem to have had a special love for La Réunion; it was a getaway favourite for President Chirac, and Jacques Brel himself sang here.

Clovis takes us high, high up the cirque to the Jardins d'Heva. Visitors, mostly walkers on holiday, stay in little green, wooden bungalows perched above the cirque and eat delicious Creole food (beans and chicken with hot rougail sauce).

We walk to the main hotel building for supper. I notice that each of the children is carrying a soft toy; Phoebe a dolphin, Gabriel his turtle, Honey a hedgehog and Lucien a bear. It's time we went home, back to London.

'I will see you for dinner,' says Clovis. 'Meanwhile, you can have the sauna.'

What, all of us?

'*Bien sûr.*'

Twenty minutes later we are all in a giant jacuzzi.

'Alice the Camel!' yells Gabriel.

'No, no, NO!' I say furiously. 'We are NOT singing and shouting.'

What can we do? I frantically think through all the quizzes, tricks, games and diversionary tactics Pip and I have used throughout the trip to engage our children across the world.

'I know,' says Pip. 'What are we all looking forward to most when we get back to London?'

The trip has been so absorbing, it has become like a person itself. And it will be sad to say goodbye to it. But after 65,000 kilometres and thirteen weeks, no one can talk of anything other than what awaits at home. Even when neck-deep in foaming, hot water 6,000 metres up on a volcano in the Indian Ocean.

'All right, Lucien, what are you looking forward to most?'

'Eating food from Sainsbury's.'

'Honey, what about you?'

'Seeing Disney, and not having mosquitoes.'

Poor Honey. She has been obliged to sleep in long pyjamas and socks every night to avoid getting bitten.

'Gabriel, it's your turn. What will you look forward to most when you're back in London?'

'Going online.'

'Phoebe?'

'Having my friends over for a sleepover. And having a PROPER birthday party.'

'Didn't you like being with the tribes on your birthday?'

'Mother!' she says, exasperated. 'How about you, then? What will you look forward to the most?'

'Having a long, hot bath,' I say.

'But you're in one already.'

'In my own house.'

Pip jumps out of the jacuzzi. 'I'm going to have a sauna,' he says. 'My back is suffering.'

'But what about you, what are you looking forward to most?'

'Being in a quiet room on my own without the kids,' says Pip with feeling as he closes the sauna door tightly.

'Awww,' says Gabriel, laughing.

'What was your best moment, then?' I say, flicking him with tepid water.

'Watching the dolphins jumping through the waves in Polynesia.'

'Being in the jungle with Paul and the black ants,' says Lucien.

'Yeah, well that's ONLY because you weren't bitten,' says Honey.

'Hearty, what about you?'

'The dolphins, too.'

'You can't have that. That's my moment,' says Gabriel.

'What else, Honey?'

'Oh, all right. The planes. Going on all those plane trips. And having those little pouches they give you full of crayons. What was your best moment, Mummy?'

'I don't know. Actually, I think it was arriving at Saint Pierre et Miquelon. BEFORE we realised nobody knew we were coming,' I laugh. 'God. Bliss followed by horror.'

Two days later, it's almost our last night and we are eating at a seaside bistro in the little town of Saint Paul. Outside, the rollers from the Indian Ocean crash sequentially along the shoreline. Inside, there are Toulouse-Lautrec posters; La Goulue, the Moulin Rouge, the classics. High on the wall is a television, which is broadcasting a local French weather report. It is windy in Biarritz, apparently.

Beside the bistro is a small *tabac*, selling Hollywood chewing gum, *Le Monde* and *Paris Match*. Or you can pick up a copy of the local rag and find out what time the next Air France flight is to Paris-Orly Airport. Rather like buses, there are seven flights a day.

Pip and I are drinking Evian and a glass of Côtes du Rhône alongside plates of salade niçoise. The children are drinking Orangina and eating croque-monsieurs.

A pair of cabaret singers set up in the corner. They start off with Bee Gees standards and Simon and Garfunkel. As the sun goes down behind the ocean, they pitch into a classic; 'La Vie En Rose', by Piaf.

'All right, so we know what we're looking forward to most. But what will you all miss most about the trip?' says Pip.

'Messing around in the car all the time,' says Phoebe.

'Hotels,' says Gabriel, ever the bon viveur.

'Seeing all the strange animals like turtles in the water,' comments Honey.

'Lucien?'

'I don't know. NOT speaking French. I hate French.'

'But what will you miss the most?'

'Putting my head down on your knee and sleeping in the planes.'

'Mon chéri?' I ask Pip.

He tips his chair back. 'I don't know. The light. The water. The fact that we were never really far away from the sea, wherever we were. The wide, wide open spaces. Places like Langlade. Places you never really knew existed.' He smiles.

'And being just here, us, the family, together on our adventure.'

'You're right. That's what I'll miss too.'

We did it, I think happily. Now we must leave this crazy alternative universe behind, and return to the real world. Because the DOM-TOMs are not a real world; at least, they are only real in the sense that they are maintained by the very real sense, by the French, of the continuing greatness of France.

Is it confidence that makes the French so insistent about the pre-eminence of their culture; or the opposite – a creeping fear that it might be wiped out by other, more dominant cultures, leaving eternal France to ring-fence itself with a single, giant apellation contrôlée? The truth is, it's probably a bit of both. And something else, I consider, as the singers croon the peerless words alongside the ocean roar. For the urban French, typically living in apartments which look onto formally arranged boulevards with clipped trees and ferociously swept pavements, there might be some balm in the notion that they could, if they wanted, simply depart to a wilder version of their own country and live on a riverboat in the middle of the jungle. After all, wouldn't you want your own pocket wilderness?

Honey's diary: *We didn't see half of the rainbow.*
We saw the whole of the rainbow.

Rosie Millard's journey can be watched on YouTube.
Type in 'Rosie Millard' and enjoy!

Tout Sweet

Hanging up my High Heels for a New Life in France

KAREN WHEELER

NEW LIFE

LOVE ?

TOUT SWEET

Hanging Up My High Heels for a New Life in France

Karen Wheeler

ISBN: 978 1 84024 761 9   Paperback   £8.99

'an hilarious account of a fashion guru who swaps Prada for paintbrushes and Pineau in rural France'
MAIL ON SUNDAY Travel

'Perfect summer reading for anyone who dreams of chucking away their Blackberry and downshifting to France'
FRENCH PROPERTY NEWS

In her mid-thirties, fashion editor Karen has it all: a handsome boyfriend, a fab flat in west London and an array of gorgeous shoes. But when Eric leaves, she hangs up her Manolos and waves goodbye to her glamorous city lifestyle to go it alone in a run-down house in rural Poitou-Charentes, central western France.

Acquiring a host of new friends and unsuitable suitors, she learns that true happiness can be found in the simplest of things – a bike ride through the countryside on a summer evening, or a kir or three in a neighbour's courtyard.

Perfect summer reading for anyone who dreams of chucking away their BlackBerry in favour of real blackberrying and downshifting to France.

A Chateau Of One's Own

Restoration Misadventures in France

SAM JUNEAU

A CHATEAU OF ONE'S OWN

Restoration Misadventures in France

Sam Juneau

ISBN: 978 1 84024 641 4   Paperback   £8.99

'*Hilarious... Engaging tale... A refreshing warts-and-all account of what follows that impulsive buy*'

SCOTTISH SUNDAY EXPRESS

Sam and Bud were ordinary first-time homebuyers in their early thirties. Their intention in moving to France was to create a simple life and spend more time with their children. The home they actually bought was an impressive seventeenth-century chateau in the Loire valley with over thirty rooms, 156 windows and 40 acres of land.

With only modest savings, the couple launched the challenging project of restoring this crumbling monster of a building to its former glory and opening a bed and breakfast in the process. This is the hilarious story of behind the scenes at a B&B that required constant disaster relief: think *Fawlty Towers* in an extraordinary setting.

A Chateau of One's Own will appeal to those like Sam and Bud who want to escape from the rat race, who work hard and have hardly enough time to play. It's the perfect read for anyone considering a grandiose home makeover project and for all of us who dream of a life in France.

a delicious love story, with recipes

LUNCH
in
PARIS

ELIZABETH BARD

LUNCH IN PARIS

A Delicious Love Story, With Recipes

Elizabeth Bard

ISBN: 978 1 84953 154 2   Paperback   £8.99

A *New York Times* and international bestseller, and recipient of the 2010 Gourmand World Cookbook Award for Best First Cookbook (USA)

HAS A MEAL EVER CHANGED YOUR LIFE?

'This is amazing,' I said. 'You have to give me the recipe.'
'There is no recipe,' he said, smiling. 'I use whatever I have. It never tastes the same way twice.'
I had no way of knowing, that first damp evening in Paris, how this man, and his non-recipes, would change my life.

Part love story, part wine-splattered cookbook, *Lunch in Paris* is a deliciously tart, forthright and funny story of falling in love with a Frenchman and moving to the world's most romantic city – not the Hollywood version, but the real Paris, a heady mix of blood sausage, *pains aux chocolats* and irregular verbs.

From gutting her first fish (with a little help from Jane Austen) to discovering the French version of Death by Chocolate, Elizabeth Bard finds that learning to cook and building a new life have a lot in common. Peppered with recipes, this mouth-watering love story is the perfect treat for anyone who has ever suspected that lunch in Paris could change their life.

Have you enjoyed this book?
If so, why not write a review on your favourite website?

Thanks very much for buying this Summersdale book.

www.summersdale.com